# 100 g

# RANCH
# VACATIONS
## IN NORTH AMERICA

© 2003 Jeff@JAGPhotoInc.com

**The Top Guest and Resort Ranches
with Activities for All Ages**

# GAVIN EHRINGER

The Globe Pequot Press

GUILFORD, CONNECTICUT

Text design by Nancy Freeborn
Photo layout by Sue Preneta

Library of Congress Cataloging-in-Publication Data
Ehringer, Gavin.
    100 best ranch vacations in North America / Gavin Ehringer.
      p. cm. — (100 best resorts series)
    ISBN 0-7627-2597-4
    1. Dude ranches—United States—Guidebooks. 2. Dude ranches—United States—Directories. 3. Dude ranches—Canada—Guidebooks. 4. Dude ranches—Canada—Directories. I. Title: One hundred best ranch vacations in North America. II. Title. III. Series.

GV198.95.E47 2003
796.46'0257—dc22
                                                                              2003056986
Manufactured in the United States of America
First Edition/First Printing

The prices and rates listed in this guidebook were confirmed at press time. We recommend, however, that before traveling you call establishments to obtain current information.

# *100 Best*
# RANCH
# VACATIONS
## IN NORTH AMERICA

# A PHOTO ESSAY

**Scott Valley Resort and Guest Ranch**

**Scott Valley Resort and Guest Ranch**

**Scott Valley Resort and Guest Ranch**

**Hidden Creek Ranch**

**King Mountain Ranch**

**Hidden Valley Ranch**

**The Homeplace Ranch**

**King Mountain Ranch**

**Rimrock Dude Ranch**

**The Historic Pines Ranch**

**Hidden Creek Ranch**

**Hidden Creek Ranch**

**UXU Ranch**

**Echo Valley Ranch & Spa**

**Skyline Guest Ranch**

**UXU Ranch**

**Triangle C Ranch**

**Bitterroot Ranch**

**Hidden Valley Ranch**

**Scott Valley Resort and Guest Ranch**

**Bitterroot Ranch**

**Triangle C Ranch**

**C Lazy U Ranch**

**Lost Creek Ranch & Spa**

**Bitterroot Ranch**

**The Hills Health Ranch**

**Triple Creek Ranch**

**The Hills Health Ranch**

**Hidden Creek Ranch**

**Hidden Creek Ranch**

**Rock Springs Guest Ranch**

Photo credits: p. i © 2003 jeff@JAGPhotoInc.com; p. i (background image) © PhotoDisc; p. iii © Jane Lidz/Hidden Creek Ranch; pp. iv-v © Chilcotin Holidays Guest Ranch; p. vi (top) © Ben Smith/Kathy Tash/K Bar L Ranch; p. vi (bottom) © Mark Mathews; p. vii (top and bottom) © Mark Mathews; p. viii © Jane Lidz/Hidden Creek Ranch; p. ix courtesy of King Mountain Ranch; p. x (top) courtesy of Hidden Valley Ranch; p. x (bottom) © Homeplace Ranch; p. xi (top) courtesy of King Mountain Ranch; p. xi (bottom) © 2003 jeff@JAGPhotoInc.com; p. xii © Rimrock Ranch; p. xiii courtesy of The Historic Pines Ranch; p. xiv (top and bottom) © Jane Lidz/Hidden Creek Ranch; p. xv (top) courtesy of Hamilton Bryan/UXU Ranch; p. xv (bottom) courtesy of Echo Valley Ranch & Spa; p. xvi courtesy of Skyline Ranch; p. xvii courtesy of Hamilton Bryan/UXU Ranch; pp. xviii-xix © Triangle C Ranch; p. xx (top) courtesy of Bitterroot Ranch; p. xx (bottom) courtesy of Hidden Valley Ranch; p. xxi (top) © Mark Mathews; p. xxi (bottom) courtesy of Bitterroot Ranch; p. xxii © Triangle C Ranch; p. xxiii courtesy of C Lazy U Ranch; p. xxiv courtesy of Lost Creek Ranch & Spa; p. xxv courtesy of Bitterroot Ranch; p. xxvi (top) © The Hills Health & Guest Ranch; p. xxvi (bottom) courtesy of Triple Creek Ranch; p. xxvii (top) © The Hills Health & Guest Ranch; p. xxvii (bottom) © Jane Lidz/Hidden Creek Ranch; p. xxviii © Jane Lidz/Hidden Creek Ranch; p. xxix courtesy of Rock Springs Guest Ranch; p. 1 © Triangle C Ranch; p. 191 courtesy of Echo Valley Ranch & Spa; spot art throughout © ClipArt.com

# CONTENTS

# CANADA

# INTRODUCTION

The horse is a vehicle that not only can carry us but that can carry us back to a simpler time. For many that journey begins at a guest ranch.

The guest ranch experience dates back more than a century and a half, when well-to-do easterners and foreign guests would travel to the sparsely populated environs of the western United States to view its scenic wonders and enjoy its open spaces. Many came West to share in the great adventure of the cowboy, an American icon whose mythology was already being written even as these rugged men were still driving cattle up the trails out of Texas.

Teddy Roosevelt was one of those early "dudes," and he often credited his days spent out West for transforming him from a pale, sickly individual into a robust man with abundant health and self-confidence. Doubtless, the modern guest doesn't anticipate such a dramatic makeover. But still, spending a week's vacation outdoors, participating in rigorous activities, or just lazing along a sunny fishing stream not only has a certain restorative value, but a transformative one, too.

I know, because dude ranches played a big role in my life. For several years I worked as a guest ranch wrangler in the Colorado Rockies. My experiences spanned the entire range of adventures one can find among the huge variety of guest ranches. At one extreme was a ranch at which guests stayed in a century-old bunkhouse with neither electricity nor indoor plumbing and dined on meals cooked on an authentic wood-stove. That was real cowboy stuff.

At the other extreme I spent a season working at the C Lazy U Guest Ranch (featured in this book), a five-star, five-diamond resort facility with a top-shelf bar, chef-prepared meals, a spa, indoor pool, an extensive western art collection, and its own tennis pro.

Whether your idea of the perfect guest ranch vacation includes sleeping on a bedroll underneath the stars or resting your head on a goosedown pillow beneath a hand-stitched quilt, chances are you'll find your kind of place in these pages.

No two guest ranches are alike. Most are family-owned, and much of the owners' personalities are invested in their properties. My goal was to select a broad variety of guest ranches so that you might find one tailored to your interests and inclinations.

I've picked traditional working ranches where guests ride herd side-by-side with real cowboys. New age ranches are also included, where you can luxuriate in full-service spas or focus on activities to enhance the body, mind, and soul. For the adventurous there are ranches that emphasize thrilling activities like river rafting, rock climbing, and mountain biking. There are sportsmen's ranches and ranches with championship golf courses. Ranches for gourmands and ranches that serve home-raised beef cooked on an open fire outdoors. Ranches on both coasts, in the scenic Rockies, and in Canada.

One thing that ties all these places together is their hosts' hospitality and dedication to service. The guest ranch tradition grew out of the Code of the West, where the doors were always open to strangers and a place was set at the table. That same spirit pervades today's guest ranches, which offer a vacation experience unlike any other and second to none.

## Being a good dude

The word "dude" might at first seem uncomfortable to wear, but it will soon fit you like an old flannel shirt. In the Old West to be a dude simply meant that you were an urbanite or an Easterner. There's no shame in that: As one ranch hand aptly said, "We were all pilgrims once."

But there are good dudes and bad dudes. Remember, you're there to share in the ranch lifestyle, and the more willing you are to take an active role with enthusiasm and a sense of adventure, the more likely you will enjoy the experience.

Ease into the experience during the first few days. You've probably got some stress to unload before you begin to properly enjoy your vacation. Get a feel for how things are done, the pace and rhythm of the guest ranch. As you become a part of the place, you can step up your level or interaction. But at first, take things slow and easy.

One thing about ranchers and cowboys: They aren't too sympathetic to whining. After a day in the saddle, you're likely to be sore. Don't be surprised when the ranch wrangler tells you that riding the next day is the best way to get the kinks out. He's right.

While some ranches are set up to pamper their guests, many are not. You may be expected to learn to saddle and unsaddle your own horse or take part in camp chores. "Hands-on" can be a wonderful and enriching experience, so don't pass on such opportunities.

Furthermore, you might want to leave the modern devices you're accustomed to using behind. A guest who is constantly yapping on his cell phone or a kid who spends his entire vacation playing video games on his personal console rather misses the point of the ranch vacation. I once took a family from Florida to a beautiful mountain valley in the Rockies and was somewhat startled when, having set up camp, the father sat down to watch a handheld television set. I was quite pleased that there was no reception in this remote wilderness, and it wasn't long before he'd turned his attention to the herd of elk streaming across the mountainside just a few hundred yards from camp.

## What to Pack

Nearly every guest ranch has its own list of suggested items to bring for your trip, particularly if you're going on a pack trip, where weight and bulk are considerations. Of course, weather is a factor too. You're packing list for a fall trip in Wyoming will be considerably different than for a spring trip in Arizona.

Still, there are basic items that nearly every guest should plan to bring.

• **Riding boots.** Many ranches require that guests wear flat-soled cowboy boots for riding, as a safety measure. The cowboy boot heel is designed to keep your foot from slipping through the stirrup, while the sole helps maintain good contact with the stirrup. Buy quality cowboy boots for everyone in the family, and be sure to allow a week or two to break them in so that you won't develop sore feet on your trip.

In addition to the traditional leather-soled cowboy boots, many western wear stores offer crepe-soled cowboy boots which are more comfortable to stand and walk in. If you have back or leg problems, these might be worth investing in.

• **Cowboy hats.** Although you don't need a cowboy hat, you do need some sort of head covering. Remember, you'll be spending a good portion of the day outdoors, often at high altitudes where solar rays can be intense. A baseball cap or a floppy-brimmed golfers' hat may serve you well.

That said, a cowboy hat is ideal. Its broad brim shadows the face and neck and serves as a personal umbrella in a rain shower. In summer an inexpensive straw hat will serve you well. For spring and fall trips, you might prefer a wool or animal-fur felt hat, which provides greater warmth. You may also wish to add a "stampede string," a thin chin strap that will keep your hat from flying away during a sprited gallop or if the wind kicks up.

• **Rainwear.** Mountain weather can be unpredictable, so be prepared with lightweight, quality rainwear. Some ranches provide guests with riding slickers or rain suits but having your own is a good idea.

• **Jeans.** Jeans are the standard riding pants in the West, and you'll want to pack several pair. Buy "boot cut" styles to fit over your riding boots, and buy them 2 to 3 inches longer than normal, because while riding they tend to hike up your leg. You want them to have a few wrinkles above your boot, and the hem should reach your boot heel when you're standing. Buying jeans that are loose in the seat will make mounting and dismounting easier.

Cotton jeans can be worse than useless when they get wet. Consider taking along some wool pants (excellent varieties can be found in military surplus stores, as well as at outdoor outfitting shops). They'll keep you warm even when wet.

• **Layering.** Weather can change considerably in the mountains, from near-freezing temperatures in the morning to 90-degree heat at midday. Having several layers of light clothing is the best way to adjust to changing climate. Lightweight pile sweaters, undershirts, vests, and rainproof shell overcoats should all be included in your suitcase.

• **Sun protection.** Take along a good sunblock—you'll need it.

• **Sunglasses.**

• **Insect repellent.** One that contains DEET is recommended.

• **Skin-care lotion, lip balm, and essential toileteries.**

If you plan to take part in specific recreational activities, such as river rafting, fishing, or mountain biking, you should find out what clothing and gear will be needed.

## What Not to Pack

• **Spurs and riding chaps.** Most guest ranchers frown on inexperienced riders using spurs, which can be irritating or downright dangerous to horses when used incorrectly. As for chaps (leather leggings worn by riders), they do offer great leg protection, but in most cases will not be necessary.

## Selecting a Guest Ranch

First, get your priorities in order. Is your heart set on visiting Yellowstone National Park during your guest ranch odyssey? Or is getting in several rounds of golf important? Will your children be happy in structured,

age-appropriate activities, or would you rather they spend as much time sharing experiences with you as your vacation will allow? Do you want to ride herd on a cattle drive, or would you prefer spending more leisure time poolside?

Look over the various listings and photos; these will give you an idea of whether the ranch leans in the direction of a posh resort or is more "down home"—or somewhere in between.

Be attentive to the activities. Horseback riding is the center of nearly every guest ranch experience, but many ranches also offer a broad palette of others things to do. Some ranches have structured recreational programs, while others leave guests to explore and plan their day on their own schedules.

If you have children, you'll want to look at ranches with kids' programs or teen programs. Day care is offered (and noted) at several facilities; others may require that you bring a nanny. Some ranches are for adults or mature teens only.

I've tried to provide an index of costs associated with your guest ranch stay. Although prices are listed on a per-day rate, the general practice is to offer multi-day packages. In most cases the ranches listed in this book follow the American Plan, which includes food, lodging, and activities. Others offer a modified American Plan, which generally includes meals and lodging, with activities charged separately, or a European Plan, which is an a la carte approach. The type of payment plan is noted for each listing. Prices, however, are subject to change, and factors such as length of stay, accommodations, extra activities, transportation, and more can affect the price you actually pay. Be sure to get specifics about your costs and what is and isn't included in those costs.

## Price Index

| | |
|---|---|
| $ | Less than $100 per person, per day |
| $$ | $100–199 per person, per day |
| $$$ | $200–299 per person, per day |
| $$$$ | $300–399 per person, per day |
| $$$$$ | More than $400 per person, per day |

# SOME COMMON QUESTIONS
## TO ASK ABOUT YOUR RANCH STAY

## Rates

What are the rates, and what do they include?

What are your policies on tipping and gratuities?

Do you offer discounted off-season rates?

Do you offer senior or children's discounts?

What is the preferred method of payment?

Is there a deposit, and if so, when is payment required?

What happens to my deposit if I am forced to cancel?

## Horse programs

What learning opportunities do you provide?

Will we be allowed to groom and saddle our horses?

Are individuals assigned one horse for their stay?

Are there opportunities to trot, canter, and gallop?

Is there any arena instruction?

Can you accommodate English riding?

What is your policy for children riding?

Are riding helmets available or provided? Are they required?

Are there opportunities to be involved with cattle work?

What safety training do your wranglers have?

How do you address emergency situations, and how far is the nearest medical facility?

Can I bring my own horse?

How much time each day can we expect to spend riding?

What are your weight limits for riders?

## Activities

What activities, besides horseback riding, are offered?

Which activities carry extra fees?

What equipment does the ranch provide?

What cultural or sight-seeing opportunities are available near the ranch?

## Children

Describe the children's program, if available.

How old must my kids be to ride?

What child care is available?

Can kids take part in adult activities?

Do children dine separately?

What are the qualifications of child care providers?

What activities can families participate in together?

## Cattle work

Does a ranch stay include participation in cattle work?

Do you offer opportunities to do such things as branding or roping?

Do you have arena activities, such as roping or team penning contests?

Describe any programs you have for trail herding.

## Backcountry packing

Do you offer backcountry pack trips?

If so, what are the costs?

Where do your pack trips go, and how many days are they?

What type of accommodations do you provide for pack trips?

What clothing and gear do you suggest for pack trips?

How many guests are allowed per pack trip?

What emergency evacuation plan do you have for guests if they are injured on a pack trip?

What type of camp food do you serve?

## General

Do you have an activities planner to help with off-site arrangements?

Do you have staff or visiting naturalists?

Do you provide off-site transportation, or should I plan on bringing a rental car?

What is the ranch elevation, and do I need to take any health or safety precautions due to altitude?

I have family members who don't wish to ride or fish. Will there be other things for them to do?

What are your policies on liquor?

Can you accommodate special diets?

What is your smoking policy? Do you have nonsmokers' rooms?

Can you provide guest references?

# UNITED STATES

# CRYSTAL CREEK LODGE

## Dillingham, Alaska

For some people, the Alaskan wilderness represents the paramount adventure. Here, the mountains are bigger, the animals are more abundant, and the streams, rivers, and lakes teem with ravenous, plump fish. For those people, the only answer to their guest-ranch search is Crystal Creek Lodge, located in southwest Alaska near the town of Dillingham. This region, known as Bristol Bay, is world renowned for its runs of wild Pacific salmon and thriving resident populations of rainbow trout, arctic char, arctic grayling, northern pike, lake trout, and Dolly Varden trout. In other words, it's a fisherman's paradise.

Strictly speaking, Crystal Creek Lodge isn't a traditional guest lodge. Fishing, not horseback riding, is the focus here. You'd be far better off investing in some new waders rather than a pair of cowboy boots if you book a trip. But if fishing, hunting, wilderness photography, or wildlife observation get your blood pumping, you'll have come to the right place.

Selected as the 1997 Orvis-Endorsed Guest Lodge of the Year, Crystal Creek Lodge offers a very upscale version of "roughing it." The lodge is indeed remote, perched as it is on Lake Nunavaugaluk, which is bordered to the north by the 1.7-million-acre Wood Tikchik State Park and to the west and south by the 4.3-million-acre Togiak National Wildlife Refuge. Given such a vast wilderness to explore, Crystal Creek relies on float planes to ferry guests to choice trophy-fishing locales and glorious nature areas guaranteed to awe any guest.

Despite its remoteness, the Crystal Creek Lodge is replete with modern amenities one might expect in a world-class destination resort. A spacious 11,500-square-foot lodge houses guests in generously sized rooms, complete with queen- and full-sized beds, full baths, and daily housekeeping service. Amenities include spa, sauna, and licensed bar. If you forget any gear or tackle, the lodge has a full complement of rods, reels, and tackle (as well as waders, in a variety of sizes) that are selected to comply with the day's fishing adventure.

Originally built as a salmon-hatching facility at a cost of $25 million, the lodge was converted into a sport fishing "camp" in 1987. It opened for business in 1988. Hosts Dan and Lori Michels combine skills essential to the fluid operation of this resort. Both are avid and lifelong outdoorspeople and shooting-sports enthusiasts. Dan's background in hotel management helps provide the attention to detail that makes guests rave about the service. His guiding abilities earned him the title of 1993 Orvis Guide of the Year, and if that weren't enough, he is also a commercially rated seaplane pilot and a licensed U.S. Coast Guard captain.

Lori is no less talented. She is a licensed commercial pilot, licensed U.S. Coast Guard captain, and the founder of Sky Trekking Alaska, an adventure travel-flight operation that she and Dan also operate, which perfectly augments their guest-lodge operation.

## Crystal Creek Lodge

P.O. Box 872729
Wasilla, AK 99687–2729
Phone: (800) 525–3153; (907) 357–3153
Fax: (907) 357–1946
E-mail: info@alaskaonthefly.com
Web site: www.alaskaonthefly.com

**Owners/Operators:** Dan and Lori Michels

**Accommodations:** 20 to 24 guests. 14 guest rooms, each with either 2 firm, double-sized or one queen-sized bed, carpet, blackout blinds and a full, private bath.

**Meals:** All food is offered by choices from a menu, then prepared and served to order in a beautiful lakeside dining room. Full breakfast menu. Box lunches have sandwiches made to order, along with homemade salads, home-made baked desserts, chips, and fresh fruit. Prepared when requested, shore lunches are fresh salmon with various side fixings prepared stream side by your guide. Special dietary needs are accommodated on request. The dinner menu offers a choice of 3 different items each evening: usually a beef dish, a chicken or pork dish, or a salmon or halibut dish, all with starch and vegetable sides. Fresh salad greens, homemade breads, and homemade desserts are served each evening. An extensive wine list and full-service bar are also available.

**Activities:** Fly, trolling, and spin fishing are the primary activities. Guests enjoy a fully-equipped tackle room and expert equipment advice. Upland bird and waterfowl hunting, in season; please inquire as to dates. Crystal Creek Lodge's Sky Trekking Program is an Orvis-Endorsed Expedition designed for guests who desire an active outdoor program that places less emphasis upon fishing or hunting.Guests who come primarily to fish or hunt are welcome to participate in all activities. Activities include bear, caribou, walrus, and other marine-mammal viewing; puffin and other bird viewing; and numerous natural interpretation opportunities. Other activities include beachcombing the Bering Sea, hiking the Wood-Tikchik State Park, and kayaking in magnificent Silver Horn, a freshwater fjord, and visits to local Eskimo villages to learn Yup'ik culture and to buy rare and beautiful crafts. One or more days of fishing can be incorporated into the itinerary. All fishing or hunting guests are welcome to participate in a Trek activity.

**Amenities:** Amenities include spa, sauna, heated room for drying wet waders and clothing, completely stocked fly-tying bench, meeting/video screening room, and licensed bar. Capacity is not based upon bed space but upon the aircraft-to-guest ratio of 1 aircraft for every 4 guests and guide-to-guest ratio of 1 guide to every 2 guests. Sporting clay range available to guests, complete with guns, ammunition, and shooting instruction if desired. Beginners welcome!

**Special Programs:** "Family Adventure Week" early in the season is a great opportunity to include children. Please call for details. Half-day shooting courses supplement daily fishing and activity programs. Sky Trekking provides an exciting alternative to hunting and fishing. Participants fly out from the lodge each day with a pilot/guide.

**Rates:** $$$$$ Full American Plan. Includes guided float-plane transportation, guide, and equipment.

**Credit Cards:** None. Personal checks or money orders accepted.

**Season:** June to September

**Getting There:** Guests should arrange air transportation to Dillingham. Lodging and dining advice for the Anchorage leg of the journey can be obtained by contacting the lodge headquarters. Transfers between Dillingham and Crystal Creek Lodge are provided.

**What's Nearby:** The Crystal Creek Lodge is a self-contained vacation destination. Activities originate and are centered around the lodge itself. Sky Trekking packages offer trips to adjacent wilderness areas and to nearby Eskimo (Inuit) villages.

# SCOTT VALLEY RESORT AND GUEST RANCH

## Mountain Home, Arkansas

The Scott Valley Resort and Guest Ranch is an anomaly in the Ozarks: a guest ranch where Southern hospitality and the Wild West collide. But with gracious hospitality, owner-operator Kathleen Cooper makes it all work. That a guest ranch has survived and thrived here is surprising, especially considering that when Kathleen and her now-deceased husband, Tom, bought the ranch on a whim back in 1986, Kathleen had only ridden three times, including two rides in a pony ring, and Tom had only been on horseback once.

What the Coopers didn't know, however, they were more than willing to learn. Presently, they have a rock-solid herd of Missouri fox-trotters that were raised and trained on the ranch. Everyone here goes out of his or her way to create an unforgettable ranch experience. Testament to the staff's exceptional efforts is Scott Valley's appearance on the *Family Circle* magazine list of Top Family Resorts three times in the 1990s. It has been featured in enough tourism and travel magazines to fill a small library and was even selected a "four paw" resort by the publication *Pets Welcome* (and yes, you can bring your Yorkie).

Affordable family fun is the key to Scott Valley's success. Both couples with kids and single parents will appreciate the facilities, which include a large playground and a petting zoo. Kids especially thrill to the horse-drawn hayride tour of the ranch and the evening ice-cream socials.

"In the summertime, if you don't like children, you probably won't like it here," confides Kathleen. "We want people to feel like they're at home, not at a motel."

Despite this (or perhaps because of it) a good number of Southern travelers stop by the ranch for the night, for the ranch has earned a reputation far and wide for its friendly ambience and exceptional home cooking.

Although the emphasis at Scott Valley is on riding, the ranch offers a wide variety of recreational activities. One can angle in a world-class trout habitat along the banks of the White and North Fork Rivers or go for a lazy canoe trip. Sports enthusiasts can play tennis, volleyball, badminton, or horseshoes or can try their luck on the "Crolf" links. ("Crolf" is a homespun combination of croquet and golf.)

Don't expect a concierge or bellhop here, but you'll always find a helpful ranch hand to help you. And don't expect The Ritz Carlton, either. Think instead of a Holiday Inn, circa 1955. The cabins are very tidy, but simple, and are intended for sleeping and bathing. Clean white exteriors and front porches are concessions to the sometimes muggy summer weather. There are no in-room televisions or phones to bother you here! It's a ranch philosophy that such modern conveniences distract people from socializing, so leave the cell phone at home (or, at least, leave it in your suitcase).

Horse riders take advantage of the wooded 640-acre spread, which features pleasant views of area peaks and altitudes that won't leave one breathless. Although not as rugged as the western mountains, the Ozarks are thickly wooded and are distinguished as being among the oldest mountains in North America. Riding groups are broken down by riding ability, not age, and each rider keeps the same horse during his or her stay. It's not unusual for your horse to greet you in the morning, as the horses are given the run of the ranch when not on the trail.

Guests may also take advantage of area attractions that include Blanchard Springs Caverns and the Ozark Folk Center. Water-sports enthusiasts will enjoy Lake Norfork, a vast water body with 550 miles of shoreline. There, one can jet ski, sail and even scuba dive.

Guests who seek seclusion can stay at the Hilltop Hideaway, a small enclave that includes a barn, a fenced grazing area, a swimming pool, catch-and-release fishing pond, and an outstanding 360-degree view of the mountains. Groups who stay there can cook and take care of their own needs or participate in horse rides and activities at the main ranch. It's the ideal spot for horse owners, who can bring their own mounts and enjoy the Ozark mountain scenery with friends and family.

## Scott Valley Resort and Guest Ranch
P.O. Box 1447
Mountain Home, AR 72654
Phone: (870) 425–5136
Fax: (870) 425–5800
E-mail: svr@centurytel.net
Web site: www.scottvalley.com

**Owner/Manager:** Kathleen Cooper

**Accommodations:** Guest capacity, 65. 28 1- and 2-bedroom, motel-style guest cabins with full bathrooms and showers. Groups and families may request the Hilltop Hideaway, a complex that provides scenic serenity. Conference space available during the off-season.

**Meals:** The food here is plentiful and basic, focusing on local staples such as Arkansas-grown beef and poultry and seasonal fruits and vegetables. Notes the owner, "The food is made the way people used to cook—before they just opened the microwave and threw in the little pan." Special dietary needs addressed with advance notice.

**Activities:** Daily scheduled horseback riding grouped by ability. Experienced riders should visit in spring or fall, when especially lengthy advanced rides are held and the emphasis shifts from families to adults. Water sports include canoeing, tubing, jet skiing, scuba, sailing, and fishing on nearby lakes and streams. Recreation on the ranch includes tennis, volleyball, a fitness room, shuffleboard, Ping-Pong, and "Crolf," a game of croquet-golf. 18-hole golf course nearby.

**Amenities:** Heated pool, recreation room, extensive nearby water-sports opportunities, children's playground, and petting zoo. Horse-drawn hayrides. Regularly scheduled evening entertainment.

**Special Programs:** Hilltop Hideaway allows guests to set their own agenda. Groups there can provide for all of their own needs, they can have food and horses delivered from the main ranch, or they can fully participate in the regular ranch programs.

**Rates:** $$–$$$ American Plan. Children under age 2 stay free. Discounts for seniors, military members, and groups. Multiday and week-long stays preferred.

**Credit Cards:** VISA, MasterCard

**Season:** March through November, including Thanksgiving and Easter. Hilltop Hideaway available year-round.

**Getting There:** The ranch is located 6 miles south of Mountain Home, just off state Highway 5. Nearest large airports are in Little Rock (156 miles south) and Memphis (196 miles east), although a small airport in Fort Smith is closest.

**What's Nearby:** Lake Norfork is one of the major recreational water bodies in the South; the bass fishing here is world-class, as are the water sports. Trout fishing on the White and Norfork Rivers. Blanchard Springs Caverns, the Ozark Folk Center, and Village 1890. Branson, Missouri, the entertainment capital of the South, is within a day's drive.

# CIRCLE Z RANCH

## Patagonia, Arizona

Circle Z Ranch is the southernmost ranch in Arizona, just 15 miles from the Mexican border. It is also the oldest continuously operating guest ranch in Arizona, having welcomed dudes since 1926. The ranch is something of an aviary super highway for migrating birds from Central America, and astute bird-watchers may encounter any of fifteen species of hummingbirds! (Special feeders are scattered around the ranch grounds to help coax the birds within easy seeing range of guests.)

The ranch is nestled in the foothills of the Santa Rita mountain range, which pro-vide a scenic backdrop to this historic high-desert ranch. Guests get a sense of stepping back in time, as this region hasn't changed much since the days when Apache Indians and Spanish conquistadors rode these hills. One reason the area was consid-ered vital to both groups is Sonoita Creek. Bordered on both sides by ancient cotton-wood trees, the waterway forms a desert oasis. Much of the land surrounding the 5,000-acre spread has been set aside for preservation: The ranch is rimmed by the Coronado National Forest, a Nature Conser-vancy preserve, a state park, and several large cattle ranches.

Although the Circle Z is an actual work-ing cattle ranch, the focus of its managers, Jerry and Nancy Holmes, is clearly on their guests. Attention to meeting the needs and expectations of visitors is one reason why more than 70 percent of the Circle Z guests are return customers.

Riding is the main emphasis of the activi-ties at Circle Z. The horses here are gentle and well-bred, and the majority are born, raised, and trained right on the ranch. Care-ful attention is paid to matching horse to rider, and in most cases, once you've been assigned a horse and gotten familiar with it, you remain paired with that mount for the remainder of your stay. Riders take part in the groom-ing and saddling of the horses, giv-ing them extra opportunity to get to know and bond with the animals. Experienced wranglers lead small groups of riders on twice-daily rides. More experienced riders may opt for a ground-covering excursion, whereas beginners participate in a slower-paced tour. It's your option to ride in the morning, the afternoon, or both. In January, there is a special session called Ardent Rider's Month, dedicated to individuals wanting ample saddle time and extra emphasis on riding technique.

A seemingly endless network of trails provides a great deal of scenic variety. One day, you may find yourself exploring color-ful red-rock canyons; the next day's ride may take you through rugged mountain terrain, or you might explore the gentle, rolling range land or take a ride along the ever-flowing Sonoita Creek. No matter where on the ranch you go, you're likely to encounter a variety of native flora and fauna. The land here is populated by stands of cacti and pine forests and is home to a variety of desert and woodlands animals—deer, wild boar, bobcats, rabbits, quail, and coatimundi (a small tree mammal similar to a raccoon)—that thrive in this environment. Be sure to take along a pair of binoculars.

If some of the scenery seems strangely familiar to you, that may be because the Circle Z has been a favorite location for sev-eral Hollywood films, including the John Wayne films *Red River* and *Broken Lance,* and for the television series *Gunsmoke*.

Although the ranch cocktail hour is strictly BYOB, you may be invited to partake of a "saloon ride" to historic Patagonia, where you can enjoy a glimpse of the West as it once was. Just remember, you've got to ride home at the end of the day!

For the saddle sore, there are a number of other recreational choices including tennis, swimming in the heated outdoor pool, fishing in Lake Patagonia, and an 18-hole championship golf course nearby. Children will find plenty of amusements, too: Ping-Pong, pool, shuffleboard, horseshoes, basketball, and their own favorite meeting place, the Kid's Cantina. Although no specific children's programs are held at the Circle Z, children over age five can ride with their parents. The ranch has no nursery, however.

Overall, the Circle Z is a great choice for people who want to spend their vacation enjoying great desert scenery and wild animals, warm, sunny weather, and a lot of quality time in the saddle.

## Circle Z Ranch

P.O. Box 194
Patagonia, AZ 85624
Phone: (888) 854–2525
Fax: (520) 394–2058
E-mail: info@circlez.com
Web site: www.circlez.com

**Managers:** Jan and Al Gotland

**Accommodations:** 7 adobe cottages provide lodging for 40 guests; 27 separate rooms, each with its own bathroom. A variety of bed sizes and arrangements provide flexibility for guests. Wood-floored rooms open to porches or patios.

**Meals:** The emphasis here is on healthy foods rather than the typically heavy guest-ranch fare. Fresh vegetables and homemade breads and desserts complement main courses such as mesquite-grilled steaks and regional southwestern dishes. Meals are served in the dining room or patio of the main lodge, affording a beautiful panoramic view of the nearby hills.

**Activities:** Riding on an endless variety of trails is the outstanding feature at the Circle Z. Twice-daily rides except Sundays, when rides go out only on holidays. Experienced and friendly wranglers lead small groups of riders. You may choose rides for the morning, afternoon, or both at the pace with which you are most comfortable. Unstructured activities include birding and nature hikes. Side trips to nearby Patagonia, ghost towns, old mining sites, the Old West tourist towns of Tombstone and Bisbee, and the border shopping town of Nogales can be arranged. Fishing in Lake Patagonia. Golf at an 18-hole course in Patagonia.

**Amenities:** Outdoor heated pool, all-weather tennis court, recreation room, Kid's Cantina, adult piano lounge, and a variety of table games and outdoor games—pool, Ping-Pong, shuffleboard, basketball, horseshoes.

**Special Programs:** Ardent Riders Month in January provides a special opportunity for equestrians. No specific children's programs, although children are welcome. Weekly overnight pack trips.

**Rates:** $$–$$$ American Plan. Reduced rates for preteens and toddlers under 5. Off-season discounts.

**Credit Cards:** None. Personal checks accepted.

**Season:** November to May

**Getting There:** Nearest major airport is Tucson International, also Nogales International in Mexico. Located off Highway 82, 60 miles south of Tucson and 15 miles north of the Mexico/U.S. border.

**What's Nearby:** Old West towns of Tombstone and Bisbee. Mining ruins, artisan village, ghost towns, Spanish mission, and border shopping in Nogales. The Nature Conservancy maintains a preserve adjacent to the ranch.

# GRAND CANYON
# BAR 10 RANCH

## Wash, Arizona

Imagine not only being able to enjoy a gratifying ranch vacation, but being able to do so on the rim of one of the world's greatest natural wonders, the Grand Canyon. That, in a nutshell, summarizes the Bar 10 Ranch experience.

The Bar 10 may qualify as one of the most remote ranches in the "lower 48": it's an 80-mile trip from St. George, Utah, the nearest sizable town, down a dirt road to this northern Arizona desert oasis. Most visitors fly in, and the Bar 10 originally got into the dude-ranch business as an adjunct to its main business: providing air service to Grand Canyon visitors.

For those of you who don't mind spending time off the main highway, the seclusion of the Bar 10 Ranch may be just your

style. The ranch serves as a jumping-off point and a destination for excursions into America's mightiest canyon. A typical guest will opt to take a scenic rafting trip down the Grand or to explore the chasm via a helicopter ride. Pack trips are another option. Regardless of the mode of transportation, nobody misses the opportunity to get an up-close-and-personal view.

Back on the ranch, however, one can find more than enough activities to fill the time. In addition to daily horseback rides, guests can participate in numerous activities that include skeet shooting, horseshoes, volleyball, and desert hiking. In the evenings, the ranch entertainment includes country/western entertainers (complete with dance-hall girls) and boisterous con-

## HOME ON THE RANGE

The Bar 10 is hidden in a side canyon of the Grand Canyon known as Whitmore Wash. Explorer John Wesley Powell, the namesake of Lake Powell, was the first man to negotiate the Colorado River through the Grand Canyon. Powell came across the wash in the 1870s. He learned from an early Mormon mercenary that it had been the site of a massacre involving three Anglos who'd gone awry of the local Native Americans. One of those would-be settlers was James Whitmore, whose memory was honored by Powell when he gave the area the name Whitmore Wash. Sandwiched between the Utah border and the north rim of the Grand Canyon, which isolates the land from the rest of that state, the stretch of land here came to be known as the "Arizona Strip."

The Heaton family's rich history on the Arizona Strip runs deep. Their story begins in the late 1800s, when an itinerant cowhand named George Lytle was assigned the task of overseeing the Mormon Church's cattle-ranching operations here. Lytle's daughter married Gilbert Heaton, whose father had walked all the way from Illinois seeking a new life out west. Gilbert and his bride settled in southeastern Nevada, but the pull of the Arizona strip proved strong. Their son, Tony, moved to St. George and fell in love with a fellow schoolteacher named Ruby. Ranching ran deep in both of their souls, and eventually they returned to found the Bar 10 in the very place where the Heaton family had laid down roots a half century before.

versation around the large fireplace "pit."

A unique feature of the ranch is the sleeping arrangements: In addition to dormitory-style lodging in the six large sleeping rooms of the main lodge, guests can also choose to sleep out under the cover of their very own Conestoga wagon! A total of thirteen wagons provide an unusual experience that will have folks back home marveling in disbelief. Each wagon sleeps two adults.

Because so many of the guests use the Bar 10 as a jumping-off or pickup point for Grand Canyon trips, the guest list is highly variable. Although extended stays are common, it is also possible to make your stay an overnighter, one that will leave you rested, refreshed, and ready to tackle the gorge. The ranch will make all arrangements for extended horse pack trips, river-rafting excursions lasting from three to nineteen days, and aerial tours of the region.

But the Bar 10 is far more than a way station for eager adventurers; it is a real working ranch with close to 60,000 acres of

**Grand Canyon Bar 10 Ranch**
P.O. Box 910088
St. George, UT 84791
Phone: (800) 582–4139; (435) 628–4010
Fax: (435) 628–5124
E-mail: reservations@bar10.com
Web site: www.bar10.com

**Owners/Managers:** Tony and Ruby Heaton

**Accommodations:** Choose from bunkhouse-style rooms (4 persons to a room) or opt for the privacy and uniqueness of sleeping in the West's original mobile home—a Conestoga Wagon! The Bar 10 can accommodate 45 to 60 guests, with larger groups able to participate in day tours.

**Meals:** Meals are served buffet style. Dinner is prepared in Dutch ovens. A typical dinner consists of tender beef, potatoes, fresh vegetables, rolls, and a homemade dessert. A plentiful sandwich bar and "cowboy breakfast" of eggs, sausages, toast, etc., keep the troops fueled for the day's activities. No alcoholic beverages are served; guests may bring their own, however.

**Activities:** Active outdoor action is the essence of the Bar 10 experience. Tour packages and ranch activities include white-water rafting on the Colorado River, cattle drives, horseback rides, ATV treks, horseback pack trips, and scenic flights in the Grand Canyon region. On the ranch, guests enjoy evening shows, skeet shooting, hiking, and a variety of recreational sports.

**Amenities:** Able to host conference groups and engage participants in challenging outdoor activities. The main ranch includes The Trading Post, a gift shop where guests can find such necessary items as sunscreen and river supplies, as well as the usual T-shirts, snacks, and souvenir items. The ranch serves as an important aviation destination in the area and has the facilities to refuel and provide service for light aircraft.

**Special Programs:** Numerous different packages allow guests to custom-tailor their own adventure. Tour packages include river rafting, ATV trekking, horseback riding, horse pack trips, and more. No specific children's programs, although children may participate in most activities (kids under 8 are discouraged from river rafting, however).

**Rates:** $$$ American Plan, plus a la carte activities for day guests. Packages all-inclusive except for airfare and helicopter tours. Inquire about package rates, off-season rates.

**Credit Cards:** VISA, MasterCard

**Season:** Open May through April

**Getting There:** Most guests fly in on small chartered planes or helicopters. The ranch reservationist will help arrange travel from Las Vegas, Nevada, a 50-minute flight one way, or the Bar 10 can provide an interpretive van tour from either St. George, Utah, or Las Vegas. Driving, which involves a 2½-hour, 80-mile drive over dirt roads from St. George, is not recommended for those travelers without high-clearance, 4-wheel-drive vehicles.

**What's Nearby:** Most trips originate in Las Vegas, the entertainment capital of the West. The main draw is, of course, the Grand Canyon.

territory that is home to 400 head of Bar 10 cattle. When not managing ranch affairs, owners Tony and Ruby Heaton and their children can inform guests on the day-to-day travails and triumphs of actual working cattle ranchers. If you wish to play cowboy, you can take part in scheduled cattle gatherings. If motorized transportation is more your preference, the ranch also offers ATV trips lasting from two hours to an entire day.

In the evenings, staff members provide homegrown entertainment in the form of a patriotic Wild West show that includes singing, dancing, country fiddlin', humorous cowboy poetry, even a gunfight. A slide show that recounts the historic develop-ment of the Bar 10 is another favored part of the evening festivities.

Given the ranch's remote location, nearly all guests opt to arrive and depart in small aircraft. When planning your trip, the Heatons can advise you on how best to coordinate your travel. The ranch has its own airstrip, suitable for light planes and helicopters, most of which fly out of Las Vegas. For some guests, getting to this remote and secluded ranch is an adventure all its own!

If serenity and proximity to the Grand Canyon coupled with plenty of adventure sound like your kind of vacation, your only choice is the Grand Canyon Bar 10 Ranch.

# TANQUE VERDE RANCH

## Tucson, Arizona

Tanque Verde Ranch ranks among the most luxurious resort destinations in Arizona, making it the ideal spot for those who prefer being pampered to "roughing it." Located in the upper Sonoran Desert on the outskirts of Tucson, Tanque Verde benefits from striking views of the Rincon Mountains and the huge and majestic saguaro cactus indigenous to this region of the Southwest. The 640-acre ranch is bordered by Coronado National Forest land and by the Saguaro National Park, affording guests an unlimited opportunity for exploration.

There are any number of ways to explore this unique and fascinating natural landscape during your visit. The ranch offers miles of hiking and mountain-biking trails and features one of the largest horse herds of any Arizona guest ranch. Rides go out daily, and individuals may choose easygoing walking tours for beginners or loping trail rides for the more experienced. Other "specialty" rides are also available, including breakfast rides to the Old Homestead, half-day picnic rides that stop in a scenic grove of trees, and riding lessons that focus on improving the skills of beginners and advanced riders alike.

For those persons who prefer mounts of a more mechanical sort, the ranch offers Specialized mountain bikes, riding helmets, and gloves. The mountain-bike excursions are led by experienced biking guides who will teach you the essentials of negotiating rough terrain in safety.

Slower paced hikes are the best way to become familiar with the fascinating Sonoran Desert environment. Staff naturalists lead guided nature walks, giving people an up-close-and-personal tour of the native flora and fauna. And if your hike doesn't reveal all of the desert creatures you'd hoped to see, you can continue your education at the ranch nature center, where many live animals are on display.

Back on the ranch, you can find facilities that rival those of most any posh resort. Tanque Verde has five Omni artificial turf tennis courts (one of them lighted for evening play) and a staff pro to help you hone your serve and volley. You can also get in a game of pickup basketball or volleyball or spend the afternoon wetting your line in a catch-and-release pond. Fitness buffs will appreciate the extensive spa facilities, which include an indoor and an outdoor pool, sauna, whirlpool baths, and fitness room.

Don't worry about bringing a bunch of extra sports equipment: Everything you need will be provided by the ranch. And did we mention golf? Guests at Tanque Verde can tee up at one of several nearby courses for an additional fee.

Although the wide variety of activities certainly encourages one to be active, inevitably you'll want to just kick back and relax. You may wish to request an in-room massage by a staff massage therapist (at an extra charge, of course) or simply relax on the broad veranda of the ranch's main lodge with a fine glass of wine (Tanque Verde maintains an extensively stocked wine cellar, along with an assortment of domestic and imported beers).

In the evenings, you can become engrossed in the crystal-clear night sky while learning the constellations with a guest astronomer or listen to a lecture by one of the staff naturalist/historians. There are also country-dancing parties and a bingo night.

Kids aren't excluded from the action, as Tanque Verde offers one of the most complete supervised children's programs of any guest ranch in the country. Children from ages four to six make up the "Buckaroos" program, whereas those aged seven to eleven make up the Wrangler Kids. The younger group participates in supervised horse riding in an arena setting, while the older kids gain proficiency on more advanced rides and on the trail. Children are also led on other activities that include tennis, swimming, nature programs, arts and crafts, and games.

## Tanque Verde Ranch
14301 East Speedway
Tucson, AZ 85748
Phone: (800) 234–DUDE; (520) 296–6275
Fax: (520) 721–9426
E-mail: dude@tvgr.com
Web site: www.tvgr.com

**Owners:** The Cote Family

**Accommodations:** 74 rooms and suites, fully air-conditioned, each with telephones and full private bathrooms. Most have fireplaces and patios. Desert and mountain views. Rates vary according to room size. Smaller standard rooms with one queen-sized bed or two twins are perfect for two people. Mid-priced rooms are larger, generally with two queen-sized beds and a shared courtyard, but no fireplace. Large deluxe rooms have two queen-sized beds or a king, fireplaces, and private patios, some of which have sitting areas with sofa sleepers. There are also 1-bedroom suites, all with fireplaces and patios.

**Meals:** Chef Mark Shelton, who was recently voted Arizona chef of the year, oversees the preparation of the Tanque Verde kitchen. Meals go well beyond standard ranch fare and are more on a par with a luxury resort hotel. Guests can enjoy weekly evening cookouts and barbecue rides, fully catered. Most other dining takes place in the main dining room overlooking the outdoor pool and the Rincon Mountains. Breakfast includes typical menu items plus a buffet of chilled juices, fresh fruits, yogurts, breakfast breads, and cereals. Examples from the dinner menu include carved roast prime ribs of beef au jus, game hens tandoori, poached filet of fresh salmon with lemon and tartar sauce, vegetable-filled egg rolls, fresh steamed asparagus spears, country mashed potatoes with chives, and French onion soup. Drinks are served in The Doghouse Saloon, with wine and beer available at all meals.

**Activities:** With 120 horses, Tanque Verde has one of the largest guest strings in the state. Trail rides are divided into slow and fast rides; children ride in their own groups, although adults have the option of joining them. Advanced riding lessons available.

Mountain biking is another favorite activity, and the ranch provides all bikes, gear, and guides. Tennis with an on-site pro, swimming, fishing, hiking with resident naturalists, stargazing with an astronomer, spa services, basketball, volleyball, and golfing off-site at select Tucson courses.

**Amenities:** Historic ranch property dating from the 1860s. Spanish-style architecture. Natural history museum. Conference facility with 6,800 feet of meeting space. Gift shop. Tennis courts, outdoor and indoor pools, spa with exercise room, whirlpool baths, and saunas. Most rooms features "kiva" style fireplaces and patios.

**Special Programs:** Comprehensive supervised kid's program (ages 7–12) focusing on introduction to horseback riding, games, recreational activities. Pack trips available certain times of the year (inquire for dates).

**Rates:** $$$ American Plan. Rates vary according to season and room size.

**Credit Cards:** VISA, MasterCard, Discover, American Express

**Season:** Year-round

**Getting There:** Easy, quick access to Tucson International via Speedway Road. Located 15 miles east of the city on Speedway. Call to arrange shuttle service.

**What's Nearby:** Saguaro National Park, downtown Tucson.

# ALISAL GUEST RANCH RESORT

## Solvang, California

Central California's ranching traditions date back to the earliest days of Spanish settlement. And although the heyday of big-spread cattle ranching has largely passed, the 10,000-acre Alisal Guest Ranch is a stalwart throwback to that bygone era. The rooms lack telephones and television sets, but that doesn't mean that California's premier guest ranch is lacking in creature comforts. Far from it. This is a full-service resort and conference center that stands up against some of the great resort properties throughout the world.

Two 72-par championship golf courses have been carved out of the rugged Santa Ynez Mountains and carefully tendered and developed to provide golfers an especially scenic playing experience. A shaped pool, hot tub, and brick-red patio (complete with cabanas) offer the perfect place to relax outdoors. A 100-acre lake is ideal for anglers, and one can get fly-casting lessons from experienced staff. The lake is also a good place to take a sail or paddle a canoe or kayak or try sailboarding. The Alisal maintains its own flotilla of paddleboats and sailing craft as well as a few small outboard-motor-powered boats. The Alisal is further blessed with an abundance of wildlife. Equipped with a sighting lens and *Alisal Field Guidebook,* you can partake of a guided nature hike to the southern edge of the lake, on a trail rich with flora and fauna. Teeming with a variety of birds, deer, and wildlife, these nature walks are favorites

with photographers. For the gustatory explorer, there's a winery tour that visits up to twenty-five of the region's exceptional vintners.

Horseback riding, of course, is at the center of the activities here. Each day is jam-packed with scheduled trail rides, and there's even an early-morning kids' ride for children aged seven to twelve. The ranch maintains a mixed-breed herd of one hundred equines, so finding one suitable to one's riding skills is never a problem. A maximum of six people per riding group ensures personalized attention from the Alisal's expert guides. Be sure to take an early morning breakfast ride to Adobe Camp, where you'll be greeted with hot cakes on a griddle and a singing cowboy!

Rodeo action is a popular Alisal tradition, and guests can participate in a slate of activities including team penning, cattle sorting, pole bending, and steer "branding" (presumably without the hot irons). You'll also enjoy a quick-draw shooting demonstration or exhibitions by the rodeo-savvy Alisal wranglers.

In addition to serving individual guests, the Alisal hosts conference groups, providing activities and planning for golfing and tennis tournaments, fishing derbies, and team-building outings. If you are looking for a unique corporate or small-business getaway, the Alisal's conference advisers will go out of their way to satisfy your group's every need.

## Alisal Guest Ranch and Resort

1054 Alisal Road
Solvang, CA 93463
Phone: (800) 4–ALISAL; (805) 688–6411
Fax: (805) 688–2510
E-mail: sales@alisal.com
Web site: www.alisal.com

**Manager:** David Lautensack

**Accommodations:** 150–250 guests (150 conference attendees); 73 modern cottages ranging from 1-room studios to two-room suites, each with private covered porches. All include fireplaces and refrigerators. Daily maid service and nightly turndown service. No phones or television sets in rooms but available in public areas.

**Meals:** The Alisal's proximity to California's wine country and the sophistication of California diners are reflected in the care taken in food preparation and service. Although the menu varies daily depending on the availability of local and seasonal foods, one can expect meals to satisfy a gourmand replete with fresh seafood, aged and tender meats, fresh vegetables, and fruits. In summer, lunch is served poolside, and luncheon facilities are also available at golf clubhouses. An exceptional wine menu complements the chef-prepared meals.

**Activities:** 2-hour trail rides go out twice daily and are separated by ability. Advanced riders may schedule longer excursions, and arena riding instruction is available to riders of all levels. Biweekly breakfast rides and weekly rodeo competition for guests. Private lake suitable for fishing, boating, and windsurfing. Equipment available. 2 golf courses, the private Ranch Course and the public River Course, offer par-72 tournament-quality layouts with PGA-certified professionals available for instruction. Tennis, nature hikes, mountain biking, volleyball, game room, billiards, and outdoor recreational facilities.

**Amenities:** Heated outdoor pool and whirlpool; 7 tennis courts and tennis pro shop; 2 championship golf courses, clubhouse, and pro shop; 90-acre private lake; ranch rodeo arena; adults-only library; fine dining facilities (evening attire required for dinner); Oak Room Lounge with stone fireplace and comfy leather lounge chairs, nightly dancing, cocktail service, and live music.

**Special Programs:** Kid-friendly facilities include a year-round petting zoo and kid-specific riding lessons. Kids' program includes daily arts and crafts instruction, games, and evening entertainment. Special holiday events such as the Easter Egg Hunt and a visit from Santa Claus at Christmas. Extensive conference facilities (including 6,000-square-feet conference space) and special group activities and sports tournaments available. Consult with the Alisal conference planner when making plans.

**Rates:** $$$$ Includes room, breakfast, and dinner. Activities sold individually and as seasonal "activity packages." Two-night minimum stay.

**Credit Cards:** VISA, MasterCard, American Express, Diner's Club

**Season:** Year-round

**Getting There:** Commercial airline service to Santa Barbara, 35 miles from ranch. Also, Los Angeles International, 2½ hours by car. Inquire about ground transportation to and from the Santa Barbara Airport.

**What's Nearby:** Local wineries, shopping, art galleries, and the historic Solvang Danish Community.

# DRAKESBAD GUEST RANCH

## Chester, California

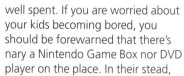

Do you have fond memories of a particularly special childhood camping trip? If so, the things you remember most were probably the simple ones: catching your first fish, sleeping under the stars, or spying a doe and her fawn as they grazed. Drakesbad Guest Ranch is the kind of place where memories like these are made. The ranch, which is more than a century old, is located in a place that is about as off-the-beaten path as you can get in the most populous state in the West.

Hidden away in a remote corner of Lassen Volcanic National Park, Drakesbad appeals simply for its simplicity. The ranch was founded by E. R. Drake, who sold the property to the Sifford family in 1900. (They named it Drakesbad for the warm waters fed by natural hot springs). At present, the ranch is operated by a concessionaire and is part of the National Parks System. Not much has changed since its creation—kerosene lamps still provide most of the ambient lighting, and the outdoor pool is still heated by the hot-springs waters.

The pace here is similarly simple, with an unstructured schedule that allows guests plenty of time to form their own explorations or simply slow down and revel in the tranquility and peacefulness of this particularly scenic mountain valley. Activities are in keeping with the "old-timey" feel of the place: horseback riding, fishing, and simple outdoor recreations such as volleyball, badminton, horseshoes, croquet, and hiking.

Drakesbad is best suited to those who wish to commune with nature, who don't need constant action and activity to find contentment, and who think that spending an hour staring at a starry sky is an hour well spent. If you are worried about your kids becoming bored, you should be forewarned that there's nary a Nintendo Game Box nor DVD player on the place. In their stead, however, is a supervised kids' program for children under the age of twelve. The program runs three days a week and includes enough activities to satisfy all but the most jaded mall-going preteens. In all likelihood, your kids will find the hiatus from the typical multiplex suburban habitat to be a wonderful growing experience.

Guests here tend to create their own nightly entertainment, too. Bring along a few good books, take time out to play some board games, and enjoy the camaraderie of an outdoor campfire. The musically inclined might want to pack along a guitar or mouth organ and stage an impromptu sing-along.

Situated at an altitude of 5,700 feet, the ranch is surrounded by stands of pine trees and aspen groves. Wildflowers abound in spring, and fall brings a particularly colorful display. Guests are advised to pack carefully, as cool weather and rainstorms are not uncommon, even during the height of summer. You'll be pleased to know that the ranch is "green certified" and maintains a rigorous program of energy conservation and resource recycling.

Overall, this historic property provides the perfect environment for a relaxing vacation unencumbered by the trappings of modern living. It harkens back to a time when life was simpler and compels its guests to clear their own minds and focus on the important things—family, friends, and the awesome beauty of unspoiled nature. Really, what more could one want?

## Drakesbad Guest Ranch

Lassan Volcanic Natural Park
Warner Valley Road
Chester, CA 96020
Alternative (year-round) address:
2150 Main Street, Suite 5
Red Bluff, CA 96080
Phone: (530) 529–1512 ext. 120
Fax: (530) 529–4511
Web site: www.drakesbad.com

**Managers:** Ed and Billie Fiebiger

**Accommodations:** Guest capacity, 75. 13 cabins, 6 lodge rooms, some with full baths, others with half baths (a bathhouse is provided). Rooms are furnished with attractive pine furniture and have hardwood floors. Electricity is limited; kerosene lamps provide a warm, homey, ambience and authentic Old West feel. Daily maid service provided.

**Meals:** Breakfast and dinner served in the main dining hall, with either a midday buffet meal or sack lunch on the trail. Menu varies according to seasonal and local availability. Emphasis is on nutritious foods, simply but carefully prepared. Special diets accommodated with advance notification. Weekly cookouts feature steaks, ribs, and hamburgers and hot dogs for children.

**Activities:** Horseback riding is available on a daily basis: Guests must make reservations the night before the ride. Length depends on the individual's ambitions: short, 2-hour rides or all-day excursions. All rides are conducted at a walk; no "fast" rides are offered. Lake fishing, hiking, and swimming in the naturally heated hot-springs pool make up the bulk of the activities. This is a ranch best suited to the relaxation minded and those wishing to spend unstructured time amid a tranquil wilderness.

**Amenities:** A rustic, turn-of-the-century ranch house best appreciated for its sparcity of amenities. Electricity is used sparingly, with kerosene lanterns and few electrical appliances or gadgets. Spring-fed pool and naturally heated spring water bathing. Simple but comfortable bedrooms. Modest collection of books and games are provided for guests' entertainment.

**Special Programs:** Supervised children's program for kids ages 6 to 12 available 3 days per week.

**Rates:** $$ American Plan prices include lodging and 3 daily meals; horseback riding extra. Due to limited space and high demand, guests must book their trips months in advance. Make initial inquiries in February in order to book summer dates. Reduced rates for children 2 to 11. Prices slightly higher for "bungalow" cabins and rooms with private baths.

**Credit Cards:** VISA, MasterCard. Personal checks accepted.

**Season:** Early June to October

**Getting There:** Ranch is located 120 miles south of Redding on State Highway 36 in Chester. Commercial airline service to Reno, Redding, or Sacramento.

**What's Nearby:** Red Bluff, a charming community with a renovated downtown historic district, antiques shops, and dining. Other attractions include Boiling Springs Lake, Devil's Kitchen, and the Pacific Crest Trail.

# HOWARD CREEK RANCH
## Westport, California

While most of the ranches featured in this book cater to, and even emphasize, family vacations with children, the Howard Creek Ranch Inn has distinguished itself as a romantic getaway for adults. "This is one of the most romantic places on the planet!" wrote a reviewer in the *San Francisco Chronicle*.

Indeed, as a romantic destination, its location on the scenic Mendocino Coast of northern California is idyllic, with its craggy cliffs, sandy beaches, and high bluffs offering views of the largely unspoiled shoreline. This is the place for anyone who has ever dreamed of riding free alongside crashing ocean waves or who is seeking the perfect place to propose marriage.

Howard Creek Ranch has been in existence since 1867, when the pioneering Howard family homesteaded a substantial land grant on California's lonely northern coast. The original ranch was supported by sheep, cattle, and a blacksmith shop. The current owners, Charles and Sally Grigg, have preserved and improved many of the oldest buildings, earning the ranch a nomination for the National Historic Register by Mendocino County. The original farmhouse (circa 1871) is a showcase for antiques, and each room is uniquely themed and painstakingly decorated with lush redwood trim, carefully matched color themes, and quirky antiques and contemporary furnishings that support the essential "feel" of each room.

The overall impression is one of an utterly charming turn-of-the-century farm, augmented by well-tended flower gardens and a lush coastal landscape (a stark contrast to the arid guest ranches typical of the American West). A swinging bridge spans Howard Creek, which flows to the Pacific just 200 hundred yards away. The beach is wild and rugged, full of rough-hewn boulders and brimming with tide pools.

The activities here are leisurely as opposed to rigorous: strolling the gardens, inspecting the tide pools, whale-watching, or swimming easy laps in the solar-heated swimming pool, followed by a relaxing massage. A trip to Medocino, one of California's more picturesque towns, is almost mandatory, as is a visit to the fabulous vineyards and wineries that have made northern California a world leader in quality wines.

Howard Creek Ranch offers a surprisingly accomplished and complete riding program, thanks to instructor Lari Shea, winner of the prestigious Tevis Cup 100-mile Endurance Race. Riders can explore the coastal highlands, visit a local cattle ranch, or opt for that once-in-a-lifetime opportunity to ride on a lovely sandy beach. In addition to standard western breeds, Appaloosas and quarter horses, Shea maintains a group of Russian-bred Arabian horses, a preferred breed for serious endurance enthusiasts. These sweet-faced and beautiful horses make for impressive mounts and outstanding photographs. Both Western and English tack are available for riders.

Howard Creek Ranch is quite a departure from the standard Western guest ranch but an alternative that may be just what a romantically inclined couple desires. All in all, it is the perfect haven for lovers.

## Howard Creek Ranch

40501 North Highway One
P.O. Box 121
Westport, CA 95488
Phone: (707) 964–6725
Fax: (707) 964–1603
Web site: www.howardcreekranch.com

**Owners/Managers:** Sally and Charles Grigg

**Accommodations:** Capacity, 22. Lodging varies from guest rooms and suites in the Old World style ranch house and the artistically renovated Carriage House to individual and secluded cabins, some with meadow views and two with an ocean view. Decor reflects an early California-inspired influence, with antiques and lovely embellishments. Some rooms have decks, microwave ovens, televisions with VCRs, and refrigerators. Most are trimmed with redwood, and most have glass-doored wood stoves. Renovation of the historic ranch buildings continues to be an ongoing project, with Charles (Sunny), a master craftsman, doing all the work using old-growth redwood.

**Meals:** As a bed and breakfast, the ranch serves only that meal. Breakfast is a hearty farm meal with fresh juice, omelets, bacon, sausage, hot cakes, fried potatoes, grits, and baked apples with granola and whipped cream. Coffee is strong and early. Tea is available any time. Menus change daily. Vegetarians gladly accommodated.

The staff will be glad to assist you in making dining plans and can recommend a broad spectrum of excellent restaurants in the Mendocino area.

**Activities:** Mendocino County is a hiker's paradise, with miles of shoreline and stands of the huge and stately redwoods indigenous to the area. The staff at Howard Creek will gladly assist you in planning hikes and provide directions to popular trail heads, or you can simply spend your time exploring the 60-acre ranch or strolling the shore. Horseback riding is provided by Lari Shea, who operates the concession on an "a la carte" basis. Be sure to make reservations. Seasonal whale-watching, bird-watching, tidal-pool exploration, swimming in the solar-heated pool, hot tubbing, wine-country tours, and relaxation round out the list of activities.

**Amenities:** The ranch offers farm animals, award-winning gardens, fireplaces/wood stoves, a 75-foot swinging footbridge over Howard Creek, a hot tub, sauna, and a German masseuse by appointment. Accommodations include cabins, suites, and rooms furnished with antiques, large comfortable beds, and handmade quilts and have views of the ocean, mountains, creek, or gardens.

**Special Programs:** No children's programs or other special programs, and visits with children are not emphasized.

**Rates:** $–$$ European Plan. Horseback riding is separate, as are other activities. Price varies by accommodations. Reduced winter rates available.

**Credit Cards:** VISA, MasterCard, American Express

**Season:** Year-round

**Getting There:** The ranch is located 3 miles north of Westport, on State Highway 1. Nearest commercial airport is in San Francisco, 150 miles south. Private car or rental necessary.

**What's Nearby:** Mendocino, with quaint shops and excellent restaurants, art galleries, theater performances, and concerts; Sinkyone Wilderness (the Lost Coast), 2 miles north, offers excellent hiking; the redwood forest just a few miles north of the ranch is an excellent spot for a picnic.

# HUNEWILL CIRCLE H GUEST RANCH

## Bridgeport, California

Hunewill's Circle H takes one back to the original concept of the western guest ranch: a working ranch whose owners invite "dudes" to share in their rural lifestyle. If your goal is to experience the life of a cowboy (with or without all the strenuous work that goes with it), the Hunewill Circle H Guest Ranch is your kind of place.

Hunewill Guest Ranch is located just east of Yosemite National Park, so plan on staying an extra day to explore that national treasure. The ranch itself is situated in a broad, green valley in the very heart of the rugged Sierra Nevada. The 26,000-acre working cattle ranch is family owned and operated by the Hunewills, the actual descendants of the original family that homesteaded the ranch in 1861. The Hunewills began hosting guests in the 1930s, but they never lost sight of the land's original purpose. Presently the Hunewill Ranch supports a herd of 1,200 cows and 120 horses, as well as sheep, llamas, and four pigs.

As a true working ranch, the emphasis here is on riding and cattle work, which the guests are welcome to participate in as they wish. One need not stick solely to well-trodden trails: With its huge acreage, lush meadows, and timbered woodlands, the ranch invites guests to range free and wide. It is, in short, a horseman's paradise. Horses are carefully chosen to match riders' abilities (guests may also bring their own), and groups are similarly separated so that inexperienced riders can take it slow and easy, while seasoned riders can trot, lope, and canter to their heart's content.

A favorite for riders of all abilities is an early-morning breakfast ride on Robinson Creek. Those who want to spend lots of time in the saddle can take part in an all-day ride to the fringes of Yosemite National Park and the Hoover Wilderness. Anyone not acquainted with ranching will likely be fascinated just watching as young foals and yearlings are being gentled in the corral or seeing the herd of saddle horses come thundering into sight during the daily morning roundup.

Activities are traditional and, for the most part, homespun: There's a talent night, family dance night, barbecues on the creek, and fishing in the many creeks and ponds of the adjacent Toiyabe National Forest and on the ranch itself.

The Hunewills are avid fly fishermen and have been in the process of revitalizing trout habitat on the ranch. They recently opened their "ice pond" to anglers. This very special fishing hole is available by reservation only and at additional cost, and only for fly fishing with appropriate equipment. Anglers who want to experience true catch-and-release trout fishing in a pristine lake environment will definitely want to inquire about this opportunity.

Given its age and location, it is not surprising that a distinct Victorian flavor characterizes the ranch buildings. The main lodge is a stately Victorian constructed in 1880; guests are housed in simple but clean white duplex cottages, each with private baths, porches, and through-doors for large families.

Overall, the Hunewill is a great place to enjoy a real working cattle ranch and to share time with a friendly and authentic western family whose roots in this beautiful place go back six generations. So, pull on your boots and jeans, set your hat low on your head, and get ready for the time of your life, cowboy.

## Hunewill Circle H Guest Ranch

(winter) 200 Hunewill Lane
Wellington, NV 89444
Phone: (775) 465–2201
(summer) P.O. Box 368
Bridgeport, CA 93517
Phone: (760) 932–7710
E-mail: hunewillranch@tele-net.net
Web site: www.hunewillranch.com

**Owners/Managers:** The Hunewill Family

**Accommodations:** Capacity, 45. Duplex cabins, each unit with 2 rooms, carpeting, electric or gas heat, private bathroom, and porch.

**Meals:** 3 meals served daily. Family-style dining features traditional western dishes. Twice-weekly outdoor barbecue.

**Activities:** The ranch program is centered on horseback riding. Rides go out in the morning and afternoon, with riders divided into groups of beginning, intermediate, and advanced riders. Most of the rides take place in large, open meadows. Guests may be invited to help out with cattle chores, such as moving cattle between pastures. Hayrides, roping lessons, and weekly "gymkhana" (games on horseback). Other activities include fishing, nature walks, and recreational games. Cross-country skiing, snowshoeing or downhill skiing at June Mountain Ski Area in winter (guests must bring their own equipment).

**Amenities:** On-premises laundry facilities, masseuse by appointment.

**Special Programs:** No formal children's programs, although kids are welcome to join in all ranch activities. Children under age 6 may be "babysat" by a kids' counselor during adult riding times and also may be led on pony rides in the corral. For those who want to get hands-on ranch experience, the ranch offers several special events guaranteed to challenge advanced equestrians. Guests learn to rope, part out a cow, track a cow and not get lost, and explore "cow logic," among other things. Fall roundup, fall cattle work, fall cattle drive, fall color ride, and spring cattle work are some of the special events offered.

**Rates:** $$ American Plan, includes 3 meals per day, lodging, and horseback riding. Discounts for children under 12 and for nonriders. Off-season reduced rates, special package rates during fall and spring cattle work.

**Credit Cards:** None. Personal checks accepted. Advance deposit required.

**Season:** May through mid-September

**Getting There:** Commercial airlines fly into Reno-Tahoe International Airport in Reno, Nevada. The drive from Reno to Bridgeport, along the scenic eastern Sierra, takes approximately 2½ hours. The ranch does not provide transportation between Reno and Bridgeport. Rental cars and bus service, however, are available in Reno. Private planes can land at the Bridgeport Airport.

**What's Nearby:** Yosemite National Park, ghost towns, hot-springs spa, and the town of Bridgeport and the resort communities of Lake Tahoe and Mammoth Lakes (each within 1 hour's drive).

# RANKIN QUARTER CIRCLE U RANCH

## Caliente, California

Southern California brings to mind sandy beaches, the teeming metropolis of Los Angeles, and the world-famous Hollywood hills. But long before it became a cultural melting pot and mecca for "the beautiful people," southern California was ranching country. The Rankin Ranch came to be in those halcyon days, way back in the 1860s. In those times, if travelers happened by the ranch, they were welcome to stop in for a meal and a bed before moving on. That was simply the way of the West. Nowadays, the Rankin Ranch remains much as it has always been: a friendly place as ideal for human habitation as for the white-faced cattle brought here by Walker Rankin more than a century ago.

Located inland from all the hubbub of the coast, the Rankin Ranch is managed by Bill and Glenda Rankin, who continue the guest-ranching tradition started by Bill's mother, Helen, in the mid-1960s. The entire Rankin family is involved in the ranch, and that family familiarity overflows to the guests who come here to stay. It's not unusual for families to return year after year, their feeling of friendship growing with each visit.

As one might expect of a place where family roots go back many generations, the Rankins are big on family values. To make guests with children more comfortable, they offer a fully supervised kids' program that includes arts and crafts projects, games, swimming, nature hikes, and visits to the barn, where kids can befriend new-born calves. The ranch is an ideal place for family reunions and holiday celebrations, and the Rankin clan will do their utmost to make those special events memorable.

The Rankin spread takes in a full 30,000 acres, making the opportunities to ride and explore quite extensive. Riding is conducted at the walk, with the exception of occasional easy lopes in the open areas. The Rankins still maintain herds of cattle, and guests are sometimes invited along to help herd cattle amid the pastures or for other ranch work. Bear in mind, however, that this is neither an everyday or every week activity.

A typical ride will take you through meadows of wildflowers, past pine-scented forests, and through mountain trails past sweet-faced Hereford cattle grazing on green grasses made greener by under-ground springs and creeks. You'll have an opportunity to ride out and have lunch along the trail or join your young children for a shorter morning ride. Most of the twice-daily rides last an hour, but you'll also have the opportunity for more saddle time, particularly if others share your enthusiasm.

Besides riding, the list of activities is quite varied. Of course, many guests simply enjoy hiking and exploring the land, so far removed from the noise and congestion of modern life. Others bring their mountain bikes, which can be ridden for hours down the quite rural byways. A 7-mile loop trail that takes in the entire valley is a favorite excursion. For the less athletic, there's a stocked fishing pond (bring your own pole and tackle), and if you bring in a fat trout, the ranch cook will prepare it for you. There's also a hot tub for soaking sore muscles, a macadam tennis court to make them sore again. Of course, there's the obligatory hay-wagon ride, and twice-weekly outdoor barbecues with tip steaks, chicken, corn-on-the cob, beans, salad, and all the trimmings. Certainly, an event to look forward to!

**Rankin Ranch**
P.O. Box 36
Caliente, CA 93518
Phone: (661) 867–2511
Fax: (661) 867–0105
Web site: www.rankinranch.com

**Managers:** Bill and Glenda Rankin

**Accommodations:** Capacity 30–40. Guests stay in duplex-style cabins (14 rooms total), which can serve as individual units for couples and small families or as contiguous units for larger families. Cabins are air-conditioned, with wood-panel walls and carpeting. Most units have a queen, twin, and a daybed suitable for up to 5 individuals. A newly constructed cabin is somewhat roomier and more luxurious, with enough bed space for 8 people. All cabins are situated in private locations and are surrounded by beautiful oaks and pines.

**Meals:** 3 daily meals included in all-inclusive ranch price. Meals are held in the spacious Garden Room. The Rankins pride themselves on their family recipes and offer a cookbook for guests who wish re-create the ample meals back home. Weekly barbecue and hayride. Special lunch rides. Vegetarian diets served at guest's request.

**Activities:** Horseback rides twice daily, with longer day rides available by request. Tennis, recreational sports (volleyball, shuffleboard, Ping-Pong, and horseshoes). Fishing in a private stocked pond. Mountain bikers should bring their bikes. Guests may be invited to help in the cattle work. Evening entertainment includes dances, pool tournaments, hayrides, barbecue, a talent show, and horse races.

**Amenities:** Hot-tub bath, recreation room, heated swimming pool, tennis court, children's petting zoo, archery range, ranch library.

**Special Programs:** Extensive kids' program with supervised activities. Activities include arts and crafts, swimming, nature hikes, picnics, pony rides, and games. Program is for kids between the ages of 6 and 11; babysitting for infants available with advance notice.

**Rates:** $–$$$ American Plan. Children's rates. Rates vary depending on accommodations and season, with higher rates for the deluxe "Chimo" cabin lodging.

**Credit Cards:** VISA, MasterCard, American Express, Discover

**Season:** Late March through October

**Getting There:** Inquire for driving directions, either from LAX or from San Francisco or Sacramento.

**What's Nearby:** Gold Rush era town of Havilah; white-water rafting on the Kern River.

# AMERICAN SAFARI RANCH

## Fairplay, Colorado

Infamous as the home of Kyle, Cartman, and the rest of the *South Park* gang, the real South Park is in fact one of the most inviting and beautiful places in Colorado. Located in Colorado's high country, South Park is a broad, green agricultural valley flanked on either side by the jagged, snow-covered peaks of the San Juan and Front Ranges of the central Rockies. The region abounds with wildlife, from pronghorn antelope to deer, elk, bighorn sheep, and the lovable marmots that inhabit the highest alpine meadows. You'll even see buffalo, as many ranchers in this region raise and nurture American bison, a healthful, low-cholesterol substitute for beef.

Set amid this fascinating and scarcely populated mountain valley is the American Safari Guest Ranch, whose name reflects something of the flavor of this full-service dude ranch. Just as any visitor to East Africa anticipates the sighting of native species, those who come "on safari" in Colorado will be thrilled to encounter many native species as they ride through the scenic trails on the ranch and its adjoining public lands. And ride you will, with one of the best riding programs anywhere.

Voted "Best Horseback Riding in Colorado" by the *Denver Post*, American Safari actually discourages riders from going nose-to-tail on narrow trails in favor of exciting rides over varied terrain in which riders learn how to handle and guide their horses. This is real ranch riding augmented by private riding lessons, horsemanship clinics in the arena, games on horseback, and more. Guests who like to ride and want to improve their skills will truly appreciate the expert help and guidance that is part of the American Safari Ranch experience.

In addition to horseback riding, the ranch offers a wide variety of typical guest-ranch activities: barn dances and bonfires, cowboy sing-alongs, hayrides, horseshoes, and trail hiking. Located in "Colorado's Playground," the ranch also offers many nearby activities such as trout fishing in gold-medal streams and rivers, white-water rafting, fairs, festivals, and rodeos. Part of the fun of any visit to this area is the town of Fairplay, a charming mountain town with great shops and restaurants. While there, you can stop by the South Park Museum and get a feel for early Colorado history and tour the wonderful South Park Main Street, a re-created Victorian-era town with authentic clapboard sidewalks, hitching rails, and frontier-style businesses.

There's no lack of entertainment back at the ranch, either. Ranch workers keep busy creating chuckwagon barbecue cookouts, Wild West shows (with a staged shootout at the OK Corral), karaoke, Western dancing, and a variety of live entertainment.

Kids have a great time here, as there are a number of activities scheduled throughout the day. From hikes to pony rides, to games and learning activities, children will find plenty to do without having to resort to a video-game console (sorry, no Nintendo or XBox Games here!). Even the kitchen goes out of its way to accommodate kids with their favorite foods during the dining hour.

Guests to the ranch enjoy comfortable lodgings in the modern log cabins, which include private baths, over-sized rooms and beds, and great mountain views. Vacationers who prefer to arrive by RV can also camp on the premises, which include twenty-five acres of camping and RV sites (be sure to ask if this interests you). Campers who opt for horseback riding camp for free.

**American Safari Guest Ranch**
P.O. Box 128
Fairplay, CO 80440
Phone: (719) 836–2431
E-mail: ride@americansafariranch.com
Web site: www.americansafariranch.com

**Owner/Manager:** Stan Kopunec

**Accommodations:** Capacity, 75. Guests stay in modern log cabins, all with private baths, or in the lodge, which includes over-sized hotel-style rooms, private baths; 3-bedroom suites available for large families.

**Meals:** Typical western-style fare served family style. Special requests and dietary needs accommodated with advance notice.

**Activities:** Horseback riding with trail riding, arena lessons, private lessons, games on horseback, and horsemanship clinics. Advanced riders may explore the ranch without a guide; others are accompanied by ranch wranglers, who encourage riders to really take control and learn the basics of riding in open country. A great program! A variety of outdoor recreational games (volleyball, horseshoes, etc.), evening entertainment, hiking, golf driving range, nearby fishing, river rafting, and sight-seeing in historic Fairplay.

**Amenities:** Campground for tent campers and RVs (prices based on stay, with activities charged separately; campers who rent riding horses stay free). Corporate meeting facilities, with group barbecues and conference rooms.

**Special Programs:** Children's program with daily activities, pony rides, hikes, and more.

**Rates:** $$–$$$ Full American Plan. Package price includes dining, lodging, and horseback riding. Nonriders packages available. Discounted children's rates, discounted early and late-season rates. Off-ranch activities charged separately, by arrangement. Very flexible program allows guests to custom-tailor their activities.

**Credit Cards:** VISA, MasterCard, American Express. Personal or traveler's checks accepted.

**Season:** May 1 to October 31

**Getting There:** Located 1 hour from Denver or Colorado Springs. Rental car from Denver International or Colorado Springs Airport recommended.

**What's Nearby:** Fairplay, the South Park Historical Museum, Breckenridge Resort, Colorado Springs, and Denver.

# ASPEN CANYON RANCH

## Parshall, Colorado

With its log cabins, sawbuck fences and old-timey lodge, the Aspen Canyon Ranch looks like a movie set for an old John Ford western, which, in its own way, simply adds to the charm of this rustic yet thoroughly modern guest ranch situated high up in the mountains along the Continental Divide.

Aspen Canyon Ranch borders the Arapahoe National Forest, creating a peaceful and secluded retreat well away from the hustle and bustle of a typical tourist-trap vacation. It truly is a place where getting away from it all has meaning. The Williams Fork River flows through the ranch property, creating a haven for wildlife as well as a perfect place to wet a fishing line. Located at an altitude of 8,400 feet, the ranch benefits from cool summer afternoons and evening temperatures that are just nippy enough to make a roaring campfire inviting.

A network of trails adds great variety to the horseback program at Aspen Canyon. Bridle paths meander through meadows of alpine wildflowers and stands of pine and fir trees as well as groves of quaking aspen, of course. Adventurous guests may be asked to ford streams or climb to high mountain passes that offer stunning, isolated views of the central spine of the Colorado Rockies. Rides are matched to the individual's abilities and interests, and for riders wishing to improve their equestrian skills, arena lessons are available at no additional cost. And if you want to play at being a rodeo cowboy or cowgirl, the wranglers will be glad to show you how to toss a rope or time you on a dash through the barrel-racing course. The ranch also hosts a weekly "gymkhana," where guests take part in various games on horseback.

Although horseback riding is central to the Aspen Canyon experience, the menu of other activities is ample. Off-site trips include rafting on the wild white water of the Colorado River, ballooning in Grand County, and visits to the quaint former mining town of Breckenridge. One can also get some fly-fishing instruction on the banks of Lost Creek or in any of three stocked fishing ponds, or just relax in a hot tub located mere feet from your cabin—and within hearing range of the burbling river.

If shooting sports are your fancy, the ranch offers a skeet-shooting range. Rugged outdoorsmen can rough it during an overnight campout. Country-music lovers can learn the latest steps and line dances during evening get-togethers. And golfers and tennis players can avail themselves of nearby facilities, too.

Come wintertime, the ranch offers a superb family gathering place for ski trips and snowmobiling adventures. Several world-class ski resorts, including Breckenridge, Winter Park, Keystone, and Arapahoe Basin offer skiers and snowboarders of all levels plenty of terrain to explore, while nearby Sol Vista, whose gentle slopes are ideal for instruction, is the perfect spot for first-timers.

Owned and operated by Steve and Debbie Roderick and their four kids, Aspen Canyon Ranch doesn't run on a squeaky-tight schedule but allows guests to set the agenda. By tailoring the experience to the individual, the ranch accommodates vacationers looking for high-energy adventure or low-effort relaxation. It's entirely up to you!

The Aspen Canyon Ranch is somewhat small by Colorado standards, with a capacity of 40. For persons looking for an intimate ranch vacation where you can set your own pace and enjoy scenic grandeur in a "set" befitting a John Wayne western, it may be just the place.

## Aspen Canyon Ranch

13206 County Road #3, Star Route
Parshall, CO 80468
Phone: (800) 321–1357; (970) 725–3600
Fax: (970) 725–0044
E-mail: acr@rkymtnhi.com
Web site: www.aspencanyon.com

**Owners/Managers:** Steve and Debbie Roderick

**Accommodations:** 40 guests. Guests may stay in 3 4-plex log cabins situated along a bank of the Williams Fork River. Each cabin is furnished with handmade log furniture, stone fireplaces, and comfortable bedding quilts. Large families and groups may reserve the Cliff House, a spacious 3-bedroom log home tucked away into a mountainside. Conference facilities for up to 40.

**Meals:** Family-style dining takes place in the rustic main lodge, which is tastefully decorated with antiques, western art prints, log furniture, and a vast stone fireplace. Evening fare might consist of savory pot roasts, egg-and-sausage casseroles, and pecan-crusted chicken breasts. For a break from the routine, guests may take part in a sunset trail ride ending in a mountaintop "cowboy" cookout.

**Activities:** Horseback riding is the center of ranch activities and guests are encouraged to take part in grooming and saddling their own horses. Groups are separated by ability, and additional arena instruction is available at the guest's request. Other arena activities include gymkhanas and practice roping events. Guests may take part in numerous off-site activities that include golf, tennis, hot-air ballooning, river rafting, and shopping excursions to Winter Park or Breckenridge. Wintertime activities include alpine skiing, cross-country skiing, and snowmobiling. The ranch has a skeet-shooting range and several trout-fishing ponds. Fly-fishing guides are available at the guest's request. Mountain bikes are also available, or one can simply explore the area on foot. Evening activities include talent shows and country dancing.

**Amenities:** Comfortable lodge with lounge (guests must bring their own liquor); streamside hot tubs; cabins with natural-gas fireplaces, refrigerators, coffeemakers, porches, and patio swings.

**Special Programs:** Kid's Canyon offers a fully supervised program of activities and services for wee buckaroos. Kids 6 and over may take part in gentle trail riding, with pony rides for kids under 6. Also, arts and crafts, bicycle riding, games, fishing, panning for gold, water activities, and the kids' rodeo. Babysitting is included at no extra charge, so adults can sneak off and go golfing or river rafting.

**Rates:** $$–$$$ Reduced rates in June and September. Reduced rates for children 3–16; children under 3 are free. Reservation deposit required.

**Credit Cards:** VISA, MasterCard, Discover

**Season:** June 1 through September 27

**Getting There:** Nearest commercial airport is Denver International, where rental cars available. Drive distance is 90 miles. Shuttle service from airport to ranch by reservation. Call for rates and a reservation form. Amtrak service is also available to Winter Park, with stops in Granby. A shuttle can pick up guests at the train station.

**What's Nearby:** Historic mining town of Breckenridge and the modern resort town Winter Park. Golf courses and tennis courts also available.

# BAR LAZY J GUEST RANCH

The Bar Lazy J opened way back in 1912, which makes this quaint ranch on the banks of the Colorado River one of the West's oldest continuously run guest ranches.

At the Bar Lazy J, the old-time Western style is genuine, with nary an air of contrivance. The log cabins are authentic, right down to the chinking, as are the knotty-pine interiors and vintage western furniture. The spacious log-cabin style main lodge is adorned with real wagon-wheel chandeliers, and the wild-game trophy heads that preside over the lodge's grand dining hall are real, too.

Every guest ranch has its own character, and the Bar Lazy J is best typified as "cowboy meets river rat." Its prime location on the banks of the Colorado gives visiting anglers ample opportunity to work the eddies and pools for German and rainbow trout. You'll be hard-pressed to find better fishing habitat than the ¾ mile of private river controlled by the Bar Lazy J. This stretch of river has been designated as "Gold Medal" trout-fishing habitat. A catch-and-release philosophy ensures that the fat, sassy fish you catch today will be there to challenge the next angler a week later. The fishing allure is so strong here that the cabins are named for popular fly patterns.

For those persons without a fisherman's patience, there is another way to enjoy the river: white-water rafting. Be sure to inquire about this thrilling activity, which is additional to the standard American Plan guest rates. Golf and tennis are also available at off-sight facilities and at extra charge.

Horses, however, are part of every package, and owners Cheri and Jerry Helmicki take great pride in their horse program. They offer two rides a day with groups broken up by ability. The ranch has a string of sixty well-cared-for and well-trained horses that are surefooted and mountain-fit. Each rider is assigned a horse at the beginning of the week, a practice that helps the rider to bond with his or her mount. A horse-sense orientation takes place on the first day, followed by a morning or afternoon ride. Riders can choose from a slow, sight-seeing walk to a more enervating "fast" ride—or somewhere in between.

When you decide it's time to give your horse (and yourself) a rest from the trail, you can take a ride on a mountain bike or enjoy a leisurely afternoon sightseeing via the ranch tour van or opt for a more rugged tour of the backcountry via Jeep; or you can stretch your legs with a hike along the miles of trails. Your hosts will go out of the way to adapt their schedule to your wishes.

In the evenings, everyone gathers around the campfire for a sing-along or joins in the popular country-western dance class. Other evening activities include hayrides, a rodeo, and a very high quality variety show that gives the Bar Lazy J's very talented staff a chance to show off.

Of course, you may just want to relieve your aching saddle soreness by soaking in the hot tub or join other guests in a lively game of stud poker. And when the socializing gets to be too much, you can find a quiet place to yourself by the river and gaze at the stars. There are fancier guest ranches than the Bar Lazy J but few that can match its down-home authenticity and western spirit.

**Bar Lazy J Ranch**
P.O. Box N
Parshall, CO 80468
Phone: (800) 396–6279; (970) 725–3437
Fax: (970) 725–0121
E-mail: BarLazyJ@rkymtnhi.com
Web site: www.barlazyj.com

**Owners/Managers:** Cheri and Jerry Helmicki

**Accommodations:** 42 guests in 12 log cabins plus the Ranch House, suitable for groups of 16. Screened porches, fireplaces, on-premise laundry, river views.

**Meals:** Family style. Vegetarian diets and other dietary needs accommodated with advance notice. All meals accompanied by homemade breads and pastries.

**Activities:** Horseback riding for all levels of riders; Jeep rides, hiking, fishing, mountain biking, and sight-seeing. Additional activities at added cost include golf, tennis, and white-water rafting.

**Amenities:** Jacuzzi hot tub, children's play set, rec room, outdoor swimming pool, volleyball court, river-front lodging.

**Special Programs:** Children's Ranch Fun program includes a variety of activities tailored to children's interests including hiking, fishing, arts and crafts, games, and for kids ages 8 through 12, guided trail rides. Arena horse rides for younger children.

**Rates:** $$ Reduced rates for children under 13; add $200 per person per week for Ranch House accommodations.

**Credit Cards:** VISA, MasterCard, Discover. Personal check, traveler's check, or cash preferred.

**Season:** Late May through September

**Getting There:** Located in Parshall, 15 miles west of Granby in Grand County. Driving distance from Denver International Airport, approximately 120 miles. Amtrak service from downtown Denver arrives in Granby daily. Van service from Denver International available by arrangement at additional charge.

**What's Nearby:** Lake Granby, Winter Park Ski Area, and Sol Vista Ski Resort. All offer summer recreation and some shopping.

# C LAZY U RANCH

## Granby, Colorado

Since 1946, the C Lazy U Ranch has set the standard for luxurious guest-ranch vacations. One point of particular pride for the owners, the Murray family, is the recognition their ranch has garnered for superlative service, facilities, activities and overall attention to guest satisfaction. The C Lazy U has consistently earned both the Mobile Travel Guide Four-Star Award and American Automobile Association Five-Diamond Award; it is the only guest ranch to consistently earn the highest marks from both organizations.

What makes the C Lazy U so special? Let's begin with its location. The ranch lies just west of the Continental Divide, whose soaring 14,000 peaks and lesser mountains separate the country's watersheds into distinct basins. It's said that a droplet of water that falls on the west summit of the mountains will eventually flow to the Pacific Ocean; one that falls on the east side flows all the way to the Gulf of Mexico! Some of that water meanders down through the C Lazy U, and, interestingly, the ranch derives its name from that very water course. If one stands on the broad deck of the main lodge, one can see where the Willow Creek cuts out the letters *C* and *U*.

Ranch guests are treated to outstanding views of the Indian Peaks Wilderness and Rocky Mountain National Park. Open year-round, the ranch can be toured on horseback or, in winter, on cross-country ski equipment furnished by the ranch. In both cases, experienced guides can be relied on to help instruct, inform, and entertain guests.

Although horses are the focus during summer months, riding is but one of a dozen scheduled activities that guests may request. Nearby Winter Park Resort affords some of the best mountain-biking trails in this bike-crazy state. One can find especially scenic hiking on or off the ranch. There's a skeet-shooting range, where one can test one's skill at bagging clay pigeons; or the staff can arrange a tee time at a nearby mountainside golf course, where you're likely to find your golf ball traveling 10 or 20 yards farther than usual, thanks to the thin mountain air.

Anglers who seek the tranquility of fly casting can practice on the banks of Willow Creek or arrange a special guided trip to several gold-medal tributaries of the mighty Colorado River. Ranch guests may also schedule wild white-water rafting trips,

## FIVE-STAR HORSE PROGRAM

Horses form the foundation of the C Lazy U experience. At the beginning of your vacation, you will be assigned your own horse to ride. Provided you get along with your mount, you'll form a bond during the week—you may even be tempted to take the horse home with you! (You can't, of course, but the staff will do its utmost to pair you up the next time you return).

Though western riding is the accepted standard, English equitation is an option. You can choose your ride based on your ability: slow, easy rides perfect for beginners and fast, loping rides for experts. The guest-to-wrangler ratio is low: Groups seldom number more than 8 riders. Adults and children ride in separate groups except during the weekly "family ride."

although these and other off-premises excursions come with an extra charge.

If you'd rather stay put on the ranch, you can while away a few hours with the tennis pro on one of several tennis courts, or you can swim laps in the heated indoor/outdoor pool. A Jacuzzi and masseuse are also available to relax saddle-sore muscles.

Winter guests mainly come to avail themselves of exceptional powder skiing for which Colorado is famous. Novices will be most comfortable at the family-friendly Sol Vista Resort; intermediates can find close to one hundred trails at Winter Park, one of the most popular ski areas in the state. Adjacent Mary Jane offers challenging steeps and moguls for experts looking for a thrill. On the ranch, you can perform pirouettes on the skating pond or schuss through the native pines and spruce trees on more than 25 kilometers of groomed cross-country trails. Around dusk, the

## C Lazy U Ranch

P.O. Box 379
Granby, CO 80446
Phone: (970) 887–3344
Fax: (970) 887–3917
E-mail: ranch@clazyu.com
Web site: www.clazyu.com

**Owners:** The Murray Family

**Accommodations:** 40 total units. AAA Five-Diamond and Mobil Four-Star award-winning accommodations. Rooms vary in size and décor, ranging from rooms with twin beds to multiroom suites. 75 percent include fireplaces; Jacuzzi-equipped suites also available. Guest capacity is 110; conference-group capacity is 80.

**Meals:** Dining takes place in the grand dining hall of the main lodge; outdoor barbecues held poolside twice-weekly in summer. All meals served family style. A typical menu includes aged prime rib, fresh Rocky Mountain trout, or rosemary rack of lamb, fresh-cooked vegetables, home-baked breads, and desserts. Special diets can be accommodated with advance notice. Wine service with dinner; bar stocked with top-shelf liquors, wine, beer.

**Activities:** More than 100 saddle horses graded and selected to suit individual riders. Trail groups are divided into fast and slow rides; children typically ride in separate groups from adults. English tack and advanced arena riding lessons available. Additional activities include hiking, fly fishing, tennis, swimming, skeet shooting. Off-premises activities include river rafting, mountain biking, and golf. Winter activities include cross-country skiing, telemark skiing, ice skating, indoor and outdoor horseback riding, sleigh rides, and alpine skiing at either Winter Park Resort or Sol Vista Ski Area (additional costs for off-premises activities).

**Amenities:** Indoor sauna and Jacuzzi, tennis courts, paddleboats, basketball court, exercise room, heated indoor/outdoor pool, business center, game room, bar, complimentary shuttle service to all off-site activities.

**Special Programs:** Activity programs for children and teens. Children seated separately for lunch, dinner. Special weeks for families with children under 3. Adults-only schedule each fall. Ask for additional details and dates.

**Rates:** $$$–$$$$ Full American Plan. Off-season and group discounts available. Several off-premises activities and some on-site activities billed separately.

**Credit Cards:** None. Personal checks, traveler's checks only.

**Season:** Summer, June–September; winter, mid-December–March

**Getting There:** Located 97 miles west of Denver/Denver International Airport (DIA), approximately 30 miles from Kremmling Airport (private planes only), and 10 miles from Granby Airport (private planes only). There are many airline and ground transportation options for guests of C Lazy U, including private shuttle services serving Winter Park/Sol Vista and Amtrak rail service to Granby.

**What's Nearby:** Winter Park Ski Resort offers some of the best skiing in North America and includes shopping, restaurants, ski instruction, and ski equipment. Nearby Sol Vista provides a host of winter and summer activities including skiing and golfing.

ranch team of Belgian draft horses is hitched to a sleigh and blanketed guests can tour the premises to the jangle of real sleigh bells.

Winter or summer, the C Lazy U staff goes to great lengths to entertain its guests. Everyone from horse wranglers to house cleaners are hired for their extra skills: Many are college students with musical training, foreign-language skills, rodeo experience, and other talents. The staff puts on regular evening shows that include sing-alongs, skits, and dances. During the day, wranglers and guests take part in weekly "showdeos," which test rider's skills in fun and safe arena events.

As one might expect, the lodging here is simple yet sumptuous. Guests may choose from hotel-like rooms, suites, or deluxe cabins with multiple rooms that are best suited to families. Rooms do not have televisions or telephones, although most have fireplaces. Deluxe rooms feature Jacuzzi tubs and small refrigerators stocked with cold beverages.

For vacationers looking for a luxurious and pampered ranch vacation experience, the C Lazy U cannot fail to satisfy.

# DROWSY WATER RANCH
## Granby, Colorado

Nestled in a protected valley amid pine, fir, and aspen trees, Drowsy Water Ranch pretty much defines the ideal of what a western dude ranch should be: tranquil and secluded, with spectacular vistas, and just enough luxury to make "roughing it" pretty darn comfy.

Picturesque red-roofed outbuildings flank the rustic main lodge, affording guests great privacy despite everything being within a moment's walk. The staff is chosen for their cheerfulness, skill, and variety of talent, giving the ranch an upbeat and friendly ambience. And the variety of barnyard pets and a playground make this a children's paradise.

Owners Ken and Randy Sue Fosha and their two sons, Justin and Ryan, are hands-on ranch managers who take great pride in their 640-acre spread, conveniently bordered by thousands of acres of the Arapahoe National Forest. They've remodeled the cozy ranch cabins, which are located near the banks of Drowsy Water Creek. Guests tend to congregate at the main lodge, a log-style great house with a huge stone fireplace and decorative southwestern accents. It's a good place for card playing or just getting acquainted with one of the books in the ranch library collection.

Drowsy Water offers a typical program of horseback riding, steak fries, square-dancing parties, Jeep trips, hayrides, and evening staff entertainment get-togethers. Those persons who enjoy river rafting or golf can partake of those activities by special arrangement. Other activities include boating and lake fishing at one of several high-country lakes and reservoirs.

If you enjoy fly fishing, you can work the pools of Drowsy Water Creek, which abounds with brown and rainbow trout, or you can schedule a trip to the mighty Colorado River, which offers scenic stretches of gold-medal trout habitat. During the fall hunting season, the ranch is open for big-game mule deer and elk hunts in the adjacent Elk Mountain and Cabin Creek areas. Confer with the ranch for information on game licenses and hunt camps.

The horse program is second to none, with more than one hundred horses available. Riders are matched to their mounts according to skill level and are given opportunities for daily instruction in the arena and on the trail. Riders can break out of the "head-to-tail" monotony of some guest ranches, and the better riders are given free rein to trot and gallop during guided trail rides.

Children are attended to and entertained by handpicked counselors, most of them college-aged students with an interest in child development and education. After an activity-filled day, children and teens are reunited with their parents for scheduled evening activities such as dances, hayrides, fireside marshmallow roasts, and staff shows.

## Drowsy Water Ranch

P.O. Box 147
Granby, CO 80446
Phone: (800) 845–2292; (970) 725–3456
Fax: (970) 725–3611
Web site: www.drowsywater.com

**Owners:** Ken and Randy Sue Fosha

**Accommodations:** Capacity, 60. Guests stay in newly renovated cabins featuring covered porches. Cabins accommodate anywhere from 2 to 9 individuals; each has its own bathroom. The sleeping lodge includes an additional 8 rooms, all with private bathrooms.

**Meals:** Many opportunities for trailside dining, as well as group dining in the main lodge. Meals vary from western favorites to gourmet creations and include a lavish salad bar and homemade breads, pastries, and desserts. Special diets accommodated with advance notice.

**Activities:** Lake and river fishing, Jeep tours, chuckwagon meals on the trail, horseback riding and instruction, rec room, arts and crafts for kids, evening dances and staff shows, nature hikes, and guest "gymkhana" rodeos with games on horseback. Off-site activities include river rafting, golf, tennis, guided fly fishing, and boating and giant waterslide at additional cost.

**Amenities:** Outdoor hot tub, outdoor pool, petting zoo, children's playground, and comfortable main lodge with entertainment hall.

**Special Programs:** One of the best children's programs in the country, offering a wide variety of supervised activities. Seasonal hunting trips available. Adults-only season in early September.

**Rates:** $$$$ Special weekly rates. Reduced rates for children under 5 and for additional guests based on double occupancy. Off-season rates 10 to 15 percent lower than peak-season rates.

**Credit Cards:** None. Personal checks, traveler's checks, and cash only.

**Season:** June–September 14

**Getting There:** Nearest commercial airport, Denver International, approximately 120 miles. Limousine service from airport available by reservation. Amtrak train service from downtown Denver to Granby, with a shuttle pickup available to and from the ranch.

**What's Nearby:** 2 18-hole golf courses, watersports in nearby lakes, shopping and dining in Winterpark and Granby. Close to Rocky Mountain National Park.

# THE HISTORIC PINES RANCH

## Westcliffe, Colorado

Situated at the base of Colorado's Sangre de Cristo range, the Historic Pines Ranch benefits from a scenic backdrop that rivals Wyoming's Jackson Hole. Fortunately, the small, quaint ranching and farming town of Westcliffe, Colorado, remains relatively undiscovered. You can always find a parking place on Main Street, even on a "crowded" weekend afternoon. And yet there's still plenty to see and do, with a full summer schedule of arts and crafts fairs, rodeos, and a highly regarded jazz festival.

The Historic Pines Ranch is very much a part of the friendly Westcliffe community, having served as an inviting destination for more than one hundred years. The original lodge was built in the 1890s. Guests will be amazed to learn that this large and comfy building was actually ordered from a Montgomery Ward catalog at an original price of $900 (not an unusual order prior to the turn of the twentieth century). The lodge remains true to that period with Victorian antiques and decor. The newly renovated guest cabins befit a region of mixed settlement and history: Design themes include Victorian, Southwest/Spanish, Western, and the "catch-all" style, Country. Most of the rooms offer mountain or valley views.

This lovely little ranch benefits tremendously from its Southern Colorado location, which ranks among the premier tourism destinations in the West. Using the ranch as a base, guests can take a white-water rafting adventure on the mighty Arkansas River or embark on a pack trip in the majestic sawtooth Sangre de Cristo Mountains, whose peaks tower thousands of feet above the valley floor and reach altitudes in excess of 14,000 feet.

In addition, tours can be arranged to the Great Sand Dunes National Monument, a

## GENUINE WESTERN GHOST TOWN

Custer County, Colorado, has a peculiar and fascinating history, one you'll surely learn more about at the Pines Ranch. Briefly, the valley was settled by a colony of German immigrants who set off from Chicago to make a better life for themselves. Soon after their establishment, silver was discovered in the valley. A silver rush ensued. In 1880 in Custer County alone, close to $2 million in silver was mined. Things could not have looked brighter. Silver Cliff, with a population of 5,040, was the third-largest town in Colorado, falling behind only Denver (with 35,629 residents) and Leadville (14,820). But when the U.S. government changed to a gold standard, silver prices plummeted and the town was nearly abandoned.

Nearby Westcliffe was founded as the terminus of a railroad spur—a wealthy individual owned the land west of Silver Cliff, and the rail line ensured its development. To this day, the two towns (which are side by side and virtually indistinguishable) maintain separate governments and identities.

Among the oddities in Custer County is a purportedly haunted cemetery. Visitors describe floating lights of different colors that can be seen at night. The cemetery was featured in a 1963 *National Geographic* article and remains a favorite "haunt" for area residents and visitors.

fascinating geological site whose dunes are among the tallest in the world. Other interesting side trips include visits to the Royal Gorge, a steep and impressive chasm formed by the Arkansas River, and the Gold Rush town of Cripple Creek, whose gingerbread Victorian buildings now house an active casino-gambling scene. Finally, one can enjoy Colorado's second-largest city, Colorado Springs, which is home to the famous U.S. Air Force Academy, the Broadmoor Hotel, the United States Olympic Training Center, and scenic Garden of the Gods Park. Many people stay an extra day in Colorado Springs (90 miles from the ranch) as a way to commence or wrap up their Colorado dude-ranch vacation.

Of course, one need not ever leave the Pines Ranch to have a perfectly wonderful and memorable vacation. Equine activities take precedence here. The ranch has close to seventy horses to ensure that each guest is matched to a cooperative mount. They will proudly tell you that more than one-third were raised and trained right on the ranch. Typically, one can rub the adorable

**The Historic Pines Ranch**
P.O. Box 311
Westcliffe, CO 81252
Phone: (800) 446–9462; (719) 783–9261
Fax: (719) 783–2977
E-mail: howdy@historicpines.com
Web site: www.historicpines.com

**Owner/Manager:** Dean Rusk

**Accommodations:** Guest capacity, 40. The renovated 1890s lodge has 4 guest rooms that are well-suited to couples or singles, providing a "bed-and-breakfast" atmosphere amid Victorian decorations and antiques. In addition, there are 4 guest cabins built on a duplex design, all newly decorated. Each cabin quarters includes a private bath, television/VCR, and living room.

**Meals:** Buffet-style chuckwagon meals served 3 times daily. A typical dinner meal might be chicken-fried steak, homemade mashed potatoes, cooked vegetables, and carrot cake. Well-stocked salad bar. Snacks and the "endless cookie jar" available throughout the day. Weekly breakfast ride. BYOB, nonalcohol bar The Sundance Saloon serves as a soda fountain where guests can enjoy sodas, floats, and milkshakes. Special dietary needs accommodated with advance notice.

**Activities:** 70+ saddle horses, many raised and trained on the ranch. Guests are encouraged to get involved in grooming, saddling, feeding. Daily trail rides, arena practice, advanced instruction on request. Overnight and extended pack trips in the Sangre de Cristo Mountains. Pond and stream fishing,

guest rodeo competition, evening dances, and staff talent show, "tea time" with local storyteller, campfire sing-along. River-rafting packages. Ranch employees available to help plan unaccompanied sidetrips to various southern Colorado tourist sites. Shopping in nearby Westcliffe and Silvercliffe.

**Amenities:** Historic ranch buildings. Indoor swimming pool, hot tub, and saunas. Riding arena. Victorian tearoom. Daily maid service. In-room television with VCR and video collection. On-premises laundry.

**Special Programs:** Children's programs for kids aged 2 to 8 include counselors and activities including scavenger hunts, nature hikes, and arts and crafts. Pony rides in a controlled arena environment; children aged 7 and over may participate in adult rides.Other programs: high-country pack trips, river-rafting trips, and Cow Camp, a backcountry cattle-herding trip. Inquire for details.

**Rates:** $$–$$$ American Plan. Off-season and group discounts. Children's rates. Packages of 2-, 3-, 5-, and 7-day stays.

**Credit Cards:** VISA, MasterCard, Discover, American Express

**Season:** May through October

**Getting There:** Located 90 miles south and west of Colorado Springs near the town of Westcliffe. Most guests rent cars at the Colorado Springs Airport; ground transportation to the ranch available at extra cost.

**What's Nearby:** Arkansas River rafting, Royal Gorge, Great Sand Dunes National Monument.

ears of a recently born colt or filly.

Extra care is taken to orient the rider to horseback riding before a mount is selected. The riding program progresses gradually, allowing riders to work up to the all-day trip to the alpine Lakes of the Clouds, a high-altitude alpine excursion that is truly breathtaking and unforgettable. Guests may be separated by ability and are welcome to help with the grooming, feeding, and saddling of the animals. Guests wanting additional riding practice and instruction can request lessons at no additional charge.

Arena activities allow further equestrian-skills enhancement. A favorite activity is team penning, a competition in which riders try to separate a group of cattle from the group and herd them into a pen. For persons truly interested in cattle work and "the cowboy experience," inquire about the special four-day Cow Camp trips in the Sangre de Cristo.

Back at The Pines, guests can fish in a stocked pond, join in evening square-dance and country-swing lessons, take part in the campfire sing-along, and enjoy a staff talent show and even join in the performances, if they wish. The ranch offers an indoor, heated swimming pool and hot-tub baths for relaxation.

# THE HOME RANCH

## Clark, Colorado

The Home Ranch is truly a place where riders learn to be horsemen. In addition to its role as a guest-ranch vacation destination, the Home Ranch is home to the Colorado Center for Equestrian Learning. There, expert clinicians work with riders of all abilities, stressing the relatively new but widely accepted method of resistance-free riding. In short, the goal of such instruction is to help humans understand the psychology and the instincts of horses and to use these insights to form more comfortable, safe, and constructive partnerships. It's the ideal experience for persons who are contemplating buying a horse, as well as those who already own horses (you can even bring yours with you, so it can take part in the training, too).

For visitors who simply want a pleasant guest-ranch experience, the Home Ranch offers great daily trail riding. During orientation at the barn, you'll learn some basic horse-savvy safety lessons before being paired with a mount matched to your skills and even your personality. Half-day and all-day trail rides, which are scheduled throughout the week, will take you into the Routt National Forest, a million-acre forest preserve featuring high-country meadows and scenic vistas.

For the more ambitious rider, the ranch clinics offer "basic training" in everything from saddling and groundwork to obstacles and the popular "Working Cattle 101," in which you gain a cowboy's cow know-how. Many of the instructors are certified riding instructors, and all have been through the clinics so often that they know the material by rote.

No matter what your goals, ranch manager Ken Jones's enthusiasm is bound to spill over to your attitude toward horses. A lifelong horseman raised on a Montana ranch, Jones gets excited about teaching. "I've ridden thousands and thousands of miles on trails, and that's great. But I hate to see horses head-to-tail and the people sitting there like passengers on a train. I feel there's so much more to riding. That's the aspect I love and what got me interested in these riding clinics," he says.

But exceptional horses and instructors aren't the only things that make the Home Ranch special. Guests can also enjoy fishing, hiking, and alpine skiing and snowshoeing treks, depending on the season. The cabins are amply appointed with wood-burning stoves, small refrigerators, and hot tubs on the porches. For guests who prefer individual rooms in the lodge, there's a sauna, hot tub, and swimming pool. Such appointments have earned the ranch the Mobil 4-Star Award, a mark of distinction among guest-ranch and resort properties, and one that is given only after a facility meets very rigorous and exacting standards.

One of those standards is dining, and the Home Ranch's head chef, Clyde Nelson, is recognized as one of the nation's best. Every meal, from sit-down dinners in the dining room to breakfast buffets and outdoor cookouts, is guaranteed to satisfy the most discriminating tastes.

The entertainment is very good, too. Ken and his crew provide plenty of fun with evening entertainment around the campfire and in the barn loft, where you may be treated to a performance by Cowboy Ken and the Ranch Hand Band (or by their alter egos, "The Moist Towelettes"). It's a hoot and a holler—just what a good guest ranch evening should be.

## The Home Ranch

P.O. Box 822
Clark, CO 80428
Phone: (970) 879–1780
Fax: (970) 879–1795
E-mail: info@homeranch.com
Web site: www.homeranch.com

**Owners:** Ken and Cile Jones, Steve and Ann Stranahan

**Manager:** Ken Jones

**Accommodations:** Capacity, 45. Well-appointed log cabins located in a grove of aspens create a feeling of privacy. Each has a woodstove, hot tub, and covered deck. A main lodge houses guests on 2 levels. Large families may request a 2,500-square-foot, 2-story log cabin. Nightly turndown service, robes, and fresh flowers.

**Meals:** A true gourmet experience—head chef Clyde Nelson came to the ranch in 1989 and has been featured in *Food and Wine, Bon Appetit, Travel and Leisure, Gourmet,* and *Condé Naste Traveller.* The ranch employs a full-time baker whose ovens produce fresh breads, pastries, and desserts. All meals are served family style at a set time in the dining room or, in summer, at the location of the day's activity. If you are leaving the ranch for a day of fishing, hiking, or riding, your sack lunch will be made to order by the Clark Store deli. Children generally are served in a separate dinner seating. BYOB liquor, wine, and beer.

**Activities:** Natural horsemanship is an important part of Ken Jones's horse program. Trail rides in neighboring Routt National Forest, along with cattle work and arena clinics. Guests are welcome to bring their own horses or ride the exceptionally bred quarter horses raised and trained on the ranch. Fishing and fly casting in a stocked pond on the ranch or on the Elk River, along with all-inclusive fly-fishing instruction. Hiking is a favorite summer activity, and staff nature guides provide interpretive nature walks. Off-site tennis and golf can be arranged. In winter, guests may take part in cross-country skiing over 20 kilometers of groomed trails, snowshoeing, as well as winter sports activities at the world-famous Steamboat Springs Resort (although you must provide your own transportation to and from the resort).

**Amenities:** The Home Ranch is simply a beautiful place, with lovely details such as fresh flowers in vases and cozy lounge furniture. Individual cabins have their own hot tubs, while a hot tub and sauna serve lodge guests. Each room has a minifridge and wine rack as well as bottle openers, glasses, and ice.

**Special Programs:** Children can become Kiddie Wranglers as part of the all-day children's activity program (ages 6 and older). Riding begins at age 6. No children under 6 allowed. In spring and fall, the Home Ranch facility is host to many equine-related clinics including team roping, eventing, colt starting, and natural horsemanship. They hold clinics in a new 240-foot by 80-foot indoor arena as well as several round pens and 2 outdoor arenas, making this the perfect place for learning and fun. For more detailed information and a list of the current clinic offerings, visit The Colorado Center for Equestrian Learning Web site.

**Rates:** $$$$ American Plan. Children's rates available.

**Credit Cards:** VISA, MasterCard, American Express. Personal checks accepted.

**Season:** Year-round, except during the slow months of November, April, and May.

**Getting There:** Located 18 miles from Steamboat Springs. Closest airport at Hayden, Colorado, with wintertime commuter connections from Denver International Airport. Ranch shuttle available at additional charge. In summer, plan on a 4-hour drive by rented car from Denver International Airport. The ranch is approximately 19 miles north of Steamboat Springs on Highway 129.

**What's Nearby:** The ranching/resort community of Steamboat Springs, with shopping, restaurants, winter-sports activities, spas, and a host of cultural events and activities. Summertime rodeo in June and July, with shuttle service from the Home Ranch to the rodeo arena.

# KING MOUNTAIN RANCH

## Granby, Colorado

Located on the fringes of Rocky Mountain National Park and surrounded by nearly one million acres of public land, the King Mountain Ranch is an oasis of gentle, rolling parklands amid stands of pine and blue-spruce forests. When one thinks of Colorado, chances are this is the kind of scenic mountain ranch that comes to mind.

Ranch architecture reflects the Rocky Mountain aesthetic. A huge gambrel-roofed barn and wood-rail corral are the epicenter of the horse activities, while a stately lodge with huge lodgepole-pine supports provides a social center befitting, well, a king. Guests stay in the comfortable, if not opulent, guest apartments and guest rooms of two large, hotel-like buildings adjacent to the main lodge.

It's not likely you'll be spending much time in your room, however, as the ranch offers a smorgasbord of activities from horseback riding to fishing to river rafting, tennis, and golf. There's even the option of going hot-air ballooning!

Despite its remote location, the ranch is but a twenty-minute drive from the myriad attractions of Grand County, one of the most heavily touristed areas in the state. Golfers can loosen up at either of two world-class courses: the Pole Creek Golf Club or the Grand Lake Golf Club. These courses cut their way through stands of pines trees and feature mountain streams and unsurpassed views. Pole Creek was rated as "The #1 place to play golf in Colorado" by the prestigious *Golf Digest* magazine.

If you prefer putting around the ranch, there are plenty of other recreational options. Among King Mountain's many amenities are an indoor swimming pool, trap- and skeet-shooting range, billiard and Ping-Pong tables, and (believe it or not) a bowling alley. Fishing is another option.

Guests can choose to angle in the well-stocked ranch ponds or venture farther afoot and access some of the gold-medal trout habitats of area streams. Either way, you'll have plenty of opportunities to wet your line and collect scrapbook photos of the fat trout you caught (you'll need a camera, as the ranch supports the catch-and-release philosophy of fishing).

At the center of the King Mountain experience is the horse program. The ranch is surrounded by miles and miles of trails, ensuring that each day's ride affords new vistas and opportunities for wildlife viewing. Rides are broken down by ability and confidence, so you can be assured of spending trail time with individuals of similar abilities.

Vacationers wishing to play cowboy may take part in arena sports like team penning, an exciting test of riding skills in which riders sort and "pen" cattle. All guests are welcome to take a riding lesson and hone their horsemanship in the ranch's ample riding arena.

King Mountain offers an extensive children's program for dudes twelve and under. Called The Foxes Den, the program includes activities such as treasure hunts, horseback riding, swimming, arts and crafts, cookouts, and rodeo-related activities for budding buckaroos. Kids may also take part in guided nature walks and hikes.

The action doesn't stop at sunset, either. Campfire sing-alongs, fly-fishing lessons, karaoke and line-dancing parties, talent shows, and the highly enjoyable Western Ball are just a sampling of the evening lineup. And if all the activities find guests in need of rejuvenation, the King Mountain Ranch includes a full-service spa where one can get a manicure or pedicure, facial, an assortment of body works, or a relaxing therapeutic massage.

## King Mountain Ranch

P.O. Box 497
Granby, CO 80446
Phone: (800) 476–KING (5464); (970)
    887–2511
Fax: (970) 887–9511
E-mail: hosts@kingmtnranch.com
Web site: www.kingmtnranch.com

**Manager:** Marci Smith

**Accommodations:** Capacity, 79. Large rooms in multistory buildings, all with king or two double beds and private bathrooms. Western-style decor. Most rooms open onto decks with views. Groups or large families may inquire about The King House, a secluded lodge with 8 bedrooms on 3 levels suitable for groups of 16 or more.

**Meals:** Opulent spreads typify King Mountain Ranch meals. Breakfast diners may choose made-to-order omelets, fresh fruits, cereals, and breads. Lunches feature hearty soups, salads, and sandwiches. Dinners begin in the Trail's End Lounge, where appetizers are served, followed by meals in the dining room overlooking the ranch corrals, lake, and evening sunset.

**Activities:** Horses are at the center of ranch action, and guests may choose trail rides of varying lengths and rides for all levels of skill. Extra credit can be earned via riding lessons in the ranch arena or via cattle working. On-site activities include indoor swimming, basketball, fly fishing, hiking, mountain biking, tennis, and shooting sports. There is also a full-service spa and a bowling alley. Off-site activities include golf, guided fly fishing, white-water rafting, canoeing, hot-air balloon rides, 4-wheel tours, and in winter, skiing or guided snowmobiling.

**Amenities:** 2 lighted tennis courts, indoor pool, Jacuzzi, basketball court, bowling alley, rec room, video library and big-screen television, shooting range, water-sports equipment, fishing lake. Full-service spa offers a wide variety of spa services and treatments. Group conference facilities also available.

**Special Programs:** Kid's program, The Foxes Den, includes a full schedule of activities for kids 12 and under. Occasional overnight pack trips. Breakfast and lunch rides and chuck-wagon rides. Combination fly fishing/horse-back rides.

**Rates:** $$–$$$ Seasonal rates, with off-season reduced rates available. Minimum stay of 2 nights, except in winter, when 1-night stays are possible. Reduced children's rates, with reduced rates for nannies. Specially discounted rates sometimes available on short notice.

**Credit Cards:** VISA, MasterCard, Discover, American Express. Personal checks preferred.

**Season:** Year-round

**Getting There:** Closest international airport, Denver International (approximately 125 miles). Rentals available at airport. Shuttle-bus services carry passengers to Grand County/Granby. Also, Amtrak train service is also available but requires that plane passengers obtain ground transport to downtown Denver. Once in Granby, a ranch shuttle will be dispatched.

**What's Nearby:** Granby and the well-established vacation village of Winter Park. Grand County offers a wide variety of diversions, from winter skiing (alpine and cross country) and snowmobiling to summer fishing, golfing, festivals, rodeos, hot-air ballooning, and, of course, shopping.

# LATIGO RANCH

## Kremmling, Colorado

If there's one thing that sets the Latigo Ranch apart from many, it's the feeling of intimacy. With a mere thirty-five-guest capacity, the ranch is small by western standards. And that's a distinct advantage. Latigo's well-trained staff makes its guests feel like valued family members, and by week's end, strong bonds of friendship invariably form.

The ranch is owned by two couples: Randy and Lisa George and Jim and Kathie Yost. Their attention to detail is profound, from the simple-yet-elegant cloth table covers in the dining room to the process of carefully matching horse to rider down at the corral. And their taste in decorating the ranch is simply exquisite. Comfortably ensconced in a plush leather couch in front of a massive stone fireplace, you'll feel as though you are staying in a private home rather than a guest ranch—albeit a private home with true western style and kingly proportions.

Located in a remote part of Colorado, 55 miles southeast of Steamboat Springs,

**Latigo Ranch**
P.O. Box 327
Kremmling, CO 80459
Phone: (800) 227–9655; (970) 724–9008
Fax: (970) 724–9009
E-mail: info@latigotrails.com
Web site: www.latigotrails.com

**Owners/Managers:** Randy and Lisa George, Jim and Kathie Yost

**Accommodations:** Modern log cabins, fully carpeted with electric heat; 1- and 3-bedroom units, each with a sitting room and fireplace or wood-burning stove, refrigerator, and daily maid service.

**Meals:** The Ranch kitchen provides a varied menu of cuisine, planned with your entire week in mind. For today's health-conscious guest, the ranch offers light fare along with hearty items at each meal.

**Activities:** More than 80 horses provide guests with "tailor-fit" mounts. Riders wishing to groom and saddle horses may do so, with expert assistance. Fly-fishing lessons and pond fishing, river-rafting trips, guided nature hikes, overnight pack trips, evening dances, and recreational activities. Experienced riders should ask about the fall roundup, a great chance to experience genuine cattle work. In winter, the ranch offers cross-country skiing.

**Amenities:** Recreation room, library, hot-tub bath.

**Special Programs:** Fall Cattle Roundup: Help a local rancher find, gather, and move hundreds of cattle from the high-mountain summer pastures. Long but rewarding days in the saddle. Experienced riders only. Similarly, ask about overnight campouts. Supervised kids' program with activities.

**Rates:** $$$–$$$$ American Plan, all-inclusive. Children's rates, seasonal rates available. Overnight pack trip and river rafting included in price.

**Credit Cards:** VISA, MasterCard, American Express

**Season:** Late May to October (summer), mid-December to early April (winter)

**Getting There:** 130 miles northwest of Denver, 55 miles southeast of Steamboat Springs. Airline service to Denver International Airport or Hayden, Colorado. Inquire about ground transportation arrangements.

**What's Nearby:** Kremmling, a secluded ranching community, offers limited shopping and entertainment and the occasional rodeo or equestrian event. Steamboat, an hour's drive away, offers world-class alpine skiing, a variety of shops and restaurants, and a myriad of entertainment opportunities.

the Latigo resides at an altitude of 9,000 feet and offers excellent views of the Continental Divide. The ranch is open year-round, with emphasis on horseback riding in summer and cross-country skiing in winter.

Latigo offers a plethora of summer activities including river rafting, guided fly fishing, evening cookouts, and evening dance lessons where guests can learn the latest line dance or traditional square dance. There's also a fully supervised kid's program, a recreation center and library, hayrides, and hot tub. In fall, experienced riders may take part in a special "roundup," helping a local rancher gather and move cattle to winter pasture. The ranch also offers team penning, an exciting arena competition involving cattle.

One of the greatest benefits of the Latigo ranch is the owners' interest in nature education. Be sure to take a guided nature hike; you'll be amazed at your guide's depth of knowledge. Latigo's all-inclusive package price means you won't be surprised when it comes time to settle up.

# SAN JUAN GUEST RANCH

## Ridgway, Colorado

It's hard to get away from superlatives when talking about the scenic settings of Rocky Mountain guest ranches, but it's particularly hard not to gush when speaking of a place like the San Juan Guest Ranch. The ranch is located in the San Juan Mountain Range, known as "the Switzerland of America," due to its abundance of 14,000 peaks and craggy, splendid mountain geology. It is so scenic that when renowned clothing designer Ralph Lauren decided to build a showcase ranch, he picked land just outside Ridgway, not far from the San Juan Guest Ranch.

This guest ranch would be notable for its location alone, but it is also one of the most complete guest ranches listed in this or any other guidebook. The list of activities is impressive: Jeep tours to abandoned ghost towns, fishing, trap and rifle shooting, off-site tennis and nearby natural hot-springs bathing, and hot-air ballooning. The winter menu is no less tasty: sleigh rides, cross-country skiing, snowshoeing, tobogganing, and excursions to the world-class ski village at Telluride.

Owner Scott MacTiernan runs a tight but fun ship; his exceptional talent as a host has earned him the honor of being chosen Outfitter of the Year by the Outfitters Association of America. The MacTiernan family opened their ranch in 1970 on the banks of the Uncompahgre River, and the entire family embraced the guest-ranch lifestyle and set about a rigorous program of expanding their skills and know-how to better serve their guests. Scott, for instance, is a certified riding instructor, and he imparts his knowledge to his carefully chosen staff of college-aged ranch hands. That ensures a safe and thorough program of riding instruction in which guests learn sound riding technique and horsemanship. One comes away with an even greater appreciation of the fine horses that make up the backbone of the San Juan Guest Ranch experience.

In addition, Scott has created a photographic program in which intrepid shutter-bugs can capture the outstanding fall foliage in this preternaturally beautiful corner of Colorado. Sharpshooters, be sure to ask about this special program.

Skiers may be intrigued to learn that their host is also an expert instructor, with years of experience teaching in the world-famous Aspen Ski and Snowboard School. In fall, the ranch provides guided deer and elk hunting trips both on the ranch and in the high country. Groups are limited to eight hunters, with a guest-to-guide ratio of 2 to 1.

The San Juan Ranch is big on hospitality but small in size. A maximum of thirty guests is accommodated, meaning that everyone gets personalized attention and a chance to get to know the entire MacTiernan clan. Such small size allows the ranch to do special things, such as overnight pack trips to particularly scenic mountain campsites.

## San Juan Guest Ranch

2882 County Road 23
Ridgway, CO 81432
Phone: (800) 331–3015; (970) 626–5360
Fax: (970) 626–5015
E-mail: Howdy@sanjuanranch.com
Web site: www.sanjuanranch.com

**Owners/Managers:** Pat, Scott and Kelly MacTiernan

**Accommodations:** Guests stay in a 2-story lodge with individual apartments with twin-, queen- and king-sized beds, depending on the unit. Capacity is 2 to 6 people. Rates depend on accommodations. All units have coffeemakers, sitting areas, and carpeted floors, with minifridges in most units. The San Juan Cottage, adjacent to the ranch, offers 1,600 feet of floor space for groups of 8 people and includes a kitchen, 2 full bathrooms, and 4 bedrooms.

**Meals:** Family-style dining served 3 times daily and features many locally grown and organic fruits, vegetables, and meats. Guaranteed to satisfy the most ravenous or discerning appetites. Those with special dietary demands should advise the staff prior to arrival.

**Activities:** A carefully structured riding program designed by a certified riding instructor. Rides by the hour, half day, or full day. Weekly cattle herding excursion. Jeep trips to abandoned mines and ghost towns. Nature hikes. Fishing in the Uncompaghre River or local ponds. Trap shooting and rifle range (ammo extra). Volleyball, horseshoes, and horse-drawn hayrides. Visits to natural hot springs and tennis courts in nearby Ouray, a quaint mountain town with excellent shopping and restaurants. Fall photo workshops. Winter snowshoeing, tobogganing, sleigh rides, and cross-country skiing. Alpine skiing at nearby Telluride Mountain Resort (45 minutes).

**Amenities:** 8-person hot tub, local artist's exhibit in main lodge, book and video library, comfortable leather sofas in main lodge, huge lodge fireplace, trap and rifle ranges.

**Special Programs:** Limited private hunting trips in fall and winter. Fall nature-photography workshops. Supervised children's program includes a petting zoo and activities. Optional balloon rides at additional expense.

**Rates:** $$–$$$ American Plan. Children's off-season and group rates available. Six-day minimum, except in winter, when a daily "bed-and-breakfast" stay is available. Rates vary according to level of accommodations. Certain special activities such as skiing or balloon rides are extra.

**Credit Cards:** VISA, MasterCard. Personal checks accepted.

**Season:** June–September (summer); adults-only stays in fall; winter bed-and-breakfast. Open Christmas.

**Getting There:** 5 miles north of Ouray, 42 miles east of Telluride. Airport service to either Montrose or Telluride. Denver International Airport, approximately 6 hours drive north and east.

**What's Nearby:** Picturesque mountain villages of Ouray and Telluride, a world-class resort center with skiing, golf, shopping, exceptional restaurants, spas, and some art galleries.

# SKYLINE GUEST RANCH

## Telluride, Colorado

Telluride rivals Aspen as one of the most desirable mountain destinations in the world, but the ambience of this former mining town is quite different. Whereas Aspen is chic, Telluride is funky. And while Aspenites strive to play a subtle game of one-upmanship, the folks in Telluride are much more down to earth and, well, folksy.

That spirit goes well with the Skyline Guest Ranch and its owners, Dave and Sherry Farny. The Farny family bought the ranch property in 1968, and for years, it served as base camp for the Telluride Mountaineering School. In 1981, Sherry and Dave brought that same spirit of adventure to guest ranching. Sherry even has a favorite phrase for it: mountain joy. "Mountain joy is a feeling that through the mountain environment, you have learned to stretch and expand personally, physically and emotionally," she explains.

It is difficult not to respond emotionally to the soaring 14,000 peaks of the San Juan Range that surround this majestically sited ranch. Residing in the rarified air 9,000 feet above sea level, the ranch takes full advantage of its high-country grassland meadows (a riot of wildflowers in summer) and tranquil aspen forests, which provide a fabulous color show in fall. And it's reassuring to know that the beauty of this ranch will remain unspoiled for generations to come, as the land's development rights have been deeded to the Nature Conservancy, insurance against the earthmover's blade.

As one might expect from a family of mountaineers, adventurous activities are the order of the day at the Skyline. Horseback riding, of course, is at the center of things. Mike Farny has adopted and adapted the principles of "natural horsemanship" to the guest-ranch experience.

The idea is to gain an understanding of the horse's view of things and to work with the horse based on its perspective. Guests are allowed to and even encouraged to groom and saddle as well as ride their mount as part of the communication process. Rides are divided into small groups of beginner, intermediate, and expert riders, seldom exceeding eight guests per guide. (Children may participate in riding programs once they are six years old.)

Truly adventurous guests can opt to take an overnight pack trip in the high country during summer, and in fall, the ranch offers a rugged four-day, 66-mile horse packing trip that will test your stamina but reward you with an unforgettable adventure.

In addition to horseback riding, the ranch offers mountain-biking excursions, both guided and unguided. One of the more challenging and thrilling rides is the single-track descent from Alta Mine, an old mining town located above the ranch. Skyline also offers fly-fishing instruction and guided fishing trips on the San Miguel and Delores Rivers as well as on their private lakes. Fly rods are available, and the ranch chefs will cook your catch-of-the-day for breakfast, lunch, or dinner.

Guests may also visit ancient Indian ruins at Mesa Verde National Park, take a four-wheel-drive tour over a high mountain pass, or opt for one of the special program weeks concentrating on one of the following: hiking, cattle work on horseback, harmony with horses, and fly fishing.

Hiking around Skyline encompasses everything from gentle strolls amid brilliant flower-filled meadows to strenuous treks amid snowfields and rocky terrain. Late in the week guests have the opportunity to summit a 14,000-foot peak. Treaded hiking boots are a must!

During winter, Cindy Farny hosts skiers in the six housekeeping cabins, and she operates a gourmet restaurant, open to guests and locals who make the winding drive from Telluride. Winter guests find cross-country ski trails just outside their front doors and ice skates for use on the pond in front of the cabins.

## Skyline Guest Ranch

7214 Highway 145
Telluride, CO 81435
Phone: (888) 754–1126; (970) 728–3757
Fax: (970) 728–6728
E-mail: skyline-ranch@toski.com
Web site: www.skylineguestranch.com

**Owners/Managers:** The Farny Family

**Accommodations:** 10 individual rooms are located in a wing off the expansive main lodge, each with a private bath, and queen, double, or single beds. 6 cabins are ideal for families or groups of friends, accommodating anywhere from 2 to 8 individuals. Daily maid service.

**Meals:** Skyline Ranch chefs are graduates of various culinary schools, which guarantees an unusually high quality of guest-ranch dining. Meals are prepared from scratch with fresh ingredients. Dining in summertime is family style, whereas winter guests may opt for casual or fine dining service. Typical entrees include Colorado-raised beef, fresh fish, pasta, and vegetarian dishes. Beer and wine also served.

**Activities:** Horsemanship featuring "natural riding" methods and advanced communication between horse and rider; overnight pack trips; extended pack trips; mountain biking; mountain climbs; high-alpine hikes; fly fishing; 4-wheel-drive excursions; visits to Mesa Verde National Monument. Winter activities include ice skating, sleigh rides, snowmobiling, cross-country skiing and alpine skiing at nearby Telluride Mountain Resort.

**Amenities:** Outdoor hot tub, on-premise laundry facilities; Outpost Store for necessities and gift items; phones, phone lines, and fax machines in the main office and in Spruce Lodge.

**Special Programs:** Special activity weeks offer activity-focused opportunities with intensive hiking, fishing, cattle work, and horsemanship clinics. Fall extended pack trip. No specific children's activities, although kids may participate alongside their parents.

**Rates:** $$–$$$ Cabin rates higher than lodge room rates. Rates vary by season and activities. All summer rates based on a weeklong (Sunday–Sunday) stay. Children 3–5 half price; infants stay free. No minimum stay for winter guests.

**Credit Cards:** VISA, MasterCard, American Express. Personal checks and traveler's checks accepted; deposit required.

**Season:** Year-round

**Getting There:** Most guests fly into Telluride Airport or Montrose (approximately 50 miles). Shuttle service available from Telluride Airport. Rental car and private shuttle services in Montrose.

**What's Nearby:** Telluride, a world-class resort town featuring shopping, fine dining, and an active nightlife. Golf and winter skiing at Telluride Mountain Resort.

# T LAZY 7 RANCH

## Aspen, Colorado

Long before Aspen became a magnet for international stars and billionaire businessmen, the Deane family was welcoming guests to their down-to-earth horse ranch just a few miles northwest of the historic mining village. Although Aspen has changed considerably over the decades, the T Lazy 7 remains an unpretentious and friendly destination for visitors of all types and means.

One thing that truly puts the Deanes' ranch on the level of world-class ranch experiences is its location. Besides the advantage of being a few minutes from Aspen's exceptional shopping and dining, the T Lazy 7 sits on the road to the scenic Maroon Bells, which many Aspenites claim are the most photographed mountains in North America. Although that's a difficult, if not impossible, claim to verify, there is no question that these rugged shark-tooth monoliths provide one of the prettiest picture postcards imaginable, postcards that you, as a guest of T Lazy 7, can put yourself and your loved ones in with a simple press of the shutter button.

Unlike the majority of the ranches listed in this book, the T Lazy 7 takes a somewhat more "a la carte" approach to guest ranching. Cabins are rented seasonally for 6-month to 1-year leases. More a western-style long-term rental service than a full-service guest ranch, the T Lazy 7 isn't set up to be the be-all and end-all of the visitor's vacation. It is assumed that guests will want to avail themselves of all the cultural, spiritual, gustatory, and athletic opportunities that Aspen has to offer, including the famous summer music and dance festivals, skiing, hiking, and restaurants. Guests, for instance, don't sit down to regular meals but instead prepare meals in their cabins (kitchenettes and outdoor barbecues are provided) or venture into Aspen to visit its renowned restaurants, burger bars, and coffeehouse bakeries. Guests may, however, enjoy a specially prepared ranch-style meal on the trail during regularly scheduled horseback rides with Maroon Bells Outfitters.

What the T Lazy 7 can supply, in abundance, is fun outdoor activities that take full advantage of its glorious location. In wintertime, skiers and others flock to the ranch to take part in organized snowmobile tours to the Maroon Bells. Tours begin with an orientation on a snowmobile track (and can

## ASPEN: CULTURAL MECCA OF THE ROCKIES

Aspen's world-renowned reputation as an arts mecca is well deserved: It's often said that the art scene here rivals that of cities one hundred times its size. The "Grandaddy" of the Aspen arts programs is the Aspen Music Festival and School, created in 1949 by Chicago industrialist Walter Paepcke and his wife, Elizabeth. Top musicians from around the globe come to perform in huge outdoor tents in a lovely park setting. Close to 200 events fill the schedule from late June to mid-August, including operas, orchestral concerts, chamber music, master classes, and children's events. Jazz enthusiasts can enjoy the Janus Jazz Aspen festival at nearby Snowmass Resort.

get quite racy). Afterward, riders head off the main road heading to the Bells. Lunch tours through the White River National Forest or to the Historic Ghost Town of Independence include a hot lunch featuring ranch-raised beef served in rustic cabins.

Another favorite winter activity is cross country skiing, although admittedly, the roar of the snowmobiles takes away somewhat from the enjoyment of backwoods travel on skinny skis.

The main winter draw, of course, is Aspen's world-famous skiing. There are four separate mountains within a 20-mile radius. Children can take advantage of the exceptional learn-to-ski programs at nearby Buttermilk Mountain, the best place for one's maiden ski experience.

## T Lazy 7 Ranch

3129 Maroon Creek Road
Aspen, CO 81611
Phone: The Lodge: (970) 925–4614; Maroon
    Bells Outfitters (970) 920–4677
Fax: (970) 925–5616
E-mail: tlazy7@rof.net
Web site: www.tlazy7.com

**Owners/Mangers:** Rick and Landon Deane

**Accommodations:** Guest capacity, 75. Cabins are equipped with kitchenettes and fireplaces (some have wood-burning stoves). 6-month minimum lease for cabin apartments. Three lodging units are available for nightly rentals.

**Meals:** The T Lazy 7 doesn't provide regular meals. Guests either cook in their cabins or venture into nearby Aspen or Snowmass to dine. The T Lazy 7 is well known locally for its lunch rides to Maroon Bells, as well as its winter sleigh ride dinner-dance. Special chuckwagon dining for groups by arrangement through Maroon Bells Outfitters.

**Activities:** Under new ownership, T Lazy 7 Horseback Riding is now known as Maroon Bells Outfitters. They offer lunch rides made famous by the T Lazy 7 to the spectacular Maroon Bells, or guests may opt for an early-morning ride through the Aspen groves, with views of the 14,000-foot Pyramid Peak. Back at the Chuckwagon Grounds, trail riders are treated to steaming cups of coffee and a huge cowboy breakfast of flapjacks, farm eggs, and fresh-cut fruit. Advance registration is advised; guests should inquire when making lodging reservations. Horseback riding is not included in lodging rates. The Maroon Bells Wilderness offers a fantastic opportunity for exploration and is a favorite destination for hikers and backpackers, photographers, and bird-watchers. Mountain bikes may be rented in summertime. Another popular warm-weather activity is fishing on 3 miles of streamside trout habitat. In winter, a plethora of active choices exist: skiing at world-famous Aspen Mountain, Buttermilk, Aspen Highlands, and Snowmass resorts; cross-country skiing from the ranch; snowmobiling tours (billed separately), and ice skating on the ranch's skating pond. Additional activities in the Aspen area by arrangement.

**Special Programs:** Maroon Bells LLC now offers Western Parties for up to 275 people in the 8,000-square-foot T Lazy 7 Lodge, featuring a barbecue prepared by chefs from Krabloonik Restaurant and a live band. Call (970) 920–4679.

**Rates:** $–$$$ Rate is strictly for lodging; activities, including horseback riding, are separate. Discounted off-season rates; long-term rates available.

**Credit Cards:** VISA, MasterCard, Discover

**Season:** Summer, June–September; winter, November–March

**Getting There:** Air service from Denver to Sardy Field, Aspen's international airport, located about 6 miles from the ranch. Air travelers may also fly into Grand Junction or Denver.

**What's Nearby:** City of Aspen, Snowmass Resort. Aspen area provides a myriad of recreational and entertainment possibilities, from golf and skiing to shopping, fine dining, and dozens of art museums and galleries.

In summertime, the T Lazy 7 shifts to a slower pace. Maroon Bells Outfitters' stable of more than one hundred horses stays busy throughout the warm weather as tourists head up into the spectacular mountains of the White River National Forest and the Maroon Bells Wilderness. The stable concession is operated separately from the ranch and not included in the lodging price, but it is very easy to plan your day rides with the help of the staff.

Aspen has become a magnet for fly fishermen, making stream-side real estate a valuable commodity. Fortunately, the T Lazy 7 has access to nearly 3 miles of prime trout stream along Maroon Creek, with guides available by arrangement. Anglers with lesser skills can hone their casts in the catch-and-release ponds on the ranch premises.

The T Lazy 7 appeals to the self-guided vacationer interested in both the beauty of nature and the urbanity that a world-class tourist destination like Aspen has to offer. By offering an a la carte choice of ranch activities in a truly spectacular setting, the ranch serves as a great base camp for an Aspen-area getaway.

# MOLOKAI RANCH LODGE

## Maunaloa, Molokai, Hawaii

Cattle ranching? In Hawaii? Believe it. The "Aloha!" traditions of the *paniolos* (Hawaiian for "cowboy") live to this day at Molokai Ranch in a unique blend of cattle ranching, adventure travel, and pure resort luxury. If you are seeking something a little exotic in your western ranching adventure, this is the place. After all, it doesn't get much more western than Hawaii!

Just a short flight from Honolulu, Molokai Ranch Lodge is located on the Hawaiian island of Molokai. The 54,000-acre ranch was originally given to Princess Bernice Pauahi Bishop by King Kamehameha V. For a brief while, it was a sugar plantation, and it even served as an African wildlife preserve. But for more than a century, the Molokai has been a cattle ranch, one that has spawned generations of cowboys dressed in straw hats and floral-print shirts.

Molokai Ranch is a fabulous mix of white sand beaches, expansive green pastures, seaside cliffs, and lush tropical valleys. It encompasses most of the western half of the island and has remained unspoiled and undeveloped. Over the years, the resort portion of Molokai Ranch has evolved into a favorite base camp for a wide variety of outdoor adventure activities that include mountain biking, horseback riding, ocean kayaking, hiking, shoreline fishing, and more. You can even try the thrilling and traditional native sport of outrigger-canoe surfing.

Molokai Ranch is divided into separate "camps," each with its own distinct character. An hourly shuttle service whisks guests between the various lodging areas and activity sites.

Kaupoa Beach Village is located amid palm tree groves, where deluxe canvas bungalows on wood floors look out over a broad, white sand beach. Far from being simple camp tents, these rooms offer comfortable queen-sized beds, solar-powered lights and ceiling fans, spacious *lanai* decks with deck furniture, outdoor dining areas, and private bathrooms.

Guests may also opt to stay at Molokai Ranch Lodge, a deluxe resort facility with twenty-two guest rooms, main lodge, and sleeping cottages. The feeling here is one of historic authenticity, with antique appointments from the 1920s and 1930s that give it an "old school" Hawaiian resort feel.

The horseback program offers a chance to ride amid some of the most overwhelming and beautiful scenery on earth. You may visit ancient archaeological sites while learning about the history of the *paniolos* and early Hawaiians, trek through Molokai's lush plains along the dramatic cliffs overlooking Kalaupapa, and visit historic sites whose stories are related by the ranch's native-born *paniolos*. Or, head down to the arena for the "Paniolo Round-Up" to enjoy traditional rodeo events and to take part in relatively safe but challenging contests such as cattle penning and herding.

All in all, the Molokai is a refreshing alternative to most vacation destinations—a guest ranch with Hawaiian aloha spirit and an ingrained sense of adventure.

**Molokai Ranch Lodge**
P.O. Box 259
Maunaloa, HI 96770
Phone: (800) 782–9488
E-mail: molokaireservations@sheraton.com
Web site: www.molokaipropertieslimited.com

**Owners:** Molokai Properties Limited

**Accommodations:** 200+ capacity. The 40 deluxe canvas bungalows at Kaupoa Beach Village offer the perfect blend of luxury and adventure. You'll enjoy a queen-sized bed, solar-powered lights and ceiling fan, spacious lanai with deck furniture, an outdoor eating area, private bathroom with hot-water shower and self-composting toilet, and daily maid service. The Hawaiian Lodge features 22 guest rooms, offering an eclectic combination of new and historic furniture (no 2 rooms are exactly alike). Located in the main building and in separate sleeping cottages, the rooms were designed to take advantage of unobstructed ocean views while offering privacy. All rooms include a wet bar, refrigerator, robes and slippers, cable television, and private lanai.

**Meals:** Meals are served in open-air pavilions and feature Hawaiian specialties as well as sumptuous American dishes. Breakfast, lunch, and dinner are prepared to order by on-staff chefs and feature such specialties as omelets, barbecued hamburgers, and grilled fish and steak. Boxed lunches available for daytime excursions.

**Activities:** Trail rides and activities for riders of all skill levels and abilities. Mountain biking with instruction for everyone from the novice to the expert cyclist. Guided ocean kayaking, shoreline fishing for Papio, Ulua, Ta'ape, Weke, and Uhu. Guided snorkeling and spearfishing. Sport shooting and archery range. Be sure to sign up for one of Molokai Ranch's cultural hikes. The *moolelo* (story-telling) integrated into these unique hikes brings West Molokai's cultural past alive.

**Amenities:** Exercise room, sauna, pool, shower and locker facilities, daily *New York Times,* dedicated Internet access, use of snorkels, fins, masks, Boogie Boards, beach toys, beach chairs, umbrellas, and fishing rods at Kaupoa Beach Village. Unlimited use of shuttles to and from lodging and activity sites. Concierge service, recreation areas and outdoor sports.

**Special Programs:** Activity programs for kids ages 5 to 12. Half-day and full-day Kamali'i EdVenture programs include tide-pool explorations; the Creature Feature, in which they learn about bugs; and the Menehune Mele, in which they learn the hula, play Hawaiian musical instruments, take guided hikes, and sing popular island songs. Packaged activities allow guests to tailor their vacations to their interests.

**Rates:** $$$–$$$$ Full American Plan, including transportation to and from the airport at Molokai and transportation among the various sites. Prices vary widely by accommodations and selected activities. Discounted children's rates.

**Credit Cards:** VISA, MasterCard, American Express, Discover. Traveler's and personal checks accepted.

**Season:** Year-round. High season, December through March.

**Getting There:** Direct flights from Honolulu, Oahu, and Maui. Shuttle service provided to the resort.

**What's Nearby:** The Molokai Ranch is a self-contained resort offering an all-inclusive vacation experience. Guests may wish to plan a few extra days to visit some of Hawaii's other beautiful islands.

# BAR H BAR RANCH

## Soda Springs, Idaho

Idaho's Bar H Bar Ranch is a working cattle ranch. Guests take part in actual cattle work right alongside the ranch's able cowboys. As owner McGee Harris likes to say, "When you are helping to do something at Bar H Bar, you're doing it because it needs to be done, not because you need something to do."

The Bar H Bar sprawls over 9,000 acres of forest and open pasture in the heart of the Bear Valley. The land is rimmed by snowcapped mountain peaks that provide the natural runoff supplying the Bear River, which runs through the property. McGee and his wife, Janet, limit the number of guests (generally four to eight individuals) so that everybody who visits gets personal attention and a chance to really participate in meaningful ranch work. Although there are ample opportunities to "do your own thing," the real fun of a Bar H Bar vacation is the chance to work (and play) like a cowboy.

What exactly does a working cowboy do? Well, on the Bar H Bar, you may participate in everything from mending fences to herding cattle between pastures or riding out to replenish the salt-block supply. If a sick calf needs doctoring, you may be given the task of minding the rope horse, and if a cow is giving birth, you'll be there to witness the calf being born. It's an amazing and unforgettable vacation.

When the work is done (or if you simply decide to "take a day off"), you can angle for trout or take a nature hike on the ranch. Wildlife resides quite happily with the cow herd, and your explorations on horseback or on foot are likely to reveal elk, deer, and moose as well as a variety of small game and upland birds.

Guests lodge in traditional cowboy fashion, in a restored four-room "bunkhouse." The rooms are furnished with rustic lodge-pole-pine furniture and antiques that reflect the ranch's pioneering heritage. Each room has an individual entrance and a comfortable porch where one can rest out of the summer sun. When it comes time to shower up for dinner, you may choose to do so in the clean, modernized facility, or get clean the cowboy way by taking a dip in Bear River, which runs through the property.

The Bar H Bar isn't for everyone. Small children are discouraged (the ranch recommends a minimum age of twelve), and even if you take teens, they might not be as enthralled with living the cowboy life as you are. Teens with a high degree of maturity, a good work ethic, and a desire to really dig in and experience alternative ways of life seem to be best suited to the Bar H Bar.

For vacationers who genuinely want to experience a fading way of American life, the Bar H Bar is ideal.

## Bar H Bar Ranch

1501 Eight Mile Creek Road
Soda Springs, ID 83276
Phone: (800) 743–9505; (208) 547–3082
Fax: (208) 547–0203
E-mail: barhbar@aol.com
Web site: www.barhbar.com

**Owners/Managers:** McGee and Janet Harris

**Accommodations:** 4 rooms in a refurbished bunkhouse. Private entrances and porches. Queen-sized or matched double-sized beds. Decor is rustic, with lodgepole-pine furniture and western antiques. Capacity is 8.

**Meals:** Served ranch style; guests and ranch workers dine together at a common table. 3 hearty meals served daily. Home-baked bread, pies, rolls, and desserts.

**Activities:** The Bar H Bar program revolves around real cattle-ranch work. Guests participate in the daily ranching chores, which may include everything from gathering and moving cattle to preparing cattle for shipping. Guests may opt out of the daily routine to go fishing or to enjoy an afternoon of nature hiking.

**Amenities:** The authentic cattle ranch is clean and modern but relatively spartan. Guests who expect spas and pampering will be disappointed.

**Special Programs:** None. Children over the age of 12 are welcome, but be certain that working on a real cattle ranch is something they will not become bored with and that they are self-motivated and able to entertain themselves among adults.

**Rates:** $$ Full American Plan. Family rates available.

**Credit Cards:** None. Cash and checks accepted.

**Season:** Summer: May through October; winter: December through March

**Getting There:** Nearest airports include Pocatello, Idaho (60 miles); Jackson, Wyoming (100 miles); Idaho Falls (120 miles); and Salt Lake City (184 miles). Ranch is 60 miles east of Pocatello off Highway 30 to Soda Springs. Discuss ground transportation from Pocatello with the ranch owners.

**What's Nearby:** Lava Hot Springs (swimming and hot tubs), Minnetonka Cave, natural soda-water springs, Pickleville Playhouse (melodrama), historic Mormon Pioneer Tabernacle, golfing.

# BAR H RANCH

## Driggs, Idaho

Every guest ranch finds a marketing niche. Working ranches tout their authentic cowboy experience. Mountain ranches offer exquisite scenery. Some ranches offer five-star services and facilities; others emphasize adventure sports such as rock climbing and mountain biking. The Bar H Ranch is unique in that it caters only to women.

Ranch owner Edie Harrop is a third-generation Teton Valley cattle rancher who decided that she wanted to share her rural revelry with other women in a friendly and, we should add, supremely beautiful place. For close to two decades, the Bar H has been a haven for mothers and daughters, friends and coworkers to literally let down their hair and be cowgirls. Guests may choose to trail ride from the ranch's main lodge or embark on adventuresome overnight and extended pack trips in the breathtaking Teton wilderness along the Idaho and Wyoming border. Either way, the scenery is postcard perfect.

Harrop's partner in adventuring is Deb Thibeault, the Bar H high-country trail boss. Her extensive experience with horses and clients ensures that strong bonds will form, both with your assigned animal and with the other women who share in your odyssey.

But the adventure doesn't end with horse riding. The Teton Valley, nestled between the majestic and famous Grand Tetons and the Big Hole Mountain Range, offers a multitude of activities that include hiking, mountain biking, and fly fishing. In addition, guests are in close proximity to Yellowstone National Park, Grand Teton National Park, and the famous Jackson Hole, a western town that offers exceptional dining, shopping, and nightlife.

Thibeault leads a number of backcountry trips of varying difficulty. These special camps vary from challenging weeklong campouts in the high country to a luxurious stay at the AAA 4-Diamond Rio Rico Resort in Tucson, Arizona. Be sure to ask about these camps when making your trip plans!

For a less structured vacation, relax and enjoy a week at the ranch in a private and uniquely appointed loft. Enjoy the fully equipped kitchen, take in the sweeping mountain views from your deck, and delight in a soak in an old-time claw-foot tub. Highlight your trip with an optional trail ride in the Tetons, or ride the ranch to check cattle. If you wish, just relax, hike, fish, or sightsee.

## Bar H Ranch

P.O. Box 297
Driggs, ID 83422
Phone: (888) 216–6025; (208) 354–2906
Fax: (208) 354–8804
E-mail: barh@tetonvalley.net
Web site: www.tetontrailrides.com

**Owners/Managers:** Edie Harrop and Deb Thibeault

**Accommodations:** Backcountry guests stay in 4-person dome tents, with 2 guests per tent. Guest capacity varies according to trip length and participation. A small number of guests may be accommodated at the ranch itself; inquire about availability of the ranch loft/bunkhouse.

**Meals:** Meals on the trail consist of basic but generous camp fare. 3 daily meals, including a trailside lunch. A camp chef prepares BBQ and Dutch-oven dinners featuring garden-fresh salads and homemade desserts in the chuck-wagon kitchen.

**Activities:** Backcountry pack trips are the focus of the Bar H activities. These vary from mild to wild and include a special trip to Rio Rico Resort in Tucson, Arizona, a full-service spa and resort. Ranch guests may partake of numerous activities, including mountain biking, fishing, and day trips to Jackson Hole. Inquire of the hosts for tourism advice.

**Special Programs:** North Leigh Canyon Camp features daily high-country trail rides from a base camp in North Leigh Canyon; advanced riders may partake of the High Altitude Camp into the Jebediah Smith Wilderness; High Country Heaven is a less rigorous program that still takes riders to the heights of the Grand Tetons; the Rio Rico trip centers around a deluxe resort in the Arizona desert, complete with spa, Jacuzzi, sauna, and outstanding recreational opportunities.

**Rates:** $–$$$ Ranch stays are structured a la carte, with horseback riding and other activities charged additionally. Ranch guests do their own cooking. Pack trips and stays at the Rio Rico Resort in Arizona are on the full American Plan.

**Credit Cards:** None. Personal and traveler's checks preferred.

**Season:** May through October

**Getting There:** Transportation from the Jackson, Wyoming, airport (or Jackson motels) to Driggs and/or North Leigh base camp is available through CART (Community and Rural Transportation). Please call (208) 354–2240 for reservations. Alternate airport destination is Idaho Falls, Idaho. CART will provide airport pickup by special arrangement.

**What's Nearby:** Jackson, Wyoming; Yellowstone National Park; Grand Teton National Park; and the Idaho towns of Driggs and Tetonia.

# HIDDEN CREEK RANCH

## Harrison, Idaho

Although the look of Hidden Creek Ranch—with its log-cabin style main lodge—is very traditional, the philosophy here is quite modern and progressive. Basically, owner John Muir and partner Iris Behr share a conservationist ethic that emphasizes the appreciation for and preservation of the natural environment. Furthermore, they've adopted the popular and somewhat revolutionary philosophy of horse training that stresses finding unity and cooperation with horses.

Although those values are not unique to the guest-ranch business, they certainly offer comfort to individuals who want to live peaceably in nature and follow the adage "Take only photographs, leave only footprints"—or, in this case, hoofprints.

Hidden Creek Ranch is nestled in a gentle valley, rimmed by rolling hills covered in stands of fir and pine trees. The environment helps protect the ranch from the extremes of mountain weather and provides a highly varied and scenic terrain over which to ride—and at Hidden Creek, you'll have the opportunity to do plenty of riding.

Appropriately, John and Iris take great pride in their horse program. Once situated on the ranch, guests are introduced to the horses. Care is taken to match horse to rider, and if the fit is good, you'll get to enjoy and bond with that same horse throughout your stay. A thorough orientation follows, and your equine education continues on the trail. A plethora of different riding activities awaits you: slow and fast trail rides, all-day rides, dinner rides, lunch rides, horse grooming and saddling instruction, wagon rides, and arena barrel-racing and cow-herding competitions. You can even learn the basics of driving a team. For serious horsemen, the ranch also offers Centered Riding Instruction and Clinics, a certified riding program designed to make you a better, more confident horseman.

For guests who don't want to spend all their time in the saddle (or for that matter, any time) there is a wide variety of additional programs and activities that will amply fill up your day. You can lake-fish, pond-fish, or take a fly-fishing lesson. There are jogging and hiking trails, an archery range, and a trap- and rifle-shooting range. If you want, you can participate in a lively volleyball game or play a more leisurely game of horseshoes. Among the favorite side trips is a boat tour of beautiful Lake Coeur d'Alene and Blue Lake, the scenic gems of Northern Idaho. (Be sure to visit the gorgeous Coeur d'Alene Resort and shop in this lovely tourist town during your stay.)

## Hidden Creek Ranch

11077 East Blue Lake Road
Harrison, Idaho 83833
Phone: (800) 446–3833; (208) 689–3209
Fax: (208) 689–9115
E-mail: hiddencreek@hiddencreek.com
Web site: www.hiddencreek.com

**Owners/Managers:** John Muir and Iris Behr

**Accommodations:** Guest capacity, 40. Authentic log cabins, each with 2 to 4 units, equipped with log furniture. Each unit has a private bath and a shower/bathtub. Covered porches complete each cabin. Most rooms have a queen-sized bed; larger units feature bunk beds and single beds, ideal for young children.

**Meals:** A classically trained executive chef oversees the kitchen, ensuring the highest-quality vacation meals. Breakfast includes ranch staples, such as huevos rancheros and biscuits with gravy, and healthful alternatives, from homemade muesli cereal to fresh fruits, fresh-baked breads, and pastries. Seasonally available fresh fruits complement hearty lunches such as quiche lorraine, stews, and turkey–black bean chili, all accompanied by an amply stocked salad bar. For a change of pace, your week also includes a barbecue cookout and a 7-course meal fit for gourmands. Dinners feature 4-course meals including salad, soups, a main course, and desserts. Special dietetic needs (vegetarian, low-fat, diabetic, or food allergies) can be accommodated with advance notice.

**Activities:** Although an extensive horseback-riding program composes the backbone of the Hidden Creek Ranch program, every riding opportunity is balanced by additional, non-equine activities. Guests may elect to learn fly fishing, go on nature hikes, or participate in gun sports, archery, boat tours, competitive arena roping classes, volleyball, and a variety of recreational games and sports. In wintertime, guests may choose to participate in snowmobile tours, cross-country skiing, snowshoeing, and downhill skiing at nearby northern Idaho resorts. Riding programs include in-depth instruction to casual trail rides, all tailored to individuals' abilities and interests. Dinner rides, wagon rides, grooming and saddling lessons, cow-herding games, and a barrel-racing rodeo are a sampling of the equestrian menu. Accomplished equestrians may wish to take part in the Centered Riding Instruction program, which emphasizes sound equitation and advanced riding skills under the supervision of certified instructors.

**Amenities:** The 7,500-square-foot guest lodge is the social center of the ranch. Relax with a book from the library or enjoy a film on video. Meals also take place in the lodge, and guests may relax with a cocktail at the bar or sit before the volcanic-rock fireplace. Fitness center offering aerobic and strength-training equipment and complemented by outdoor hot tub baths, an authentic Native American sweat-lodge ceremony, and an outdoor swimming pond. Guests may also take a swim in the beautiful Blue Lake.

**Special Programs:** A full children's program for children ages 3 to teens available throughout the day as well as during adults-only evening activities. It is up to each parent how much time they want to spend with their children and how much time the children want to spend within the children's program. Adults-only weeks available in spring and autumn. Corporate retreat programs designed to enhance communication and group problem solving. There's also the Body, Mind & Spirit program, a holistic approach to fitness, which includes instruction and participation in yoga, stretching, relaxation, fitness and conditioning, and massage. A full-service fitness center and expert staff will help you ease into a healthful program designed to benefit you long after your vacation is over.

**Rates:** $$$ Full American Plan. Rates based on a 6-night stay, double occupancy. Reduced rates for children 3–11; kids under 2 stay free. Reduced off-peak and winter rates also available. Per-person rates May–October: double occupancy, $2,165; single occupancy, $2,495; kids 3–11, $1,776; kids 2 and under, free.

**Credit Cards:** VISA, MasterCard, American Express

**Season:** Year-round

**Getting There:** Located 5 miles east of Harrison off Highway 97. Closest commercial airport, Spokane (78 miles southeast). Private airport in Coeur d'Alene, 40 miles southeast.

**What's Nearby:** Sweitzer Winter Resort, resort town of Coeur d'Alene, which includes quaint shops, art galleries, and a world-class championship golf course.

# IDAHO ROCKY MOUNTAIN RANCH

## Stanley, Idaho

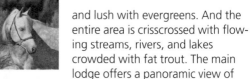

Imagine being able to go back and see the West as the Corps of Discovery's Captains Lewis and Clark did two centuries ago. It's possible at the Idaho Rocky Mountain Ranch, a historic guest ranch located in the heart of the Sawtooth National Recreation Area, the largest wilderness area in the continental United States.

This is truly a special place, ideal for individuals looking for a relaxing scenic getaway or an outdoor adventure that is truly far from the trodden path. The ranch was created in 1930 as a private retreat, available only to club members and their invited guests. Carpenters handcrafted the lodge and adjacent buildings from native lodgepole pine. The buildings have aged beautifully and provide a pleasant rusticity to the property. Edmund and Ruth Bogert bought the ranch in 1951, and it has since passed into the capable hands of their daughter, Rozalys Smith. In 1995, the ranch was added to the National Register of Historic Places as a well-preserved example of the earliest guest ranches in the American West. Guests take great pleasure in the original handcrafted furniture, furnishings such as mounted trophy animals and generations-old photographs, and decorative ironwork, while relaxing in the comfort of thoughtfully upgraded modern amenities.

Although most guest ranches can boast of beautiful scenery, this ranch is situated in one of the truly more outstanding natural areas in North America. The craggy and steep Sawtooth and White Cloud Mountain Ranges remain snow-covered throughout most of summer. The forests here are deep and lush with evergreens. And the entire area is crisscrossed with flowing streams, rivers, and lakes crowded with fat trout. The main lodge offers a panoramic view of the mighty Sawtooth Range, making it the favorite place for guests to congregate after an active day.

There are plenty of activities to keep you engaged here. The horse program is focused on wilderness exploration on well-established bridle paths. If you prefer, you can rent a mountain bike and explore under your own power. Individuals who want to get wet can take a thrilling raft ride on the Salmon River or opt for a more leisurely float down the Payette. Anglers will find excellent lake and river fishing, whereas shutterbugs can simply grab a camera and go "hunting" for the perfect shot—it won't be hard to find! After your exertions, you can relax in the ranch's large swimming pool, which is fed by local hot springs.

Large groups (eighteen or more) may wish to "rent" the meadow ranch site for a special occasion, such as a family reunion, conference, or wedding. Located near Gold Creek, a five-minute walk from the main lodge, this site offers lovely views of the Sawtooth Range and provides rustic tables and benches in a covered pavilion ideal for the sumptuous Dutch-oven meals and grilled specialties served up by the ranch's head chef.

In addition, the ranch offers conference and large-group packages that allow you to essentially "rent the ranch," custom-tailoring your activities and meals to your own program.

## Idaho Rocky Mountain Ranch

HC 64, Box 9934
Stanley, ID 83278
Phone: (208) 774–3544
Fax: (208) 774–3477
E-mail: idrocky@ruralnetwork.net
Web site: www.duderanchers.com/guest
ranches/idahorockymountainranch

**Managers:** Sandra Beckwith and Bill Leavell

**Accommodations:** 21 total units; maximum occupancy, 44. 16 duplex cabins include rock fireplaces and queen-sized beds. Some cabins have walk-through doors to accommodate families. Special Honeymoon Cabin also available. Additional lodging in 4 rooms in the main lodge. All rooms and cabins have private baths. No in-room phones, televisions, or radios, but a courtesy phone, pay phone, and office services are available to guests.

**Meals:** Guests dine in the historic lodge dining room, completed with central fireplace and quilted tablecloths. 2 seated meals a day, with picnic lunches available at extra cost. Breakfast consists of a continental buffet and hot breakfast items, fresh fruits, and fresh-baked goods. Evening dining includes a 5-course meal of appetizers, soup, salad, choice of entrée, and desserts. Entrees include specialties such as mountain trout, lamb, paella, duck breast, prime rib. Thursday night barbecue, Monday night outdoor cookout with traditional Dutch-oven meal. Special diets accommodated with advance notice.

**Activities:** Guided horseback rides, hiking, nature walks, mountain biking, fly fishing and lake fishing. Guests may arrange off-site river rafting, hikes in the Sawtooth National Recreation Area, canoeing, windsurfing, and kayak-ing. Fishermen can request a horseback ride into secluded, high-alpine lakes. Species include rainbow, cutthroat, brook and bull trout. Cross-country-ski touring in winter.

**Amenities:** Hot-springs pool; library and board games; complimentary laundry facility; day-use conference facility with catering; handcrafted furniture and original "pioneer" furnishing; cabins equipped with individual fireplaces.

**Special Programs:** No children's programs are available; children are the responsibility of their parents and participate alongside adults in ranch activities. Children's rates available, however.

**Rates:** $$ Modified American Plan. Guest price includes breakfast, dinner, lodging, and use of all ranch facilities. Additional prices charged for activities, including horseback riding, mountain-bike rental, off-site trips, etc. Inquire about activities and costs before committing to a reservation. Rates do not include 15 percent service charge/gratuity and state and local taxes.

**Credit Cards:** VISA, MasterCard (summer months only). Personal checks, traveler's checks, money orders also accepted anytime.

**Season:** October–September

**Getting There:** The ranch is 9 miles south of Stanley, on Highway 75 between mile markers 180 and 181. Nearest airports are Boise (130 miles) and Sun Valley/Hailey (65 miles).

**What's Nearby:** Sun Valley, one of the loveliest all-season resort towns in the West; nearby ghost-town tours; Sawtooth National Recreation Area.

# TETON RIDGE RANCH
## Tetonia, Idaho

When most people think of the Teton Range, they conjure images of the beautiful Jackson Hole valley and its famous resort town, Jackson, Wyoming. It's perhaps, then, a well-kept secret that the Idaho side of that same range is every bit as striking but quite a bit less crowded with showcase millionaires' ranches and SUVs. Think of it as Jackson Hole, circa 1940.

It's here that the luxurious Teton Ridge Ranch is located. Situated on 4,000 acres of private land bordered by the Targhee National Forest, the ranch offers close proximity to Yellowstone and Teton National Parks and is but an hour's drive from Jackson, with its world-renowned shopping, museums, and restaurants, not to mention two first-rate ski areas, Grand Targhee and Jackson Hole. Winter or summer, this ranch offers all the scenic beauty of the mountain West along with the amenities and gracious living afforded by a first-rate resort hotel.

Teton Ridge Ranch boasts a 10,000-square-foot main lodge of modern log-cabin design, with huge windows that look out onto stunning views. The interior is simply outstanding, with warm knotty pine, cathedral ceilings, exposed beams, and stone fireplaces. The dining room is particularly elegant, with guests seated at candlelit tables and feasting on gourmet meals prepared by professional chefs.

With a mere seven suites (five in the lodge, two in the nearby cottage) to accommodate guests, the feeling here is one of intimacy. Each of the suites features its own private deck, woodstove, king-sized bed, opulent bathroom, and even a Jacuzzi bath.

As befits such a top-shelf resort property, the menu of adventures is quite extensive. Shooting-sports enthusiasts and first-time shooters alike can hone their aim from the ranch's shooting towers or blast away on the challenging shooting clay course. In fall, guests may take part in pheasant or partridge hunting, ably assisted by trained English setters.

White-water rafting on the Snake River is another popular activity. Anglers can wet their lines in any number of rivers, including the Snake, Madison, and Teton. All are world-class fishing destinations, and expert guides will help you find the best waters. If hiking is your idea of a day well spent, the ranch offers 14 miles of marked trails.

In addition to these activities, the ranch hosts can arrange for off-site hot-air bal-

## GRAND TARGHEE WINTER RESORT

Skiing aficionados recognize Grand Targhee Winter Resort as one of the West's best-kept secrets. With more than 400 inches of snow a season, it frequently tops the lists in snow accumulation, which translates into acres and acres of fresh powder. To make things even better, Targhee offers unique Sno-Cat adventures that take advanced skiers into the backcountry, where face shots in untrammeled fields of powder are the norm.

And that's not all: Even in-bounds, the lifts are seldom crowded; the snow often remains pristine even days after a storm. Visitors can also visit the resort's ice skating rink or take a dogsled trip through stands of pine and fir trees.

looning, and guided mountain-bike rides; you can even try tandem hang gliding. Just about any outdoor adventure you can think of (with the exception of, say, surfing) can be arranged during your stay.

And of course, there's horseback riding. In addition to daytime rides from the ranch, guests may opt for overnight pack trips that take them high into the Teton mountains, where trappers and mountain men once flourished.

In winter, the resort lends itself to a plethora of sports, including cross-country skiing, snowshoeing, horse-drawn sleigh rides, and even dogsledding.

## Teton Ridge Ranch
200 Valley View Road
Tetonia, ID 83452
Phone: (208) 456–2650
Fax: (208) 456–2218
Web site: www.tetonridge.com

**Guest Services Manager:** Jan Betts

**Accommodations:** 7 total units; 14 guests. 32-day guest limit for conferences or family get-togethers. Suites include balconies, wood-stoves, oversized bathrooms, mountain views, Jacuzzi hot-tub baths.

**Meals:** 3 meals served daily. Cuisine focuses on regional specialties, such as roast loin of elk, breast of duckling, fresh fish, and locally picked wild mushrooms. Dinners include 4 courses. A typical menu: French onion soup, medallions of salmon and beef tenderloin, buttered asparagus, saffron rice, walnut-pecan wheat bread, linzertorte, raspberry coulis. Special diets accommodated with advance notice. Beer and wine served with dinner.

**Activities:** Activities are tailored to guests' desires. Horseback riding, overnight pack trips (extra), hiking, stream and lake fishing, cross-country skiing, snowshoeing, shooting sports, sleigh rides, dogsledding. Additional activities, such as downhill skiing, mountain biking, ballooning, snowmobiling, and more can be arranged at extra cost. Fall upland bird hunting available.

**Amenities:** A small but luxurious guest ranch with the amenities one would expect in an expensive resort hotel. Guest rooms feature steam baths and Jacuzzi hot tubs, reading areas. In winter, cross-country skiers can schuss on 19 miles of groomed trails. On-site masseuse.

**Special Programs:** None. Well-mannered children over 12 welcomed. Guests arrange activities and schedules through the ranch's activities planner.

**Rates:** $$$$ Full American Plan. Reduced rates during the off-season and corporate rates; 1-week minimum stay in July and August (peak season).

**Credit Cards:** None. Personal checks and traveler's checks are preferred.

**Season:** Summer, late May through October; winter, mid-December through March

**Getting There:** Closest airports are Jackson Hole, Wyoming, 45 miles; Idaho Falls, Idaho, 75 miles. Pickup or delivery to Jackson at $90 per vehicle, one way. Rental car recommended.

**What's Nearby:** Jackson Hole, Wyoming, Jackson Hole and Grand Targhee Winter Resorts, Yellowstone National Park, Teton National Park. Nearby town of Tetonia offers shopping, restaurants, services.

# TWIN PEAKS RANCH

## Salmon, Idaho

Twin Peaks Ranch is a place of great diversity, both in its natural setting and its activities. Truly, it is a place where one can live out one's adventure fantasies.

Homesteaded in 1924 as a working cattle ranch on the banks of the wild Salmon River, Twin Peaks has evolved into one of the premier guest ranches in a state rich with such destinations. The ranch also takes full advantage of its river setting, giving visitors the chance to raft some of the best Class IV and Class V rapids in the West; guests can also try their hands at running some milder rapids in a kayak. Sportsmen will love this setting, where one can fly fish on the banks or from the gunwales of an outboard boat. True nature lovers will want to thrill to the overnight backcountry pack trip through land teeming with elk, deer, moose, bighorn sheep, and even a few bears.

Twin Peaks encompasses several thousand acres of private land offering a park-like setting. Massive peaks rise several thousand feet above the principal ranch lands, adding an inspiring scenic backdrop to the ranch's open pastures and forested trails. Instead of one single ranch compound, Twin Peaks has several staffed outposts, each offering a unique experience. During your stay, you will move between the various camps, each offering different opportunities for entertainment, dining, and diversion.

You'll pack in to the North Basin, a high-mountain tent camp. The Williams Lake Lodge fishing camp gives anglers and would-be anglers the chance to lure trout in a subalpine lake. The lower-elevation Ram's Head Lodge provides overnight accommodations within hearing distance of the roaring Salmon River, the ideal stop for adventurers setting out on a two-day white-water excursion down the mighty Salmon.

All in all, Twin Peaks Ranch is an ideal place for singles, couples, and families in search of an unforgettable adventure. Your week will be crammed full of adventures as you ride the banks of the Salmon, climb to the 9,000-foot-high country camp at North Basin, fish in stocked ponds and flowing rivers, even take a few hours to learn archery and marksmanship at the archery, and trap- and skeet-shooting range. Finally, your week will end in true cowboy fashion with a Western cattle drive and horseback games in the ranch's ample arena. All the while, you'll be entertained by cowboy singers, evenings of country dancing, and even a hayride on a wagon pulled by stout draft horses.

## Twin Peaks Ranch

P.O. Box 774
Salmon, ID 83467
Phone: (800) 659–4899
Fax: (208) 894–2429
Web site: www.twinpeaksranch.com

**Owners:** Allen and Lenabelle Davis

**Accommodations:** Capacity, 55. 7 rustic cabins accommodate 2 to 4 persons each, with individual bathrooms. Deluxe cabins feature 2 bedrooms with whirlpool tubs. A 3-bedroom unit is also available, complete with full bath and game table. A suite is available at the Salmon Run Cabin.

**Meals:** Meals are served in the main lodge in a comfortable dining hall with excellent mountain views. Sojourners will enjoy trailside lunches and outdoor cookouts of barbecued steaks, corn on the cob, salad, baked beans, and cobbler. Similarly, hearty breakfasts are served out of the camp's cook tent. At the Ram's Head Cafe, guests enjoy dinners based on the original menu. In short, the dining opportunities are as varied as the activities themselves.

**Activities:** Trail rides take in the scenic possibilities of the Salmon River to the high-alpine setting of the North Basin, destination of the overnight pack trip. River rafting on the Salmon will take you to Ram's Head, a remote wilderness outpost. Fishermen can enjoy everything from stocked ponds to white-water pools, with fly-fishing instruction and out-board trolling available. Archery and shooting sports, cattle work, and an arena play-day.

**Amenities:** Singing cowboy musicians, a western dance band, western dance instruction, authentic Yellowstone open-topped tour bus, riding arena, fishing camps with tackle supplies, outdoor pool at Salmon run, hot-tub baths.

**Special Programs:** A full program is available from mid-June through August for children ages six and up. The Kids' Program includes daily horseback riding, games, petting zoo, and outdoor activities. Meeting facilities and activities for up to 55 participants available.

**Rates:** $$$ American Plan. Children's, group, off-season discounts available. Shortened stays (3 days) also available.

**Credit Cards:** VISA, MasterCard. Cash, and cashier's and personal checks accepted.

**Season:** June through October

**Getting There:** Located 18 miles south of Salmon, 40 miles north of Challis, Idaho. Located off Highway 93. Commercial air transportation to Idaho Falls, Idaho, and Missoula, Montana. Local shuttle flights available to Salmon. Complimentary airport transportation to and from Missoula and Idaho Falls airports. Inquire about the shuttle schedule.

**What's Nearby:** Missoula, Montana, a delightful and historic college town three hours north, provides an interesting opportunity for dining, shopping, and cultural events.

# WESTERN PLEASURE RANCH

## Sandpoint, Idaho

Although still a relatively young guest ranch, the Western Pleasure has a rich family history. The ranch was founded in 1940, when family patriarch Riley Wood pulled up stakes in Colorado and sought out a new beginning in the Idaho Panhandle. Since that time, the family has operated a working ranch here. In the 1990s, the ranch acquired additional acreage, and the family began searching about for new things to do with their original ranch lands. They began offering day rides on horseback. The trips grew so popular that Riley's granddaughter, Janice, and her husband, Roley Schoonover, decided to build a guest-ranch facility to accommodate their burgeoning clientele.

The ranch lodge, completed in 1995, is truly a work of art. The entire building is made of locally cut timber in the traditional log-cabin style. Modern log cabins complement the lodge, giving the entire ranch a feeling of rusticity and continuity. Each cabin accommodates up to six people and is well apportioned with a bedroom, loft, furnished kitchen, bathroom, and traditional woodstove. Additional guests stay in six separate rooms in the main lodge, whose amenities (recreation room, pool table, river-rock fireplace, and outdoor hot tub) make it a favorite gathering place for all.

Outdoors, the activity focuses on riding. The Western Pleasure horse program begins with a fun and informative riding lesson, including the careful selection of horses to match riders' abilities. Rides take full advantage of the family cattle tradition, with riders passing through pastures crowded with grazing cattle, or riders may head through the woods, where they may encounter a variety of wildlife in their native habitat. Beautiful views of the Selkirk and Cabinet Mountain Ranges and Lake Pend Oreille create lasting memories. Rides last from a moderate two hours to overnight trips lasting two days!

The Schoonovers often include guests in the actual work of a family cattle ranch, and so you may get the chance to herd the eighty pairs of cows and their calves among the various pastures. "The guest's involvement depends on where we're moving cattle," Roley said. "Sometimes it involves opening a gate and letting them into a different pasture. If we're moving them to the neighbor's leased pasture, the guests get to drive them down the road." It's simple, but can be thrilling, particularly when one of the bulls decides that he wants to put up a fuss rather than cooperating. Fortunately, experienced hands are always available to keep the bovines in line!

Nearby Lake Pend Oreille offers the opportunity for water sports, including a kayaking adventure. Golf is another option at Hidden Lakes Golf Course, 10 miles from the ranch. In winter, guests can visit nearby Schweitzer Ski Area, one of the better ski resorts in the Pacific Northwest. In the evening, enjoy a ride in a sleigh pulled by two herculean Percheron draft horses. Be sure to visit the town of Sandpoint, a century-old former mining town on the shores of 41-mile-long Lake Pend Oreille.

## Western Pleasure Ranch

1413 Upper Gold Creek
Sandpoint, ID 83864
Phone: (208) 263–9066
Fax: (208) 265–0138
E-mail: info@westernpleasure.com
Web site: www.westernpleasureranch.com

**Owners/Managers:** Roley and Janice Schoonover

**Accommodations:** Capacity, 34. 3 cabins, 6 lodge rooms. Cabins accommodate from 2 to 8 individuals. Each cabin has a loft, bedroom, bathroom, and woodstove. Main lodge has 6 guest rooms with private baths.

**Meals:** Meals are served family style in the main lodge dining room. Western fare with ranch-raised beef (prime rib, steaks) are a specialty.

**Activities:** Horseback riding is the main activity. Guests are sometimes invited to participate in cattle work. Rides based on experience: slow, medium, and fast-paced rides. Arena instruction offered. Nearby 18-hole golf course. Cross-country skiing and downhill skiing available in winter.

**Amenities:** Luxurious 10,000-square-foot main lodge made of hewn logs taken off the land; horse-drawn buggy rides; outdoor recreational game facilities, children's playground, rec room with video library.

**Special Programs:** No formal children's programs. Kids and parents play together; however, a summer-camp program, Fiddler on the Hoof, for kids is offered in July. The program teaches equitation and music instruction based on folk fiddling. Additional kid's camp programs also offered. Camps include wagon rides, BBQ dinner, western equitation, and a horse show put on by the kids.

**Rates:** $$–$$$ Full American Plan or B&B plan. Reduced rates for children 6–12. Ask about special rates for family reunions, weddings, and retreats.

**Credit Cards:** VISA, MasterCard

**Season:** Year-round. Summer packages June 1 to September 30.

**Getting There:** Nearest commercial airport, Spokane, Washington (approximately 90 miles). Located 60 miles north of Coeur d'Alene, Idaho; 16 miles northeast of Sandpoint, Idaho.

**What's Nearby:** Sandpoint, a century-old mining and logging town; Schweitzer Winter Resort; Coeur d'Alene Lake Resort and the city of Coeur d'Alene.

# EL RANCHO STEVENS

## Gaylord, Michigan

It seems as though the farther east you go, the more "western" the guest ranches become. Perhaps it is to compensate for being so seemingly out of place. El Rancho Stevens fits that mold. This ranch is so kitschy and unapologetically western in its look and feel, you'll quickly forget you are in Michigan and not, say, Wyoming.

Take the lodging, for instance. With lodge names like the Thunderbird, Double H, Frontier, and Westward Ho!, the point that this is indeed a dude ranch is hard to escape. What redeems the El Rancho Stevens is its fabulous family atmosphere, its location (on the banks of Dixon Lake), and its genuine western hospitality. If you live in the Midwest, have young kids, and dread the hassle of flying to the West, you might just want to pack up the minivan and head . . . north.

El Rancho Stevens was built in 1948 by Detroit auto engineer "Doc" Stevens and his wife, Candy, just in time for the big western craze that swept postwar America. At present, the ranch is still owned and managed by their son, Steve. The Stevens family's decades of guest-ranch experience have resulted in a comfortable, clean, well-run ship that emphasizes friendly service and a boatload of fun activities. Think of summer camp when you were a kid, and you start to get the feeling of being here.

An outstanding kids' program makes vacationing relaxing for children and their parents. Kids six to twelve take part in the Junior Wranglers, with hikes, lessons in horse care, horseback riding, games, arts and crafts, hayrides, pizza parties, and special dinners in the Roost. Baby-sitters for younger children, by arrangement.

While the kids play, their parents and older siblings can enjoy the sandy lakefront beach, cruise the lake on a variety of water craft, or fish for bass, perch, pike, tiger muskie, and walleye; the cook will even prepare your catch. A pool and poolside snack bar offer alternate recreation and lounging options. Organized water games and evening wiener roasts and cookouts on the beach extend the waterside fun.

If golf is your game, you can tee it up at one of twenty-two golf courses in and around the ranch. Inquire about the various opportunities.

Indoor activities abound, as well. There are western dance lessons, card games, bingo, children's games, arts and crafts projects, a weekly talent show, video games, and Ping-Pong and pool tables.

A variety of lodging plans and rate packages allows you to tailor your vacation to your budget. You can stay a day, a weekend, or a week. It's all up to you.

Rancho Stevens may not have the Rocky Mountains as a backdrop, but it compensates with a wonderful mixture of amenities, activities, and good ol' western fun. You—and your family—will be happy you stayed here.

**El Rancho Stevens**

P.O. Box 495
Gaylord, MI 49735
Phone: (989) 732–5090
E-mail: info@elranchostevens.com
Web site: www.elranchostevens.com

**Owners/Managers:** The Stevens Family

**Accommodations:** Capacity, 100. 30 motel-style units; additional family suites. Rooms include private baths and double beds. Suites have 2 bedrooms, full baths, and living rooms. The A-frame suites can accommodate 6; each of these units has a downstairs bedroom with private bath and 2 upstairs rooms that will sleep 4.

**Meals:** 2 seated meals daily. Lunch is served in the Silver Dollar Saloon, at additional expense. Dining is buffet and family style and includes a soup and salad bar. Kids may eat with their parents or with counselors. Cookouts and barbecues at lakeside are favorite activities. Breakfast rides are offered, too. Alcoholic drinks are served in the licensed cocktail lounge and the Silver Dollar Saloon at the beach.

**Activities:** Horseback riders and hikers can explore acres of well-marked trails on the ranch and on the adjacent state park. Rides are per-hour and are divided by ability levels. A large indoor riding arena is provided for games and instruction, as well as riding during inclement weather. Heated swimming pool. Lake swimming beach with small sailboats, kayaks, canoes, and paddleboats. Softball games, archery, and volleyball areas. Gaylord is the golf capital of the Midwest, with 22 courses. Advice and tee times can be arranged.

**Amenities:** Pool, indoor arena, game room, small watercraft, lakeside and poolside lounge furniture, recreational equipment, cocktail lounges, snack bar.

**Special Programs:** Junior Wranglers program provides a huge variety of activities for kids 6 to 12. Baby-sitters may be arranged for toddlers. Non–horse-riding guests can get reduced rates based on a modified activities program.

**Rates:** $–$$ Full American Plan and Modified American Plan (no horseback riding) available. Rates include breakfasts, dinners, one horseback ride per day, all planned activities in the children's program, use of watercraft, use of pool, and dinner. Rates vary according to accommodations and length of stay. Reduced children's rates; kids under 2 are free.

**Credit Cards:** VISA, MasterCard, Discover

**Season:** June through September

**Getting There:** El Rancho Stevens is located 244 miles north of Detroit Metro Airport; 136 miles from Saginaw-Midland-Bay City (Tri-City Airport), and 67 miles from Traverse City (Cherry Capitol) Airport. Inquire for driving directions from I–75 at exit 279.

**What's Nearby:** Gaylord, the Midwest's "golfing capital."

# TURKEY CREEK RANCH
## Theodosia, Missouri

Missouri has been known as the Gateway to the West since the nineteenth century, and the Turkey Creek Ranch might officially be proclaimed the place where the West begins. Its owners, the Edwards family, have provided a warm, western welcome for more than four decades, and that hospitality now extends down through three generations.

Nestled in the Ozark Mountains on the shores of Bull Shoals Lake, Turkey Creek Ranch provides the best of two worlds: horseback riding and summer fun on the water. The Edwardses like to refer to their retreat as "a lake resort with a dude-ranch flavor." It's appropriate that the ranch brand is a "swimming" T.

A 700-acre cattle ranch set amid rippling hills provides the perfect backdrop for exploration on horseback. The ranch maintains a solid string of western pleasure horses of various breeds, colors, and temperaments, and in a range suitable for the most inexperienced "gunsel" to the trail-hardened horseman. For novices, the ranch wranglers will provide instruction on the art of horsemanship. Then, it's off to the bridle trails, lined with colorful dogwood trees and blooming wildflowers.

When the heat becomes searing, you can head for the lake, where pontoon boats, paddleboats, canoes, and sailboats await. If waterskiing is your fancy, you can do that, too. There are also bass boats available for some serious lake-fishing action. There's even a dock where you can park your own watercraft.

For landlubbing recreationists, the ranch has a slew of amenities that include a putting green, an outdoor pool, whirlpool baths, and recreation rooms with pool tables, Ping-Pong tables, and video games.

When owners Dick and Elda Edwards first married, they bought this property with the idea of turning an old farm into an inviting guest resort. With the addition of cabins, casitas, and numerous renovations (along with the addition of five children of their own), they've achieved that, and more. The Edwards family knows how to have fun, and their enthusiasm and experience makes it easy for their guests to enjoy themselves, too. Return guests are the norm here. As one guest said, "We have such a good time there, why go anywhere else?"

## BRANSON: ENTERTAINMENT IN A SOUTHERN SETTING

Branson, Missouri, has a well-deserved reputation as the Entertainment Capital of the World. Beginning in the 1960s, the once-small Ozark Mountain town began attracting a tourist trade in search of recreation and entertainment. Soon, recording stars such as Mel Tillis, Andy Williams, and Mickey Gilley discovered the charms of the town, purchased properties, and developed hotels and show clubs, where they frequently headlined. At present, the town's various music showcases (thirty theaters in all) and casinos draw music-lovers from throughout the United States and, indeed, the world. In addition to Branson, guests enjoy Silver Dollar City, a popular theme park that opened forty years ago. While in the area, catch a show on Country Music Boulevard, the heart of the Branson music scene.

**Turkey Creek Ranch**
HC 3, Box 3180
Theodosia, MO 65761
Phone: (417) 273–4362
Web site: www.turkeycreekranch.com

**Owners/Managers:** The Edwards Family

**Accommodations:** Capacity, 150. 24 total units. Guests stay in deluxe cabins and casitas, small houselike duplexes with separate bedrooms, kitchens, microwaves, and full-sized appliances. Rooms are air-conditioned and carpeted. Units include screened porches, TVs, picnic tables, and barbecue grills. Cabins can accommodate from 4 to 10 individuals.

**Meals:** Guests can prepare meals in their own cabins or visit any of several restaurants in the area. Catering for group functions available on request.

**Activities:** Daily guided horseback trips of 1-hour duration go out throughout the day; otherwise, no scheduled activities. Hiking on wide, durable bridle paths. Most activities focus on water sports: sailing, paddleboating, canoeing, waterskiing, scuba diving. Riding and boat rentals at additional cost. Resort activities also include swimming in an indoor pool, a whirlpool, outdoor pool and children's pool, tennis, shuffleboard, volleyball, horseshoes, a putting green (golf courses nearby). Guests sometimes participate in cattle activities.

**Amenities:** Indoor and outdoor pools, whirlpool, piano and organ for entertainment, daily newspaper delivered to your cabin, a wide variety of watercraft for rent, dock, barbecue and picnic areas, scuba equipment, recreation rooms, children's playground.

**Special Programs:** No specific children's programs, although children are welcome, and there are plenty of activities they can participate in with their parents.

**Rates:** $–$$ Inquire for rates; prices vary by accommodations, length of stay. Activities such as horseback riding and boat rental are extra. Meals not included.

**Credit Cards:** None. Personal checks accepted.

**Season:** Year-round

**Getting There:** Located 47 miles east of Branson, Missouri. Nearest airport in Springfield, about 85 miles.

**What's Nearby:** Branson, Missouri, approximately 45 miles. Theme parks, casinos, entertainment, musical performances, shopping, dining.

# AVERILL'S FLATHEAD LAKE LODGE

## Bigfork, Montana

For some people, the ideal vacation involves lounging on a beach; for others, there are simply not enough hours in a day to fit all the activities they want to do. Averill's Flathead Lake Lodge is the place for the latter type of vacationers.

Situated on the banks of Flathead Lake (the West's largest freshwater lake) in northwest Montana, Averill's sprawls over 2,000 acres of the northern Rocky Mountains. An ample beachfront on the east shore of the lake makes it an ideal spot for water sports. The ranch offers everything from sailing to sea kayaking, canoeing, and waterskiing. Guests looking for an adrenaline rush can river raft or take white-water kayak lessons, whereas guests looking for a slower-paced activity can try their hand at sailing. The resort maintains everything from small dinghies to two magnificent 51-foot sloops, which transport guests on regular tours of the vast Flathead Lake. These two historic boats, the *Nor'Easter* and *Questa,* were built in the late 1920s as prototypes for America's Cup racing boats.

One favorite cruise takes wayfarers up Flathead River through a waterfowl preserve, where sightings of bald eagles are commonplace. Water skiing originates at the boat dock, and even young kids can take part, riding atop the skiffing "boogie boards."

Horseback riding makes up the second component of the Flathead Lake Lodge experience. Trails take riders through the nearby mountains as well as the ranch's private game preserve, stocked with elk and American bison. Inexperienced riders can get saddle time in a riding arena under the watchful eye of skilled instructors. The confidence this instills in guests encourages them to explore this sizable property.

Children also ride, and the ranch has an excellent Junior Wranglers program in which they learn saddling, horse care, grooming, and barn duties. They get to tag along with real cowboys and cowgirls, learning the ins and outs of caring for the large herd of horses—valuable and character-enhancing experience.

Early risers can even head out on horseback for a pancake breakfast, the perfect way to start an active day. If you'd rather sleep in, you can saddle up for the evening barbecue ride, where you will be served out of an authentic western chuckwagon.

If you're saddle sore, you don't have to ride to eat. Guests dine together in the main lodge, where the meals are served family style and include homemade baked goods. A separate children's seating makes it easier for adults to simply relax and enjoy their meals, and it's a heck of a lot of fun for the kids, too.

Of course, everyone needs some time to just read and relax. For those quiet moments, you can visit the heated pool, or walk on the beach, or just kick back in the overstuffed buffalo-hide couches close by the massive river-rock fireplace in the main lodge. You'll sleep well at night in the cozy log-style cabins, all decorated with western style. Additional motel-like "family rooms" are available in the main lodge and are ideal for small families.

Averill's prides itself on having one of the biggest menus of activities of any guest ranch in the West, and with more than five decades of experience, the folks here know how to please. Bring lots of suntan lotion and be prepared to take plenty of long, soothing baths to relax your tired muscles. You're in for a whirlwind of exciting adventures.

## Averill's Flathead Lake Lodge

P.O. Box 248
Bigfork, MT 59911
Phone: (406) 837–4391
Fax: (406) 837–6977
E-mail: dude@averills.com
Web site: www.averills.com

**Owners/Managers:** Doug and Maureen Averill

**Accommodations:** Guest capacity, 120. Total units, 31 including 13 private cabins, 15 rooms in the south lodge, another 3 sleeping rooms in the main lodge. Family rooms in the lodges provide private common areas for families; rooms have 1 queen-sized bed, 2 sleeping beds in a loft area, and a private bath. Cottages have queen or twin beds in separate bedrooms, a living room, bathroom, and a porch overlooking the lake.

**Meals:** 3 adult sittings daily; separate kid's seating. A typical breakfast menu might include eggs Benedict, hash browns, breakfast meats, cereal bar with fresh fruits, cowboy coffee cake, and juices. Lunch: salad bar, roasted chicken and potatoes, fresh fruit and vegetables, chocolate cake. Dinner: Caesar salad, herb bread, whole roasted pig, roasted baron of buffalo, twice-baked potatoes, green beans almondine, chocolate mousse. Dinner and breakfast rides and beach cookouts.

**Activities:** Horseback riding, trail riding, arena competitions, sailing, water skiing, kayaking, and canoeing, lake tours, fly fishing, lake fishing, boat fishing, rodeos, roping contests, mountain biking, rafting, golf at nearby resort, evening barn dances, more. Averill's prides itself on offering more activities than any other guest ranch—and they mean it!

**Amenities:** In-room coffeemaker, complimentary guest basket, daily newspapers in the main lodge, Saddle Sore Saloon, rec room, use of sailboats, fishing boats, water skiing, tennis courts, beach fires.

**Special Programs:** Children's Junior Wranglers program includes horseback riding, arts and crafts, fishing, games, and more. Children under 6 may ride in a supervised arena program. Child care available.

**Rates:** $$$–$$$$ Full American Plan. Children's rates, teen rates, infant rates. Most on-site activities are included in the price; a few activities are charged extra, especially off-site activities such as golf and river rafting.

**Credit Cards:** VISA, MasterCard, American Express. Personal checks accepted.

**Season:** May through October

**Getting There:** Nearest commercial airport in Kalispell, 17 miles. Contact the ranch in advance to arrange ground transportation.

**What's Nearby:** Glacier National Park, the National Bison Range.

# BEAR CREEK LODGE

Victor, Montana

The Bear Creek Lodge experience was well summed up in an article that appeared in *Condé Naste Traveler:* "Owner Roland Turney has elevated the notion of a log retreat into something of an art form: eight comfortable rooms overlooking the forest, exceptional gourmet meals, and an atmosphere of tranquil relaxation that lends itself to adventurous exploring or solitary exploration."

Turney, a former schoolteacher, has indeed stamped the ranch with his own infectious personality, from the gracious log lodge built from timber rescued after the Yellowstone fire of 1988 to the portrait of his grandfather (in full Cossack uniform) that hangs above the lodge's river-stone fireplace.

Bear Creek Lodge is, indeed, a retreat. Guests come away feeling as though they visited an old friend—one who happens to have a stunning mountain home, gourmet chefs, and a staff that caters to one's every whim. Guests can take rejuvenating hikes along the timbered banks of Bear Creek, cross paths with white-tailed deer, elk, and moose. Many guests take advantage of the Blue Ribbon fishing waters made famous in the novel *A River Runs through It.* Mountain biking, canoeing, and white-water rafting can all be arranged through the lodge, along with golf at an 18-hole championship course, tennis, or workouts at a top-drawer athletic club in nearby Hamilton.

Trail riding on horseback is, of course, a favorite activity. Guests can ride as much or as little as they like, from short one-hour jaunts to full-day trips into the Bitterroot Mountains. A local outfitter provides horses, tack, and guides. More than twenty-five trails through the woods assure that you'll never trace the same steps or see the same scenery twice during your stay—unless, that is, you want to.

Although many guests feel so comfortable that the thought of leaving the ranch itself never crosses their minds, it should be noted that this area offers more than its share of interesting diversions, all within an hour's drive. To the north is the National Bison Range, home to one of the last remaining herds of wild American buffalo. Two different wildlife refuges will satisfy bird-watchers. The historically minded will want to visit St. Mary's Mission, home of the first permanent white settlement in Montana, and the Daly Mansion, the opulent home of an early copper baron. And the Big Hole Battlefield demarcated the site of an epic struggle between Nez Perce Indians and the U.S. Army in 1877.

Bear Creek is a small place with a maximum capacity of sixteen. The owners share meals and their time with guests, giving the ranch a very personal and intimate feeling. Although not "traditional" in the sense of many guest ranches, this retreat goes to the original intent that began the guest-ranch tradition: inviting travelers into one's home to share in the wonderful blessings of God's creation.

## Bear Creek Lodge

1184 Bear Creek Trail
Victor, MT 59875
Phone: (406) 642–3750
Fax: (406) 642–6847
E-mail: info@bear-creek-lodge.com
Web site: www.bear-creek-lodge.com

**Owners/Managers**: Roland and Elizabeth Turney

**Accommodations:** Capacity, 16; Total units, 8. Guests are lodged in a beautiful log lodge, completed in 1991. Guests share a common deck, library, game room, exercise room, and sauna. Rooms complete with private baths.

**Meals:** A flexible menu to accommodate guests' activities. Menu varies appreciably, but a typical evening menu gives a sense of the care in preparation: salad of greens, feta, and pine nuts dressed with a tart lemon vinaigrette; wine-marinated chicken breast with figs and olives; wild-rice pilaf with lentils and barley; baby carrots with orange juice and cumin glaze; and pear frangipane tart with a delicate toasted-almond crust for dessert. Picnics available for daytime activities. Evening cocktail bar and wine served with hors d'oeuvres.

**Activities:** Horseback riding on wooded forest trails; fly fishing in several local rivers; hiking; mountain biking; bird-watching; backpacking; visits to nearby attractions, wildlife preserves, historic sites.

**Amenities:** Robes, hair dryers, redwood hot tub, self-service fruit, baked goods, and beverages; satellite television.

**Special Programs:** No formal children's program. Children welcome when parents or families rent the entire lodge.

**Rates:** $$$ Full American Plan. Guided service such as riding, fishing, etc., additional. 15 percent service charge not included.

**Credit Cards:** VISA, MasterCard, Discover

**Season:** March through October

**Getting There:** Missoula, 45 miles north of Bear Creek Lodge, is the nearest commercial airport. Rental cars available at the airport. Hamilton airport serves general aviation with a 2,400-foot runway, 12 miles south of Bear Creek Lodge.

**What's Nearby:** 18-hole championship golf course, athletic club in Hamilton; National Bison Range; Lee Metcalf and Otto Teller Wildlife Refuges; Daly Mansion, St. Mary's Mission, Big Hole Battlefield.

# THE COVERED WAGON RANCH

## Gallatin Gateway, Montana

Montana's Gallatin Canyon area boasts one of the most intense concentrations of guest ranches and outfitters in North America. The Covered Wagon is a stately elder citizen among that community, having opened way back in 1925. Throughout the years, it has earned a reputation as a traditional western dude escape with an authentic, rustic appeal, while constantly upgrading and modernizing to ensure that its guests remain comfortable.

The ranch is a mere 3 miles from Yellowstone National Park, amid the green mountains of the Gallatin. Wildlife thrives in this natural setting, and on any given day you are likely to spy deer, elk, moose, big-horn sheep, even black bear and the occasional mountain lion. Human activity won't impinge on the wildlife here. Guest capacity is a mere twenty-four individuals, which translates to privacy and a great deal of personal service. (Come fall, the ranch serves as the perfect outpost for big-game hunters. Inquire if you are interested in a dream hunt in Big Sky country. An outside outfitter can be arranged, as the ranch doesn't provide a licensed outfitting service.)

The Covered Wagon Ranch was handed down from the previous owner to a favorite employee, Will King. Also handed down was an ethic of ownership that King adopted, that of treating every guest like cherished family. As one might expect at home, the pace here is set by the individual guests, who may partake of a short menu of on-ranch activities, from fly fishing (a Montana staple) to hiking and, of course, horseback riding.

More activities can be easily pursued nearby, such as mountain biking, golf, tennis, and in wintertime, cross-country skiing, snowmobiling, and downhill skiing at famed Big Sky Resort. The staff will be glad to help set you up with the appropriate local outfitter or make reservations for activities such as snow-coach trips through Yellowstone Park.

Evening activities are similarly casual. Guests and wranglers often gather around the campfire to share stories, sing, and listen to the baying of coyotes and, sometimes, wolves. A rec hall is especially popular with teens, but anyone who is game can participate in billiards, Ping-Pong, and foosball.

Guests gather in the recently built grand dining room, a beautiful example of log-cabin architecture that features huge log beams and plenty of windows looking out onto the forest and the mountains. Like all things at Bear Creek, dining is an informal activity, served family style. This is a teetotaling outfit: those diners who like a beer or cocktail before or after dinner should bring their own.

Daily horseback trips take riders through the Gallatin and Madison Mountain ranges as well as Yellowstone Park. All-day rides are especially popular and include a midday break for a trailside lunch. After a full day in the saddle, you'll want to soak in the ranch hot tub to get your muscles good and relaxed for the next day's adventure. And it feels just as good after a winter's day spent snowshoeing or skiing.

## The Covered Wagon Ranch

34035 Gallatin Road
Gallatin Gateway, MT 59730
Phone: (800) 995-4237
E-mail: info@coveredwagonranch.com
Web site: www.coveredwagonranch.com

**Owner/Manager:** Will King

**Accommodations:** Capacity, 24. 10 total units, consisting of rustic, original 1- and 2-bedroom cabins, each with log furniture, private bath, and covered porch.

**Meals:** Basic, hearty American ranch cuisine (think meats, vegetables simply prepared, potatoes), served family style in a spacious, modern log-cabin style lodge. BYOB in cabins only.

**Activities:** Fly and reel fishing, horseback riding, mountain biking, hiking, and indoor recreational games. Off-site river rafting, tours of Yellowstone National Park, snowmobiling, cross-country and alpine skiing, golf, and tennis.

**Amenities:** Spacious guest ranch features comfortable furniture and a modest reading library, recreation room, hot-tub bath.

**Special Programs:** No structured kid's programs, although children are welcome guests. Mature children may ride, with their parent's permission.

**Rates:** $$-$$$ Full American Plan, with or without horseback riding. Higher rates reflect in-season visits and full horse and wrangler service. Children's rates, off-season reduced rates.

**Credit Cards:** VISA, MasterCard, American Express. Personal checks preferred.

**Season:** Summer: May through October; winter: February through April

**Getting There:** 54 miles south of Bozeman, 34 miles north of West Yellowstone on state Highway 191. Nearest commercial airports, Bozeman and West Yellowstone. Ranch shuttle available at either airport.

**What's Nearby:** Yellowstone National Park, Big Sky Winter Resort.

# KLICK'S K BAR L RANCH

Augusta, Montana

Dick and Nancy Klick offer an old-school approach to guest ranching: Keep things simple, mind the little details, and let nature exert her own powerful force and beauty on the guests. It has been a winning formula at the K Bar L since 1925, when family patriarchs Emil and Sam Klick first settled in this still-unspoiled wilderness and began guiding hunters through the backcountry.

For generations, the Klicks have been the sole residents of the Sun River Game Preserve, and they have a profound respect for and enjoyment of their remote outpost. There's no easy road into the Klick's main ranch: Guests must either take a thrilling jet-boat ride across Gibson Lake or mount up and ride a saddle horse around the lake shore, their gear dutifully carried by pack mules. Clearly, your adventure begins even before you arrive at the spectacular ranch compound.

The K Bar L is surrounded by wilderness; not only is it part of the game preserve, the trails also dip into the mighty, million-acre Bob Marshall Wilderness, perhaps the least-trodden, wild, and wonderful wilderness area in Montana. "The Bob," as locals refer to it, is wilderness most people can only imagine: rugged peaks, alpine lakes, cascading waterfalls, grassy meadows embellished with shimmering streams, a towering coniferous forest, and big river valleys.

This region of Montana includes the North and South Forks of the Sun River and the Middle and South Forks of the Flathead River. It runs for 60 miles along the Continental Divide, with elevations ranging from 4,000 feet to more than 9,000 feet. A huge escarpment called the Chinese Wall, a part of the Divide, highlights The Bob's vast untrammeled beauty, with an average height of more than 1,000 feet and a length of 22 miles. Guests wishing to see this magnificent formation up-close can opt for an extended pack trip that departs from the Klick's ranch; those preferring a shorter trip may take two- or three-day "overnighters" during their weeklong stay, including a trip to the Prairie Reef Lookout, from which you can see the Chinese Wall.

But you don't have to spend days in the saddle to enjoy the Klick's outfit. Many guests prefer to simply stay "in camp," enjoying the spacious lodge, playing volleyball, throwing horseshoes, and swimming in the natural hot-springs pool, which maintains a year-round temperature of 86 degrees.

Schedules scarcely exist here: The Klicks work with guests, planning daily wilderness horseback rides and fishing trips according to their guests' own proclivities. Fishing is a major focus here: Beginners can learn a great deal, and the Klicks have an encyclopedic knowledge of what flies work best for the more seasoned anglers.

Fall is hunting season on the ranch, and you won't find better, more experienced guides. From deer and elk to big-horn sheep and black bear, you'll find an abundance of trophy animals in this awesome and remote wilderness. And if you don't desire to shoot them, the folks here will gladly help you preserve the animals—on photographic paper.

## Klick's K Bar L Ranch

P.O. Box 287
Augusta, MT 59410
Phone: (406) 562–3589 (winter, spring); (406)
 562–3551 (summer, fall)
Web site: www.kbarl.com

**Owners/Managers:** The Klick Family

**Accommodations:** Guest capacity, 35. 1-, 2-,
and 3-bedroom cabins with traditional western ranch furniture, Indian and western furnishings, heavy wool blankets. A hydroelectric
generator powers the ranch; water comes
from natural springs. Separate shower house
and modern toilet facilities. This is a remote
property, but comfortable. Here, you'll "rough
it" in relative comfort.

**Meals:** Meals served family style. Weekly
cookouts, trail-side pack-trip meals. BYOB.

**Activities:** The horse program is at the center
of activities. Exceptional fishing as close as the
stream that runs in front of your cabin door.
Lake fishing, fly fishing, stream fishing.

Extended and overnight pack trips into the
Bob Marshall Wilderness (inquire for details).
Volleyball, horseshoes, sing-alongs, and
swimming.

**Amenities:** Natural hot-springs pool maintains a year-round temperature of 86 degrees.

**Special Programs:** Young children (under age
6) not advised. Fall hunting programs, guided
fly fishing, backcountry pack trips.

**Rates:** $$–$$$ Full American Plan. Minimum
5-night stay. Shorter stays available in June,
September.

**Credit Cards:** None. Personal or traveler's
checks accepted.

**Season:** June to mid-September; extended
hunting season.

**Getting There:** Nearest airport, Great Falls.
Ground transport with prior arrangement
(additional cost). Ranch is 35 miles west of
Augusta, 75 miles west of Great Falls.

**What's Nearby:** Yellowstone National Park.

# LONE MOUNTAIN RANCH

## Big Sky, Montana

If fine dining in a luxurious ranch setting within hollering distance of Yellowstone National Park is your idea of a perfect vacation, look no farther than Lone Mountain Ranch. Guests and journalists alike rave about the food, served in the spacious, gracious, and charming main lodge dining room, a voluminous log building decorated with elk-antler chandeliers, a massive stone fireplace, and tasteful western decor.

Doug Hare presides over the kitchen, which specializes in what Hare describes as "creative American cuisine." Here's just a taste of what you can expect (excerpted from the evening dinner menu): crab and tuna cakes served with baby greens and lemon-basil vinaigrette and topped with mango coulis; spinach salad with sautéed mushrooms, bacon and tomatoes with a toasted almond dressing and goat cheese; elk medallions and braised elk osso bucco paired with madeira mushrooms or caramelized shallot butter.

Renowned gourmet and travel publications, including *Town & Country, Travel & Leisure,* the *New York Times,* and the *Los Angeles Times,* have all heaped their acclaim on the Lone Mountain Ranch's dining. You may never want to leave the dining room!

But leave you must, and will, to partake of the equally enticing ranch activities. This is a top-shelf ranch vacation spot offering a multitude of must-do opportunities. Visit the Yellowstone Park and enjoy its natural wonders; take a hike with a llama, and learn about the native geology, history, and flora and fauna; take a canoe trip on a mountain river; and of course, spend lots of time getting acquainted with your equine buddy on dozens of forested trails. Winter guests have their pick of cross-country or downhill ski adventures, guided winter fly fishing, sleigh rides, and evening entertainment. And if you get sore from all the activities, you can schedule a session with a licensed massage therapist.

Winter or summer, guests not only get a lot of physical activity, but an enjoyable educational experience, too. Lone Mountain is renowned for its naturalist program, and all of the staff are quite knowledgeable when it comes to identifying the species in this biologically diverse region of Montana and edifying people on the natural world surrounding the ranch.

The plethora of choices doesn't end with the outdoors, however. Even before you arrive, you can select from a variety of accommodations that range from rustic bungalows to family-sized cabins. There are also six private couples' rooms in the

## WHAT IS A GEYSER?

A geyser is a plume of superheated water that erupts from fissures in the earth's surface—and the Yellowstone National Park has more of them than anywhere else on earth. About half of the earth's 800 or so known geysers can be found there. Geysers form in areas where groundwater contacts volcanic magma near the earth's surface; the superheated water is "plumbed" through silica-rich rock formations that can withstand the awesome force of an eruption.

Ridgetop Lodge, a great place to meet other sojourners or to hold a conference event. But don't dawdle—it's not unusual for spaces to be booked up as much as a year in advance.

Lone Mountain Ranch is one of the premier family-owned and -operated guest ranches in North America and well deserving of its many accolades earned in more than half a dozen national magazines and periodicals. It comes highly recommended.

## Lone Mountain Ranch
Box 160069
Big Sky, MT 59716
Phone (800) 514–4644
Fax: (406) 995–4670
E-mail: lmr@lmranch.com
Web site: www.lmranch.com

**Managers:** Brian and Kelli Wadsworth

**Accommodations:** Capacity, 80. 30 total units. 21 1- and 2-bedroom log cabins accommodate from 2 to 9 guests each; 6 additional rooms in the recently built Ridgetop Lodge. Rooms and cabins include bathrooms with full baths, rock fireplaces or woodstoves. Cabins are located near a burbling brook and feature front porches.

**Meals:** Breakfast and lunch served buffet style. Dinner menu includes a choice of numerous entrees, which vary daily. Special diets accommodated. Full-service bar. As noted, Lone Mountain serves some of the finest dining available in the guest-ranch business.

**Activities:** Fly fishing year-round; horseback riding and equitation instruction; tennis, swimming, white-water rafting; rock climbing lessons on the ranch's own climbing wall and golf off-site. Extensive naturalist program and tours of Yellowstone National Park. Extensive winter activities menu includes fly fishing, snowshoeing, sleigh-ride dinners, and more. This ranch was featured as one of the best cross-country ski destinations in North America; alpine skiing also available at nearby Big Sky Winter Resort.

**Amenities:** Video services for guests, hot tub, masseuse; conference facilities, outdoor specialty equipment shop.

**Special Programs:** Well-designed and supervised program for children ages 4 to 12; kids take part in a wide variety of activities ranging from naturalist hikes to rock climbing to horse and pony rides. Fly fishermen can participate in special fishing packages, including a 2-week fly-fishing marathon that includes Montana's top spots. Inquire if you love to fish! Winter includes several adventure packages centered on alpine or cross-country skiing.

**Rates:** $$$–$$$$ Full American Plan. Reduced children's rates, off-season rates, and winter rates. Special package rates; special nanny rates. Guided fly-fishing trips and instruction, massage therapy, photo clinics, and tours (on space-available basis), additional cost.

**Credit Cards:** VISA, MasterCard, Discover

**Season:** Summer: late May to October; winter: early December to early April

**Getting There:** Located 40 miles south of Bozeman on Highway 191; shuttle service available for guests staying 4 days or longer. Nearest commercial airport: Bozeman.

**What's Nearby:** Yellowstone National Park, Big Sky Winter Resort.

# MOUNTAIN SKY GUEST RANCH

An upscale guest ranch with a friendly, informal ambience best describes Mountain Sky. Set in the aptly named Paradise Valley, just south of Bozeman and a short distance from the north entrance of Yellowstone National Park, Mountain Sky has a long and storied history in the western guest-ranch business. One of the oldest guest ranches in the state (it opened its doors to dudes back in 1929), Mountain Sky was known as the Ox Yoke. Now, under the capable management of owners Alan and Mary Brutger, the ranch has a new name and a new face. An extensive renovation has helped to elevate this property to one of the most comfortable and modern in the guest-ranch industry.

Still, the Brutgers knew well enough not to change the very things that made this historic guest ranch inviting: Its rustic original cabins retain their charm, the horse program remains outstanding, and warm and friendly service continues to attract guests from throughout the world. Simple but elegant touches, such as fresh-fruit baskets delivered to guest rooms each day and lovely flower baskets decorating cabin porches, add a touch of distinctive graciousness and beauty to each new day.

Activities at Mountain Sky cover the usual menu of most guest-ranch vacations. Horseback riding, fly fishing and pond fishing, nature hikes, and river rafting trips make up the backbone of the daily activity list. Great care is taken to ensure that guests are entirely comfortable and engaged in the day's activities; for example, those who embark on the all-day trail ride are treated to a fabulous picnic spread and wonderful vistas of the Paradise Valley.

In the evening, you won't want for things to do, either. Each night, guests are entertained with western dances, cowboy and folk sing-alongs, special gourmet sit-down dinners, poolside barbecues, hayrides, and campfire storytelling sessions.

During the summer months, the ranch is very family oriented, with an outstanding kids' program that includes riding, arts and crafts, cookouts, hiking, swimming, and fishing. During spring and fall, however, the mood turns romantic as the ranch welcomes couples and singles looking for a tranquil escape and adventure in the company of other adults.

Individuals who are interested in improving their horsemanship won't be disappointed. The ranch divides its rides based on experience, and riding groups seldom exceed eight, giving guests and wranglers a great opportunity to work together. A variety of rides go out each day, including an early-morning breakfast ride featuring a campfire breakfast complete with fabled "cowboy" coffee. Those guests who request additional riding instruction can take part in informal classes in the arena headed by Mountain Sky's expert horse hands.

## Mountain Sky Guest Ranch

P.O. Box 1219
Emigrant, MT 59027
Phone: (800) 548–3392; (406) 333–4911
Fax: (406) 333–4537
E-mail: Use Web site
Web site: www.mtnsky.com

**Owners/Managers:** Alan and Mary Brutger

**Accommodations:** Capacity, 75. 27 total units composed of guest cabins suitable for 2 to 7 guests. Older cabins completely renovated with full-sized bathrooms; newer cabins feature large-view windows, full baths, and sitting rooms. All cabins have front porches with deck furniture.

**Meals:** Twice-weekly, 5-course gourmet meals featuring inventive continental and American cuisine; evening barbecue cookouts, poolside cookouts, buffet style breakfasts and lunches with homemade breads and breakfast pastries, breakfast trail rides. Special diets accommodated. Sample dinner menu: Duck confit appetizer with balsamic glazed apples served with warm polenta; nectarine and roasted pepper salad served with mixed greens; smoked loin of lamb and stewed summer vegetable entree; warm Valrohna cake served with homemade huckleberry ice cream and fresh huckleberries.

**Activities:** Broad horse program featuring daily trail rides, half-day and full-day rides, breakfast rides, arena instruction; fly-fishing and pond fishing; swimming in an outdoor heated pool; nature hikes; tennis. Evening western dances, sing-alongs, Saturday Showdeo performance and riding games. Guided fishing trips on Blue Ribbon waters arranged at guest's request.

**Amenities:** 2 all-weather tennis courts, whirlpool baths and sauna, full bar and wine service, comfortable main lodge with library and a grand piano.

**Special Programs:** Daily children's program includes riding, cookouts, arts and crafts, hiking, swimming, fishing. Baby-sitting service. Spring and fall adults-only programs.

**Rates:** $$$–$$$$ Full American Plan. Children's rates, off-season rates available; inquire.

**Credit Cards:** VISA, MasterCard. Personal checks preferred.

**Season:** Mid-May to mid-October

**Getting There:** Located 60 miles southeast of Bozeman, 30 miles south of Livingston. Nearest commercial airport: Bozeman.

**What's Nearby:** Yellowstone National Park (30 miles).

# 63 RANCH

## Livingston, Montana

In case you're wondering, the ranch was built in 1863, hence, its name. As one might expect of a true "Century Ranch," the 63 is as authentic as they come. A working cattle ranch situated amid the breathtaking mountain scenery of Big Sky Country, the 63 was the first dude ranch in the state to earn designation as a National Historic Site.

Paul and Jinnie Christensen welcomed their first guests in 1929. Their daughter, Sandra, and Sandra's husband, Bud Cahill, have continued the family tradition on into the twenty-first century. It would be hard to imagine a more idyllic setting for a western ranch: Bordered by the Gallatin National Forest, the ranch straddles Mission Creek Canyon and extends to the foothills of the Absaroka Mountain Range. The grassy hills are ideal for livestock, the ridges are sharp and scenic, and the ranch is situated near the banks of the Yellowstone River. Yellowstone National Park is a mere 50 miles to the south, so plan on including that in your travel plans as well.

A true working cattle ranch, the 63 invites guests to join in gathering and moving cattle, and occasionally roping them, too. Horses outnumber guests two to one, so you'll never exhaust the supply of fresh mounts. These horses are in top condition and of excellent quality, and guests are not limited to a pokey walk along a bridle trail. If cantering through the woods or across an open pasture is your desire, the folks at the 63 will be glad to oblige you. And for guests who appreciate a more leisurely ride, nobody will complain if you choose instead a contemplative ride through the woods.

There are even gentle "kid's horses" for children as young as four years of age.

In June and July, overnight pack trips limited to four guests are offered. Those taking part ride into the Absaroka-Beartooth Wilderness, an especially wild and beautiful backcountry.

Although riding is the focus here, there are numerous other diversions as well. You won't be held to a rigorous schedule. If you want to sleep in, you can do so. If you're up at the crack of dawn, you can watch the cowboys as they bring in the remuda. Fishermen enjoy Mission Creek's burbling banks, where trout jump in the pools. Please, put them back, though. The ranch adheres to a catch-and-release ethic. Kids can fish in a stocked pond, which is also an ideal place to practice fly casting. Avid fishermen can explore several nearby rivers with Blue Ribbon sections.

Photographers will be able to gather an album full of memories: beautiful sunsets over the mountains, cowboys and cattle, wildflowers and wildlife. The possibilities are as varied and endless as your imagination. Be sure to spend some time in Livingston, a picturesque ranch town with a restored historic district, restaurants, saloons, museums, and shopping.

There are dozens of other recreational activities available at the 63, from volleyball and softball games to parlor games, billiards, and square dances. Off-site activities include white-water rafting, visits to the Lewis and Clark Caverns, the Custer Battlefield, and historic Virginia City.

## 63 Ranch

P.O. Box 979
Livingston, MT 59047
Phone: (406) 222–0570
E-mail: sixty3ranch@mcn.net
Web site: www.sixtythree.com

**Owners/Managers:** Sandra and Bud Cahill, Jinnie Christensen

**Accommodations:** Capacity, 30. Guests stay in 8 individual cabins ranging from 1- to 4-bedrooms. Each has log furniture, fresh seasonal wildflowers upon arrival, baths and showers, and twin or double beds.

**Meals:** Wholesome meals, served family style, draw raves from guests. The menu operates on a 21-day cycle, ensuring that no two meals will be the same. Lean grass-fed beef from the 63 Ranch herd served along with pork, poultry, and fish; fresh fruits, vegetables, and baked breads. Sunday-night buffet. Steak barbecue on Mission Creek on Saturday evening. Special diets (low cholesterol, high fiber, vegetarian, pork-free, or food allergies) accommodated with advance notice.

**Activities:** Horseback riding is the central focus of daytime activities. Western riding instruction available, in addition to trail rides. Overnight pack trips. Fishing is a favorite pastime; guests may fish on Blue Ribbon tributaries of the Yellowstone, in Mission Creek, or in "secret" spots, by special arrangement. Request a fishing brochure. Stocked ranch pond for kids. Pond swimming, hiking, nature walks, local history lesson, parlor games, recreation room. White-water rafting off-premises. Evening entertainment includes sing-alongs, square dancing, and entertainment in the ranch pavilion. Local rodeos (ask for a schedule).

**Amenities:** Ranch "newspaper." Pay telephone, soda machine. Think simple, rather than opulent.

**Special Programs:** No formal children's programs. Baby-sitter available. Kids as young as 4 are allowed to ride.

**Rates:** $$ Rates are based on a 7-day stay and are not discounted or reduced for persons staying less than 1 week. Reduced rates for children to age 11.

**Credit Cards:** None. Personal checks, traveler's checks accepted.

**Season:** Mid-June to mid-September

**Getting There:** Nearest commercial airport, Bozeman (50 miles). Shuttle by prior arrangement, at additional charge. Car rentals available at the Bozeman airport. City-county airport with landing strip in Livingston; no charge for pickup.

**What's Nearby:** Livingston, a charming ranching town with a lively historic district. Also, Yellowstone National Park, Lewis & Clark Caverns, Nevada City (a restored mining town), Custer Battlefield, scenic Beartooth Highway. Fourth of July Rodeo, annual county fair.

# 320 GUEST RANCH

## Gallatin Gateway, Montana

A famous historic ranch, the 320 Guest Ranch is celebrating a full century of welcoming guests from all over the globe. It's not hard to understand why this pioneering guest ranch has remained in business for so long. First, its location in the Gallatin Canyon places it just minutes from Yellowstone National Park, Big Sky Winter Resort, and the million-acre Gallatin National Forest. Second, the ranch is bisected by 2 miles of the Gallatin River, which provides access to Montana's famed fly-fishing habitat. And finally, the ranch offers high-level service and upscale accommodations (it has earned the AAA Three-Diamond Award), making it one of the most acclaimed resort properties in the West.

In fall, the ranch lends itself to big-game and bird hunting; in winter, it's the perfect locale for snowmobiling, skiing, dogsled trips, and snowshoeing. In spring, the pastures come alive with wildflowers, and in summer, the high country opens itself up to horseback riding on miles of well-established trails.

Overall, the appearance of the ranch is classic, with chinked-log cabins, lodges, and lodge buildings. More than simply a guest ranch, the 320 is a full-blown western resort complete with a popular steakhouse and dancehall-saloon. Its size gives the ranch a flexibility not often found in the guest-ranch business.

Visitors are welcome to stay a day, a week, or a month! The flexibility extends to the types of guests the ranch attracts, everyone from Yellowstone visitors just passing through to international visitors enchanted with the idea of staying at a true western cattle ranch, to adventurers eager to do some backcountry snowmobiling, to soon-to-be newlyweds looking for the ideal romantic wedding site. And, of course, there are the traditional guest-ranch vacationers who are looking for an all-inclusive

## DOCTOR McGILL AND THE 320 RANCH LEGACY

Caroline McGill was a forward-thinking woman with a love of the outdoors. Montana's first woman physician and its first pathologist, Dr. McGill purchased the 320 in 1936, hoping to create a place for her patients to convalesce, and as a healthful place for friends and patients to recreate. Years before Montana received electricity, Dr. McGill installed a gas generator (made from an old Cadillac engine), which powered the ranch for more than a decade. In 1940, she built a lovely gambrel-roofed barn whose picture has appeared in publications and advertisements throughout the world.

Dr. McGill was loved throughout the region, and her staff eventually expressed their affection by building a custom home for her, with each individual marking their contribution with a small note and their name. The house, which was finished in 1955 on Christmas Day, became known as the Christmas Cabin. When McGill passed away in 1959, her extensive collection of antiques were used to create the Museum of the Rockies and to help restore the famous historic mining towns of Virginia and Nevada Cities.

package that includes dining, activities, and lodging. Such guests can choose between deluxe four-day or seven-day packages, as well as "basic" packages that include just bed and board.

During the busy summer season, the action centers on horseback riding and fly fishing. An indoor arena affords riders the chance to improve their skills and is also the site for rodeo performances and ropings. Anglers can take advantage of an on-site outfitter whose professional guides can help to provide the perfect fishing excursion (and guide you through a fully stocked fly-fishing shop). Guests may also take part in guided rafting trips on the Yellowstone and day trips to famed Yellowstone Park.

### 320 Guest Ranch
205 Buffalo Horn Creek
Gallatin Gateway, MT 59730
Phone: (800) 243–0320; (406) 995–4283
Fax: (406) 995–4694
E-mail: info@320ranch.com
Web site: 320ranch.com

**Owner/Manager:** David Brask

**Accommodations:** Capacity, 200. Accommodations are upscale and vary from single cabins to 3-bedroom cabins. Some cabins include kitchenettes and fireplaces. All have telephones and cable TV. Daily maid service.

**Meals:** Guests dine in the full-service restaurant, which serves breakfast, lunch, and dinner. Restaurant is open to the public. A full-service bar also serves adult guests.

**Activities:** Horseback riding and fly fishing are the backbone of the summer activities program. 6 rides go out daily, giving riders the choice of long or short excursions. Indoor arena hosts riding lessons, rodeos, roping events. On-site fishing-guide service can treat guests to fishing in several local rivers. River rafting through local guide service. In winter, guests may take part in snowmobile tours in Yellowstone Park (ask about snowmobiling packages), alpine skiing at Big Sky Resort, and cross-country skiing or snowshoeing on the ranch. Also available: dogsledding and sleigh rides. Fall hunting trips available. Inquire for additional hunting info and requirements.

**Amenities:** A full-service resort, the 320 includes a renowned steak house and dance hall. Weekly "cowboy" entertainment, dances, rodeos. Wedding facilities and conference facilities.

**Special Programs:** No children's program, but baby-sitting is available. Kids 6 and older may participate in activities with their parents.

**Rates:** $$–$$$ Full American Plan. Prices vary widely based on lodging, length of stay, activity level, time of year. Single rooms as low as $82; full-service Western Dream packages (all-inclusive with horseback riding, fly-casting lesson, half-day Gallatin fishing trip, continental breakfast and dinner, full access to the entire ranch), $1,586 for seven days. Similar winter package including 2-day ski pass, snowmobile excursion, sleigh ride, continental breakfast, evening dinners, $1,430. Children's discounts.

**Credit Cards:** VISA, MasterCard

**Season:** Summer: late May to early October; winter: mid-November to mid-April

**Getting There:** Nearest commercial airport, Bozeman, 50 miles. Regional airport at West Yellowstone, 34 miles. Ranch is 12 miles south of Big Sky, 36 miles north of West Yellowstone on Highway 191.

**What's Nearby:** Yellowstone National Park, Big Sky Resort.

# TRIPLE CREEK RANCH

## Darby, Montana

Triple Creek is an adults-only luxury-resort property, with all the amenities one might expect to find in a Club Med. If you want to work on your forehand lob or practice your putting stroke, there is a tennis court and a putting green. Want to take a scenic excursion in a Hummer? Or is a mountain bike more your speed? You pick. You can even knock around on a croquet pitch, work out in a full-scale weight and fitness center, or just laze around in a hammock beneath the pines. Whatever your heart desires, chances are these folks will be able to accommodate your every whim.

Situated at the foot of Trapper Peak, the ranch takes full advantage of its secluded mountain setting. This region is resplendent in native wildlife such as moose, elk, and white-tailed deer, any of which you are likely to see during daily trail rides and cattle drives experienced on the back of your own horse. While you are out on the trail, you'll be able to stop for a picnic lunch at a stunning overview that looks out on the French Basin and the Anaconda-Pintler Wilderness.

You're welcome to go off the ranch as well and visit the nearby art galleries and specialty shops of the Bitterroot Valley, a favorite haunt of Hollywood stars who maintain vacation homes in the area. Adventurers can opt for a white-water river-rafting excursion, whereas serious fishermen can partake of the Blue Ribbon trout streams of the Bitterroot, Big Hole, and Clark Fork Rivers.

Amenities abound here: Guest cabins feature wood-burning fireplaces, hot tubs, stocked wet bar, a refrigerator, satellite television with VCR, air conditioning, and room service. A variety of accommodations is available to suit different budgets.

As one might expect, guests dine in a superb setting with gourmet meals prepared by master chefs. There's a complimentary wine service and a fully stocked top-shelf bar to help you ease into happy hour.

Come winter, guests may enjoy numerous sports adventures including snowshoeing, downhill skiing, and cross-country skiing on groomed trails. Christmas comes alive with the spirit of the season: Guests can bundle up for a sleigh ride and enjoy a hot cocoa by the fireplace afterward. If you want to experience the bracing cold and the clear azure of the Big Sky state in winter, a horse and guide will be at the ready down at the corral, anxious to cut across the snow-laden meadows in search of a spectacular overview.

Triple Creek is truly a unique and inspired property, one that will create memories to last a lifetime. For vacationers looking for the ultimate in a pampered ranch getaway, this just might be your place.

**Triple Creek Ranch**
5551 West Fork Road
Darby, MT 59829
Phone: (406) 821–4600
Fax: (406) 821–4666
E-mail: tcr@bitterroot.net
Web site: www.triplecreekranch.com

**Managers:** Wayne and Judy Kilpatrick

**Accommodations:** Capacity, 48; 19 total units plus lodge suites; accommodations vary from the modest Cedar cabins to the opulent Sapphire and Stage Stop mountain homes. All cabins and suites, however, afford guests a high level of luxury amenities such as king-sized beds, fireplaces, fully stocked bar, satellite television and VCR, and daily housekeeping. Luxury cabins feature king-sized log-post beds, steam showers, and private hot tubs.

**Meals:** Rates include 3 sumptuous daily meals and picnic lunches at guests' request. Menu changes frequently, but a sample dinner menu included crab cakes or seared loin of rabbit with chipotle corn cassoulet appetizers. Entrees: grilled Pacific salmon with polenta, filet mignon with foie-gras butter and gnocchi, and free-range chicken breasts with fine herbs and polenta, all served with soup and salad. Breakfast menu items: huevos rancheros, apple French toast, biscuits and chorizo gravy, eggs Benedict, and the Ranch House Breakfast (two eggs, hash browns, bagel, toast or muffin, choice of breakfast meat).

**Activities:** A truly unbelievable array of choices: horseback trail rides and arena lessons, swimming in a heated pool, hiking, photography, fly-fishing lessons, tennis, white-water rafting, Humvee tour, mountain biking, ATV riding, cattle drives. Winter downhill and cross-country skiing, snowshoeing, sleigh rides, snowmobiling.

**Amenities:** Outdoor heated pool, tennis court and exercise facility, individual hot tubs in higher-priced cabins and a communal hot tub near the remaining cabins, putting green, helicopter pad, mountain-bike rentals, complimentary bar and wine service, room service, wood-burning fireplaces; some cabins with kitchens or kitchenettes.

**Special Programs:** Children under 16 are allowed only if the entire ranch is rented; otherwise, this is an adults-only facility. Vintners Series, a culinary and wine-tasting extravaganza combining the exceptional talents of the Triple Creek chefs with visiting Vintners staff. Wine seminars, cooking with wine classes, wine pairing and food seminar, 4-course dinners with matched wine selections, and farewell reception. Inquire for rates and dates.

**Rates:** $$–$$$$$ Full American Plan. Rates include all meals, snacks, cocktail and wine service, use of facilities, fly-casting lessons, horseback riding, tennis, putting green, and much more. Some activities, such ATV rides, snowmobiling, white-water rafting, and scenic river floats, available at additional expense.

**Credit Cards:** VISA, MasterCard, American Express, Discover

**Season:** Year-round, including holidays

**Getting There:** Nearest commercial airport, Missoula. Highway 93 to Darby to Highway 473; ranch is located just off the highway. Airport transportation to the ranch available.

**What's Nearby:** The Bitterroot Valley area offers many museums, restaurants, and specialty shops and is well worth the visit.

# WHITE TAIL RANCH

## Ovando, Montana

Some ranch owners take a very hands-on approach to hospitality, and the Wellman family—Bill and Diana—fit that mold. Prior to purchasing White Tail Ranch in 1996, the Wellmans spent nearly two decades in the resort business, a background that helps them in overseeing the small details and the large vision that make a vacation property truly special. They are here to serve you in a gracious and friendly fashion befitting this historic and lovely property.

White Tail Ranch began as an outfitting business, eventually expanding to encompass the variety of experiences and options of a full-fledged guest ranch. The overall feel is of simplicity and rusticity, but with carefully chosen appointments that make even the most persnickety city folk feel comfortable and at ease. The guest cabins are cozy structures arrayed along the banks of the trout stream that cuts through the property. They afford guests lovely views of the surrounding mountains as well as a sense of privacy. The beds have heavy quilt covers and the bedside tables are fashioned from bear boxes (boxes once used to transport bears) and pack boxes, giving the rooms just the right feeling of authenticity and Old West style.

The century-old main lodge houses the dining room and common areas, where guests congregate and socialize. An old-fashioned dinner bell calls the guests to meals, but guests also have the option of dining family style in the privacy of their own cabins. The simple, home-cooked meals are steeped in western culinary traditions and are complemented by home-baked breads and desserts.

Guest activities are organized in an informal fashion. If horseback riding is your desire, you can explore to your heart's content on all-day rides or ease into the rigors of the trail with shorter loop trips. Hiking, bird-watching, and mountain-bike touring are other favorite activities. Guests who are looking for exhilaration can take a white-water rafting trip; those who prefer more solitude can dip a line in Salmon Creek, which runs through the property, or try the challenging eddies of the famed Blackfoot River.

Winter visitors can choose from dogsledding, cross-country skiing, snowshoeing, and snowmobiling. Spring and fall offer particularly fine wildlife viewing and a chance to see Montana's lovely wilderness unfold in fields of wildflower or fantastic autumn displays. This part of Montana abounds with white-tailed deer, red fox, and bald eagles, so keep your eyes open and your binoculars close at hand.

In the evening, guests can settle in and relax amid a delightful array of parlor games, an extensive library, or join a sing-along at the piano. Enjoy a campfire with your family or just stare up at the huge sky filled with twinkling stars—more, perhaps, than you've ever seen in your life. For a special treat, inquire about visiting a Native American pow-wow meeting.

## White Tail Ranch

82 White Tail Ranch Road
Ovando, MT 59854
Phone: (888) 987–2624
Fax: (406) 793–5043
E-mail: whitetail@montana.com
Web site: www.whitetailranch.com

**Owners/Managers:** Bill and Diana Wellman

**Accommodations:** Capacity, 25. 9 total units. Guests stay in comfortable cabins along the banks of Salmon Creek. 6 rooms feature private baths; the remainder share a bath house. All have electric heat and woodstoves.

**Meals:** 3 daily seatings served family style or buffet style. Vegetarian and special diets accommodated on request.

**Activities:** Complete horse program with daily trail riding and arena instruction. Trails meander through gentle meadows and steep mountain trails with striking views. Mountain biking, hiking, bird-watching, fly fishing on the Blackfoot River, float trips. Anglers may inquire about guided trips on pristine trout waters. Additional activities at nearby Cooper Lake. Winter season includes cross-country skiing, snowshoeing, and guided or unguided snowmobiling. Dogsledding and sleigh rides, too.

**Amenities:** Hot tub, outdoor recreational facilities (badminton, croquet, volleyball, arena roping), library, parlor games, sitting room in main lodge.

**Special Programs:** Children's program offered during the day; kids take part in hikes, arts and crafts, games, swimming, and trail rides. Baby-sitting available with advance notice.

**Rates:** $$–$$$ Full American Plan. Reduced off-season rates, reduced children's rates for ages 6–14. Minimum 3-night stay.

**Credit Cards:** None. Personal checks and traveler's checks accepted.

**Season:** Summer: May to mid-November; winter: January to April.

**Getting There:** Nearest commercial airport, Missoula (60 miles west) or Helena (75 miles southeast). Airport transfer available at additional cost.

**What's Nearby:** Missoula, 1 hour's drive west, is a charming college town with art galleries, restaurants, and shopping.

# THE LODGE AT CHAMA

## Chama, New Mexico

A sportsman's paradise best describes the Lodge at Chama. Imagine befriending a wealthy billionaire and being invited to his private fishing and hunting lodge. Upon your arrival, he treats you and your partner to cocktails at a privately stocked bar. Afterward, you settle in for a gourmet meal. You're shown to your private room. The bed is luxurious, with wonderful high-count sheets and big, plush pillows. The bathroom is huge and luxurious, with thick terry robes for your comfort. In the morning, you eat a sumptuous breakfast. Your host greets you, and you are introduced to his personal fishing guide. For the next three days, you are schooled in the intricacies of fly selection, insect recognition, trout habitat, and casting technique. One afternoon, you spend time on the shooting range blasting clay pigeons to dust while your spouse takes spa treatments in an intimate salon; the next, you go horseback riding in a seemingly endless wilderness.

Minus the billionaire host, that about encapsulates the Lodge at Chama experience. This is a premier resort property located on 36,000 acres of Jicarilla-Apache–owned land in the San Juan Range of Northern New Mexico. This state's motto is "the Land of Enchantment," and you'll certainly feel as though you've been transported to a fairy-tale land of outdoor recreation and the ultimate in personal care and attention during your stay at the Lodge.

Considered to be one of the world's finest outdoor-sporting retreats, the Lodge at Chama hosts impressive hunting get-togethers in season. Guests hunt both upland birds (including wild turkey) and big-game animals including deer, elk, bear, and even buffalo.

If hunting isn't your thing, however, there are ample chunks of the year when you can simply watch and observe the native wildlife in a truly secluded wilderness setting. The 27,000-square-foot lodge building is spectacular: The exterior is a mix of smooth pine logs and impressive stone masonry; inside, the two magnificent Great Rooms feature 36-foot-tall cathedral ceilings and soaring view windows; in the evening, you'll relax in front of a 20-foot-wide see-through fireplace. All the furnishings are luxurious and inviting.

The huge rooms are appointed with plush lounging chairs and ample private decks where you can enjoy cocktails or private get-togethers. Two new suites feature see-through fireplaces, satellite TV, and French doors that open onto outstanding vistas.

Brandy and Belgian chocolates will await you at bedside after a long and luxurious bath in the huge whirlpool and sauna. If you didn't get the workout you anticipated during the day, you can also visit a full-scale health spa with the latest in exercise equipment.

Winter guests are every bit as pampered. Those who visit during the cold months can expect a wide variety of daily diversions, from cross-country skiing and snowshoeing to ice fishing and snowmobiling. The winter offers an especially good time to elk-watch, as the animals have moved down from the high country to inhabit the lowland pastures of the ranch.

## The Lodge at Chama

P.O. Box 127
Chama, NM 87520
Phone: (505) 756–2133
Fax: (505) 756–2519
E-mail: reservations@lodgeatchama.com
Web site: www.thelodgeatchama.com

**Manager:** Frank Simms

**Accommodations:** Capacity, 40. 22 total units. Guests rooms and suites located in the architecturally wonderful lodge. Oversized rooms feature private baths, satellite TV, posh linens and towels, complimentary brandy and chocolates, guest robes, and private decks. Four new luxury suites include see-through stone fireplaces and large sitting rooms.

**Meals:** True gourmet meals served in the lodge dining room. Breakfast buffet includes fresh-baked pastries, muffins, and coffee cakes; breakfast meats, eggs, French toast, and more. Gourmet picnic lunches provided for your daytime adventure. In the evening, guests are welcome to the fully stocked bar and select dinner wines from an extensive wine list. The evening dinner menu varies daily, based on the availability of seasonal and fresh ingredients and the whims of the lodge's executive chef.

**Activities:** Guided day-fishing trips; fly-fishing school (additional cost); full use of the Lodge facilities, including spa facility; sporting clay shooting, hiking, ranch tours, wildlife viewing, photography, horseback riding. Wintertime snowshoeing, cross-country skiing, snowmobiling, ice fishing, wildlife observation. All activities are guided and most are charged separately.

**Amenities:** Complimentary bar, full-service spa, exercise room, satellite TV, huge sitting rooms with overstuffed chairs.

**Special Programs:** Bear-, elk-, deer-, and bird-hunting in season. Children must be at least 12 years of age, except by special arrangement.

**Rates:** $$$$$ American Plan option, with activities included. Meals, complimentary bar, use of spa and conference facilities included in basic rate. Activities package includes the above, plus fishing, sporting clays, hiking tours, ranch tours, wildlife viewing and photography excursions.

**Credit Cards:** VISA, MasterCard. Personal and corporate checks accepted.

**Season:** Year-round

**Getting There:** Nearest commercial airports: Colorado Springs, Durango, and Albuquerque. Ranch airstrip accommodates private aircraft. The Lodge is located 100 miles north of Santa Fe, 90 miles west of Taos. Inquire for specific directions.

**What's Nearby:** Taos, with its famed native arts and fine arts community, approximately 1½-hour drive. Durango, a vibrant western town located in the southwest corner of Colorado, offers excellent winter skiing at Durango Winter Resort. Summer guests, ask about the Cumbres and Toltec Railroad, which departs from Chama and winds through the mountains of southern Colorado.

# LOS PINOS GUEST RANCH

Cowles, New Mexico

Simplicity and intimacy characterize Los Pinos Guest Ranch, a historic property set in the preternaturally beautiful Sangre de Cristo Range of the lower Rocky Mountains. If you're looking for a great escape from the pressures, schedules, and deadlines of modern living, this is the place.

Situated at an elevation of 8,500 feet, Los Pinos commands wonderful views of the surrounding peaks that are among the West's better-kept secrets. Its subalpine elevation means warm summer days of idyllic 70-degree weather and cool nights, when the thermometer often drops into the 40s—so pack plenty of sweaters! You'll definitely want them when you stray away from the lodge to gaze at the stars in one of the clearest skies you'll ever experience.

Originally built as a summer residence, Los Pinos first began catering to adventurers in the 1920s. Throughout its eighty years of operation, the ranch has remained delightfully small, accommodating up to twelve guests. Imagine having your own summer retreat in the Rockies; that's the atmosphere you'll find at Los Pinos.

Guests stay in any of four modest log cabins, each equipped with antique clawfoot tubs (perfect for soaking), front porches, and wood-burning stoves. The rooms are absent of phones and televisions, adding to the blissful serenity of the experience. You won't miss them, as there are many pleasant diversions to occupy your time. The sparkling waters of the upper Pecos River and the Mora River teem with trout and offer excellent opportunities for fly fishing. You can arrange guided half-day trips on the rivers, or you can take a rod along on a high-country horse ride that takes you to lovely high-alpine lakes.

The motto at Los Pinos is, "Where the road ends and the trails begin." A fitting motto, as trail riding and nature hikes constitute the main organized activities here. Guests take part in half- and full-day trail rides through the forests and alpine meadows of the Santa Fe National Forest. In early spring, the lower elevations unfold in carpets of wildflowers, and the profusion of color continues through the summer as the growing season works its way upward to the higher (and cooler) upper elevations. Wildlife abounds in this setting: On any given day, you may encounter deer, elk, coyotes, and birds of prey; you may even see a furry marmot whistling at you from his perch in the upper-alpine tundra.

Guests can stretch their legs on any number of excellent trails accessible from the ranch. Several choice alpine lakes can be reached on Forest Service trails. Or you may laze on the wide porch of the main lodge with a good book plucked from the McSweeney family library.

Dining is informal, but the service is superb. Fresh-baked breads, homemade soups, and desserts accompany your dinner, which the McSweeney clan describes as "contemporary ranch" style cuisine. Day hikers and riders can request packed sack lunches for the trail. If you wish to have an evening cocktail or glass of wine with your meal, you are welcome to bring your own.

There are any number of special places described in this book, all with special attributes that set them apart. At Los Pinos, those attributes can best be described as simplicity and gracious service in an outstanding and serene setting.

## Los Pinos Ranch

Route 3, P.O. Box 8
Terrero, NM 87573
(505) 757–6213
(winter address, October–May)
P.O. Box 24
Glorieta, NM 87535
Phone: (505) 757–2185
Web site: www.lospinosranch.com

**Owners:** The McSweeney Family

**Accommodations:** Capacity, 12; 4 total units. Guests stay in 4 aspen-log cabins, each equipped with a front porch, private bath, and woodstove. The main lodge, built in 1912, is the central gathering spot. A large screened porch with rustic furniture provides the perfect setting for relaxation and socializing.

**Meals:** Simple, healthful foods characterize meals at Los Pinos; fresh-baked breads, soups, and desserts accompany the evening meal, with sack lunches available for daytime activities.

**Activities:** Horseback riding, hiking, and fly fishing are the main activities here; guests take great pleasure in nature observation and simple relaxation in this amazingly breathtaking mountain setting.

**Amenities:** Ranch library, with an emphasis on nature books and local history; piano in the main lodge; the ranch emphasizes serenity over luxury.

**Special Programs:** Children over 6 years of age are welcome; no formal children's programs. Parents are responsible for their kids' entertainment and activities, but most kids gladly take part in the informal ranch activities at Los Pinos, enjoying the pleasures of experiencing and exploring nature.

**Rates:** $$ Lodging and dining included in basic costs; horseback riding and guided fishing charged additionally. 2-night minimum stay. Children's rate. Discounts for full-week stays.

**Credit Cards:** None accepted. Cash or check, please.

**Season:** June through September

**Getting There:** Nearest airport, Santa Fe. Guests fly into either Santa Fe or Albuquerque. Located 45 miles northeast of Santa Fe off I–25. Map and directions available on request.

**What's Nearby:** Santa Fe, with its fabulous art galleries, museums, restaurants, and native craft shops; nearby towns of Chimayo, Las Vegas (New Mexico), and in particular, Taos; all merit day trips. Also, the Pecos Historic Park.

# PINEGROVE DUDE RANCH

Kerhonkson, New York

New York's Catskill Mountains have been a favorite vacation destination for nearly a century, making the Pinegrove Dude Ranch a relative newcomer to the neighborhood. The ranch was opened in the early 1970s by owners Dick and Debbie Tarantino, who have made this place one of the finest resort destinations in the region. Over the years, the Tarantino family has earned numerous awards for their outstanding travel destination, including a "Ranch of the Year" award from *Family Circle* magazine.

Located in the ruggedly beautiful Sawangunk Mountains, Pinegrove abounds with wild animals, including migratory waterfowl, fox, raccoon, quail, pheasant, and a variety of songbirds. You'll definitely want to spend some quiet time exploring the ranch's 600 acres of rural countryside via the trails that intertwine across the rural landscape.

Pinegrove maintains a great string of well-trained and gentle horses, including a number of pure-bred quarter horses and Appaloosas. Rides depart hourly on ample trails offering outstanding mountain views. If you've always wanted to play cowboy, ask about participating in an authentic cattle drive on the ranch. Kids can take part in a Junior Wrangler program, as well as in daily supervised activities for children of all ages.

Pinegrove is a large resort, accommodating as many as 350 guests. As one might expect, the menu of daily activities is extensive, and the facilities offer a variety of choices to round out your vacation experience. Guests can enjoy lake and river fishing, paddleboating, rock-climbing practice on the ranch climbing wall, tennis, swimming, and complimentary golf at a nearby course. Evening entertainment includes a cocktail lounge with live music, square dances, a western saloon, a pool bar, a nightclub with an evening show, and hayrides. Kids will especially enjoy the newly added double-flume water slide!

It is nearly impossible to list all the activities offered at Pinegrove. Suffice it to say, you will always find something fun and entertaining to do here.

If you are interested in a winter getaway, Pinegrove accommodates guests who come to ski, ice skate, and enjoy sleigh rides and tubing. With two slopes, it is the ideal place for never-evers to get their "ski legs" without the crowds and the hustle-bustle of expensive winter-resort destinations. Be sure to ask about the learn-to-ski package. Alpine and cross-country ski equipment is available, so all you have to bring is your mittens!

Pinegrove is as much a full-service resort as a guest ranch, and even people who are a little horse-phobic will find plenty to do here. This is an ideal location for families who have a diversity of interests and who want to spend time together—and time apart.

## Pinegrove Dude Ranch

P.O. Box 209
Kerhonkson, NY 12446
Phone: (800) 346–4626
Fax: (914) 626–7365
E-mail: pinegrove@ulster.net
Web site: www.pinegrove-ranch.com

**Owners/Managers:** Dick and Debbie Tarantino

**Accommodations:** Capacity, 350. Guest rooms in the motel-style main lodge are large, comfortable, and modern. Sizes vary from small rooms, with double beds suitable for couples with small children, to large suites featuring king and double beds, ideal for larger families. Rooms include TVs, phones, air conditioning, and private baths.

**Meals:** 3 sit-down meals daily, extensive menu at each meal. Sunday barbecue in summer. Complimentary snack bar serving fries, franks, burgers, etc. until midnight.

**Activities:** Daily trail rides depart on the hour; riding instruction and evening riding seminars with video review; young children can take pony rides in the riding arena. Weekly cattle drive—inquire, as spaces may be limited. Fishing in a stocked pond. Boating on the ranch's lake. Other outdoor activities include tennis, swimming in a heated pool, archery, basketball, volleyball, miniature golf and boccie ball, and shuffleboard. Indoor recreation room. Evening entertainment and activities include nightclub show, country dancing, disco dancing, pool bar, game nights, live entertainment, and music. Winter activities include skiing, ice skating, sledding and tubing, sleigh rides, with equipment and ski lessons available.

**Amenities:** Game room, kid's playground, nursery, cocktail lounges and bars with live entertainment or deejays, sporting equipment, complimentary snack bar, heated pool, day camp for kids, and plenty of planned activities.

**Special Programs:** Kids' Junior Wrangler riding program, nursery, kids' activities, and teen programs.

**Rates:** $$–$$$ Full American Plan. All-inclusive package includes accommodations, meals, free snack bar privileges, cocktail parties, horseback riding, Junior Wrangler program, and use of all facilities, even complimentary golf! Reduced rates for 1-week stays; reduced kids rates depending on ages; reduced off-season rates; group and senior discounts.

**Credit Cards:** VISA, MasterCard, American Express, Discover

**Season:** Open year-round

**Getting There:** Nearest airports in New York (Kennedy) and Newark, N.J. Located 100 miles north of New York City, one mile west of Kerhonkson off Route 209. Nearest train: Poughkeepsie, 25 miles.

**What's Nearby:** Guests may wish to explore the lovely towns of the Catskill Mountains, with numerous restaurants, stores, and antiques shops.

# RIDIN-HY RANCH RESORT

## Warrensburg, New York

When the Second World War ended, Americans released their pent-up desires to travel by heading West. Postwar Americans identified with the Hollywood cowboys, who personified strength and independence and freedom. If a family couldn't find the means to head out West, they slipped out of the Bronx or Queens or New Jersey and headed for the next best thing: Ridin-Hy Ranch Resort, as western a guest ranch as you'll find out East.

Presently, Ridin-Hy remains much as it did during its heyday back in the 1950s. A year-round family resort, Ridin-Hy is owned and operated by Andy and Susan Beadnall (Susan's father started the resort in 1940). It has grown over the years but still maintains the optimistic spirit and family-friendly fun that made it a success half a century ago.

Ridin-Hy is situated in the lush forest lands of the Adirondack State Park on the shores of Sherman Lake. From the lake, one can enjoy lovely views of the Adirondacks, which rise amid one of the largest public parks in the continental U.S.—more than six million acres!

Most of the guests here are repeat customers. Some have even created their own Web sites documenting their annual visits. It's not unusual to meet fellow guests who have been coming here since they were children and now bring their own kids and even grand-kids.

What is it about Ridin-Hy that inspires such loyalty? First off, a staff that strives to make everyone comfortable and has loads of fun doing their jobs. The activities list is extensive: horseback riding, pony rides for young kids, a weekly professional rodeo and weekday guest "showdeos," fishing in either of two lakes and a rushing stream, and your choice of water activities on Sherman Lake. Enjoy a paddleboat or rowboat ride, swim in the lake or heated outdoor pool, go waterskiing or wakeboarding, or simply lounge around before taking a trip to the spa. There are also dozens of summertime games, including volleyball, softball, horseshoes, archery, or tennis on either of two private courts. As one visitor commented, "There are way more activities than anyone needs to be doing on vacation."

Even in winter, the ranch bustles with activity. Favorite pastimes include cross-country skiing, sleigh rides, ice-skating, snowmobiling, and nearby alpine skiing.

This is a large place, capable of hosting 195 guests. With more than 800 acres of private land, however, it's not difficult to find a serene place to spread out a picnic lunch and enjoy a relaxing afternoon with loved ones. When you decide it's time to socialize, there are square dances, barbecues, hayrides, and other evening activities.

This is a family-run and family-friendly ranch resort with high standards of professionalism honed over decades spent in the guest ranch business. If you live back East and want a taste of the West without the hassle of long-distance travel, you may find that you need go no farther than Ridin-Hy.

**Ridin-Hy Ranch Resort**
P.O. Box 369
Sherman Lake
Warrensburg, NY 12885
Phone: (518) 494–2742
Fax: (518) 494–7181

**Owners/Managers:** Susan and Andy Beadall

**Accommodations:** Guest capacity, 195. Rooms vary from motel-like lodges to chalet-style pinewood cottages that can accommodate anywhere from 1 to 3 families. All have full bathrooms. The main lodge, which provides a focal point for most indoor activities, features a large stone fireplace in the lounge and a central dining room with outstanding views of the lake and the Adirondack Mountains.

**Meals:** 3 meals served daily. Families dine together in the main dining room. Menu selections are ample and varied. Theme dinners include a pizza night, outdoor barbecue at pool side, and a hot-dog roast. Weekly smorgasbord dinner with sliced ham and turkey.

**Activities:** Horseback riding includes arena instruction and mountain-trail rides, with slow, moderate, and fast-paced groups. Pony rides for children also available. Weekly professional rodeo and midweek guest "showdeos." Lake fishing and river fishing, waterskiing, rowboats, paddleboats, and swimming in the lake and in a heated outdoor pool. Evening planned activities including dances, games, theme dinner, and outdoor sports. Nearby golf and alpine skiing in winter. Additional winter activities: snowmobiling, cross-country skiing, sleigh rides, and ice-skating.

**Amenities:** Guest spa, whirlpool bath, cocktail lounge, game room, water sports supplies, and boats.

**Special Programs:** Organized children's Program with children's activity director. Babysitting available. Supervised pony rides for kids ages 7 and under.

**Rates:** $–$$ Full American Plan, with or without horseback riding. 2-night minimum stay. Off-season discounts and children's rates, by age.

**Credit Cards:** VISA, MasterCard, American Express, Discover. Personal checks accepted.

**Season:** Year-round

**Getting There:** 65 miles north of Albany, 15 miles north of Lake George off Route 87.

**What's Nearby:** Lake George, Stone Bridge Caves, Fort William Henry, and Lake Placid.

# ROARING BROOK RANCH AND TENNIS RESORT

### Lake George, New York

Although the emphasis of this book is family vacations, we realize that some readers may be looking for a place to hold a conference. Although the Roaring Brook Ranch and Tennis Resort certainly will appeal to family vacationers, it is also one of the largest guest-ranch resorts in the country and an exceptional place to hold a conference, especially if you are looking for plenty of recreational activities and a western flavor.

This ranch can accommodate 300 overnight guests and as many as 1,000 conference attendees. With more than 17,000 square feet of seminar and exhibit space, Roaring Brook has hosted corporate groups ranging from the General Electric Corporation to Chevrolet to Lincoln Logs, Inc. These groups, and many more, have found Roaring Brook Ranch to be an ideal location for a memorable and productive getaway.

That said, let's talk about family vacations. Roaring Brook has long been a favorite destination for New Yorkers and New Englanders who appreciate its picturesque locale on beautiful Lake George, a particularly scenic lake that has been a favorite vacation destination for more than a century. One reason for its popularity is the plethora of off-site attractions, including Fort Ticonderoga, the racetrack at Saratoga, Howe Caverns, and "the Million Dollar Mile," a popular shopping mall.

The ranch has more than adequate facilities to please the most pampered guests, including a workout room, five tennis courts (two lighted), an indoor pool and sauna, two outdoor pools, and an extensive children's program. The horse program is particularly appealing; the ranch recruits actual cowboys from out West to serve as wranglers.

Each evening features entertainment and musical performances, often including national television and recording artists. There are two cocktail lounges, where guests mingle with one another and enjoy the live entertainment.

There are a number of recreational activities, too. You can shoot billiards, play table tennis, badminton, archery, horseshoes, or take part in a spirited game of beach volleyball.

Besides the usual ranch activities, this ranch also has an excellent tennis program. Players of all levels can improve their game with the help of the resident pro, and there are always plenty of guests ready and willing to toe up at the service line and test your ground stroke.

With close to 500 acres of property, the ranch is also a good place to take a contemplative walk and do some bird-watching. This is a full-service resort, one that you will likely want to return to over and over again.

## Roaring Brook Ranch and Tennis Resort

Route 9N South
Lake George, NY 12845
Phone: (800) 882–7665; (518) 668–5767
Fax: (518) 668–4019
E-mail: mail@roaringbrookranch.com
Web site: www.roaringbrookranch.com

**Manager:** George Greene

**Accommodations:** Capacity, 300. The ranch features 140 rooms in 9 motel-like buildings. Rooms include private baths, heat and air conditioning, TVs, and phones. Many have decks. Suites also available on a limited basis.

**Meals:** Meals are served in a commodious dining room. Expect a varied menu. Guests may also dine in the coffee shop.

**Activities:** 4 scheduled horseback rides depart daily in groups of 25 to 30; riders are grouped by experience. For new riders, group lessons are available. Tennis is probably the single most popular pastime here, and there are 5 courts, which are always in use. Other activities include swimming, recreational sports, and a popular shoreline cruise on Lake George.

**Amenities:** Workout facilities, 5 tennis courts, nightly live entertainment, indoor pool and sauna, direct-dial telephones, color cable TV in each room, nearby golf, activities director and children's counselors, many nearby attractions and tours.

**Special Programs:** Modest children's program in summer accommodates kids of all ages, but is not formalized. Activities include arts and crafts, pony rides, and games. Most kids take part in activities side by side with their parents. Nursery available by arrangement.

**Rates:** $–$$ Modified American Plan, including breakfast and dinner. European plan also available (no meals). Activities such as horseback riding, lake tours, and others charged additionally.

**Credit Cards:** VISA, MasterCard

**Season:** Mid-May to mid-October. Conferences scheduled year-round.

**Getting There:** Nearest commercial airport, Albany. Most guests arrive in private cars. Ranch is located 2 miles south of Lake George, off I–87, about 200 miles north of New York City.

**What's Nearby:** Fort William Henry Historic Site; Saratoga Springs Performing Arts Center; French and Indian War Battlefields; Fort Ticonderoga Historic Site; Frontier Town; Howe Caverns; Santa Claus's North Pole Village; cruises on Lake George; Great Escape Theme Park.

# ROCKING HORSE RANCH

## Highland, New York

There's something irrepressibly fun about this ranch, and it begins with the name. As one might expect from a place called Rocking Horse Ranch, this upstate mountain resort is a kid's paradise. But adults love it too, as there are few resorts, much less guest ranches, that offer as many things to entertain you and occupy your day as are available here.

One writer from the *New York Post* aptly described it as "the Club Med of Ranch Resorts." Here's just a sampling of the many activities you can choose from: Ride the giant waterslide, ride a horse, pilot a paddleboat, water-ski, shoot an arrow on the archery range, play a round of miniature golf, play a game of beach volleyball, play tennis, take an aerobics class. Oh, and then at night, you can country dance, disco dance, see a comedian or magic show, take a hayride, watch movies on the big screen TV, sing karaoke, or play parlor games in the game room.

Whew! Tired already? The Rocking Horse is also a great place to relax and do nothing at all. With 500 acres, it's relatively easy to find a quiet place to just stretch out and take a nap. There are two gigantic outdoor pools with waterslides for kids and adults, a wading pool for small children, and plenty of lounge furniture to kick back on. There's also lakefront property, great for watching your family learn to water-ski, and if the weather should turn cloudy, you can lounge beside the indoor pool.

Despite its playful name, the Rocking Horse takes its equine program quite seriously. There are more than one hundred horses on the ranch, giving a ratio of one horse to every four guests. Riding instruction is available. Riders are tested for ability and divided into groups of like aptitude. One-hour rides depart from the stable throughout the day. Small children can enjoy supervised pony rides in the arena.

Return guests know that losing weight is a difficult, if not impossible, proposition, as the meals are sumptuous and all-you-can-eat. The chefs update the menu regularly to ensure that you won't be selecting from the same items with each visit, but you can always count on fresh fruit and vegetables and high-quality breads and desserts.

The high standards set by the Rocking Horse have earned it numerous awards, including the AAA 3-Diamond Award and the Mobil 3-Star Award, both reflective of a high level of service.

If you take the best of western hospitality and mix it with the most efficient and attentive New York savoir faire, the result is the Rocking Horse Ranch, one of the premier resort properties in North America. If you are like most guests, you'll want to come back again and again and again.

**Rocking Horse Ranch**
Highland, NY 12528
Phone: (845) 691–2927
Fax: (845) 691–6434
E-mail: info@RHRanch.com
Web site: www.RHRanch.com

**Owners:** The Turk Family

**Accommodations:** Guest capacity, 400. 120 units divided between two motel-style buildings, the Oklahoma and the Main Lodge. Rooms sleep up to 6 people and include TVs, air conditioning, private baths, direct-dial telephones, and daily maid service. Deluxe rooms available with king-sized bed, sofa bed, minifridge, and coffeemaker.

**Meals:** Menu varies on a regular basis but always includes hearty American staples. Huge breakfast buffet, ice-cream socials, 24-hour coffee-and-sandwich shop, cocktail parties in licensed bar.

**Activities:** Horseback riding, tennis, waterskiing, paddleboating, beach and water volleyball, court sports (basketball, handball, boccie, etc.), softball games, miniature golf, rifle and archery shooting, nature hikes, evening entertainment, and much more. Extensive winter activities include on-site skiing, giant tube run, ice skating, and horse-drawn sleigh rides.

**Amenities:** 2 outdoor pools, wading pool, water slides, court sports facilities, private lake, shooting gallery, archery range, video arcade, children's playground, parlor games, fitness room, sauna rooms, nightclub. Handicap accessible with special needs accommodated.

**Special Programs:** Supervised kids' programs and activities. Day-camp program for children 4 to 12 includes sports, hikes, games, swimming, crafts, treasure hunts, and more. Children's nursery and babysitting available.

**Rates:** $$–$$$ Full American Plan. Reduced prices for kids ages 4–15, no charge for children under age 4. Special preseason summer rates; off-season rates.

**Credit Cards:** VISA, MasterCard, Discover, American Express

**Season:** Year-round

**Getting There:** Located in the mid-Hudson Valley off New York Thruway (I–87), 1½ hours north of New York City. Nearest commercial airport: Stewart International, Newburg, N.Y., about 20 miles from the ranch.

**What's Nearby:** West Point Military Academy; Roosevelt's Hyde Park Mansion.

# CATALOOCHEE RANCH

## Maggie Valley, North Carolina

North Carolina's Great Smoky Mountains are one of the most beautiful and serene places in all of North America, a fact not lost on the original founder of the Cataloochee Ranch, Tom Alexander and his wife, Judy. Tom was a timber cruiser who appraised timberlands in the Great Smoky range. When the company he worked for went bankrupt during the Great Depression, Tom negotiated some land in exchange for back pay and opened a fishing camp.

The young couple opened the original Cataloochee Ranch in the newly created Great Smoky Mountains National Park, then relocated to the present site near Burnsville. They converted a sturdy stone-and-log cattle barn into the main ranch house and went about making improvements that included the first ski area south of Virginia. At present, this graceful North Carolina landmark ranch remains a sparkling jewel overlooking the rolling hills of Maggie Valley. With an elevation of 5,000 feet, it provides Southerners and other sojourners with a cool, pleasant place to while away their summer vacations. The ranch is still owned and operated by the family, principally Tom Alexander Jr., daughters Alice Aumen and Judy Coker and their husbands, Tom Aumen and Rick Coker.

The ranch has 1,000 mountaintop acres that adjoin the Great Smoky National Park, giving guests unlimited opportunities to hike and explore. Outdoor recreation is a big industry in this part of North Carolina, particularly fishing, golfing, and river rafting. Golf fiends can tee up at any of six nearby courses, offering them a full week of golf, if that is their desire. If casino gaming is your desire, you can visit Harrah's Casino on the nearby Cherokee Indian Reservation. But be sure to give yourself plenty of time for on-site activities, especially horseback riding. It is still the ideal way to experience the lovely Smoky Mountains.

The Cataloochee is a pleasant mixture of western and southern hospitality and culture. A favorite entertainment is watching traditional mountain-clogging demonstrations or taking in a performance by local mountain musicians singing traditional and new folk songs.

In the evening, you can join in the singing around the campfire, take a pleasant ride in the hay wagon, or take a sunset dip in the heated outdoor pool. The ambience here is informal, so guests can take things at their own pace. You can cram a full day of activities into your schedule or settle in with a good novel under a shade tree and work through it undisturbed.

The Cataloochee is a modest-sized place, as far as guest ranches go. With a maximum of sixty-five guests, the ranch allows for lots of personal attention. The Alexander family has more close to three-quarters of a century of experience taking care of vacationers, and they do it with consummate grace and southern charm. You'll look hard to find a guest ranch that comes this close to perfection.

## Cataloochee Ranch

119 Ranch Drive
Maggie Valley, NC 28751
Phone: (800) 868–1401; (828) 926–1401
Fax: (828) 926–9249
E-mail: info@cataloochee-ranch.com
Web site: www.cataloochee-ranch.com

**Owners/Managers:** Alice and Tom Aumen, Judy and Rick Coker

**Accommodations:** Capacity, 65. 19 total units. Guests stay in well-appointed log cabins, some with kitchenettes, or in guest rooms in the original main ranch house. All cabins have fireplaces, refrigerators, coffeemakers, radios, and private bathrooms. The lodge is the main gathering spot here; the interior features antique furniture, a huge stone fireplace, and rustic chandeliers fashioned from oxen yokes. Conference facilities for 40 available.

**Meals:** Although some ranches claim to offer homemade foods, this one really delivers. Fresh local trout, Virginia ham, ranch-raised garden vegetables, and beef fill out the dinner menu; even the breads and desserts are homemade. Guests enjoy weekly outdoor barbecues, and the ranch hosts an annual fall wild-game feast featuring venison and elk.

**Activities:** Daily horseback rides on the ranch and in the Great Smoky National Park; creek and river fishing, pack trips, recreational games, swimming, hiking, tennis. Float trips and white-water rafting trips on nearby rivers and golfing at 6 local courses. Winter sports at nearby Cataloochee Ski Area.

**Amenities:** Conference facilities, children's playground, heated swimming pool.

**Special Programs:** No formal children's programs, but kids are welcome. Children must be at least 6 years of age to ride horses.

**Rates:** $$–$$$. Modified American Plan. Meals and accommodations included; horseback riding at additional cost.

**Credit Cards:** VISA, MasterCard, American Express. Personal checks accepted.

**Season:** April to November, late December to March

**Getting There:** Located 35 miles west of Asheville off I-40 and U.S. Highway 19. Nearest commercial airport in Asheville, N.C.

**What's Nearby:** White-water rafting, craft shops, golf courses, and recreational and historical sites, including the Appalachian Trail, Biltmore Estate, Blowing Rock, Blue Ridge Parkway, Cherokee Indian Reservation with Harrah's Casino, Chimney Rock Park, Ghost Town in the Sky, Grandfather Mountain, Linville Caverns, Mountain Heritage Center, Tweetsie Railroad, and the Cataloochee Ski Area.

# CLEAR CREEK RANCH

## Burnsville, North Carolina

Word has gotten out about North Carolina's western mountains and the fantastic vacation opportunities they provide. If you're considering a vacation in the Tarheel State, we might suggest the Clear Creek Ranch, nestled in the peaceful Blue Ridge Mountains.

Owned and operated by Rex Frederick and his wife, Aileen, Clear Creek was the realization of the couple's dream of opening a western-style guest ranch in this most southern of states. That they did in 1995, and Clear Creek has been gaining in stature as a guest-ranch destination ever since. Part of the allure is its location on the edge of the Pisgah National Forest, which offers more than 80,000 acres of forested trails, streams, and mountain vistas. Adding to that is the Fredericks—as warm and inviting a couple as you are likely to find.

Clear Creek offers the usual menu of guest-ranch activities and then some. Horseback riding, of course, is a mainstay at the ranch. Guests can ride morning and afternoon, and those who stay all week can enjoy an all-day picnic ride on the Buncombe Horse Trail. The ranch also has a heated pool and hot tub with fabulous views of the Blue Ridge Mountains. Fishing is available in their stocked trout pond, or "real pros" can wet their line in the South Toe Ridge, where you match wits with rainbow and brown trout.

Golfers will appreciate the opportunity to tee it up on one of the finest mountain golf courses anywhere, just a three-minute drive from the ranch. Thrill seekers can indulge in white-water rafting offered twice weekly, or "tube" down the South Toe, which is done almost daily. Craft tours to local artists are offered, and children just love the weekly gem-mine trip.

In addition, Linville Falls, Grandfather Mountain, and Mt. Mitchell are all just a short drive from the ranch, and the magnificent Biltmore Estate in Asheville is about an hour's drive away.

Situated at an elevation of 3,200 feet, the Clear Creek Ranch is refreshingly cool in summer, and in springtime, it is a showcase of spectacular flowers: dogwood, forsythia, tulips, daffodils, and magnificent weeping cherry trees. Fall brings a brilliant wonderland of color. Special rates are available in spring and fall, and senior citizens enjoy extra discounts on weekdays.

Evenings offer a variety of activities including karaoke singing, line dancing, a marshmallow roast, a special "Margarita" night, or a hayride and steak cookout down on the river. An end-of-the-week highlight is the Saturday rodeo and chicken-and-ribs cookout, as well as a hootenanny put on by the staff.

The overall ambience of the ranch is one of casual fun and down-home friendliness. For families or singles, it's a perfect escape, with exceptional facilities in a beautiful setting and a friendly staff eager to do all they can to make your vacation a memorable one. A return rate nearing 50 percent tells us that they have been successful!

## Clear Creek Ranch

100 Clear Creek Drive
Burnsville, NC 28714
Phone: (800) 651–4510; (828) 675–4510
E-mail: CCRDUDE@prodigy.net
Web site: www.clearcreekranch.com

**Owners/Managers:** Rex and Aileen Frederick

**Accommodations:** Guests stay in one of 3 buildings adjacent to the main lodge. The structures are all new, carpeted, air-conditioned, and heated, but have a rustic charm. All buildings have covered porches with rocking chairs and offer spectacular views of the mountains. The lodge is comfortably furnished with a massive stone fireplace and a fine library of the latest books, which are available to guests.

**Meals:** All meals are served family style with the exception of cookouts and picnics on the trail. Expect homemade soups, fresh-baked breads, pastries and well-prepared main courses. Beer, wine, and mixed drinks are available to guests in the old-fashioned "cantina."

**Activities:** Horseback riding, hiking, fishing, tubing, and swimming, plus the fun of the weekend rodeo. Nearby golf and white-water rafting are available but do cost extra.

**Amenities:** Hot tub, heated pool, game room with pool tables and Ping-Pong, conference center for business meetings.

**Special Programs:** During summer, special activities are offered for children 5 years and older.

**Rates:** $$–$$$ American Plan. Rates include lodging and all meals and activities except those noted. Reduced rates are offered for children and seniors. Rates lower in November.

**Credit Cards:** VISA, MasterCard. Personal checks preferred.

**Season:** April 1 through the end of November. Children's programs June through August

**Getting There:** Located 45 miles north of Asheville, N.C., which is also the site of the nearest airport. Pickup is available at a small additional cost.

**What's Nearby:** Biltmore Estate, Grandfather Mountain, Linville Falls and Caverns, and a wide variety of local artists. Rafting and golf available at additional cost.

# EARTHSHINE MOUNTAIN LODGE
### Lake Toxaway, North Carolina

Earthshine Mountain Lodge suffers from a bit of an identity crisis: Is it a country inn, a bed-and-breakfast, a guest ranch, or a family resort? Regardless of what it may be called, it is a wonderful departure from the conventional vacation destination.

In a review that appeared in *Southern Living* magazine, one author states: "Earthshine offers such a picture-perfect mountain getaway that L.L. Bean has photographed catalogs there." Surrounded by the rolling hills of western North Carolina's Blue Ridge Mountains, Earthshine is indeed a picturesque place. Imagine a natural-wood lodge set in a broad, open pasture and surrounded by lovely forests that show their bold colors from spring until late fall. That pretty much summarizes the eye appeal. But there's more to Earthshine than meets the eye.

Hosts Marion Boatwright and Kim Heinitsh liken a visit to Earthshine to a fairytale trip to Grandmother's farm. The seventy-acre property abuts the Pisgah National Forest, providing endless miles of trails to explore. Two favorite hikes take walkers to the scenic French Broad River and the delightful King's Falls.

Just like at Grandma's farm, guests are welcome to help with feeding the animals and are encouraged to learn traditional farm crafts such as cider pressing, wool spinning, blacksmithing, and more.

Earthshine also offers more contemporary skills development, offering physical challenges that will excite young and old.

One unique activity is the Flight through the Tree Tops Zip Course," an obstacle course in the treetops that tests one's nerve and agility—in a relatively safe setting, of course. There's also a climbing wall and a ropes course.

Horseback riding is another favorite pastime. Guests may choose trail riding or get instruction in the arena. Small children will thrill to the experience of their first horse ride in the controlled environs of the arena and under the watchful guidance of trained riding instructors. Afterward, they can meet eye to eye with a special equine resident—Liza Jane, a miniature donkey.

The lodge is a handsome hand-constructed cedar-log building with magnificent views of the surrounding mountains. Visitors stay in tastefully decorated guest rooms that reflect the regional country charm of the Appalachian Mountains. You'll really enjoy the patchwork quilts, log beds, and comfy rockers that adorn these family-friendly lodgings.

In the evening, the entire family will enjoy sing-alongs, mountain dances, Native American ceremonies, storytelling, and lots of fun games. For those who simply can't stay put, the folks at Earthshine can help guide you to exceptional white-water rafting, tennis, fly fishing, golf, and mountain biking. Don't forget to allow enough time to take a scenic drive through the Blue Ridge Parkway, one of America's most scenic roads.

**Earthshine Mountain Lodge**
R.R. 1, Box 216C
Lake Toxaway, NC 28747–9736
Phone: (828) 862–4207
E-mail: earthshine@citcom.net
Web site: www.earthshinemtnlodge.com

**Owners/Managers:** Marion Boatwright and Kim Heinitsh

**Accommodations:** Capacity, 30. 13 total units. Guests stay in the main lodge, which has private rooms, each with bathrooms, private balconies, quilts, and log furniture, or in the Sunrise Cottage, which has 3 family suites. 8 guest rooms have Little House on the Prairie sleeping lofts, a great place for kids. Kids may also stay a night in the barn loft, an experience they won't soon forget.

**Meals:** The Earthshine follows the tradition of rural bed-and-breakfast inns, or you can have an all-inclusive stay including 3 daily meals. Fruit and beverages included throughout the day. Emphasis is on fresh, healthful foods (vegetarians gladly accommodated). Fresh local trout is a specialty. Sunday brunch.

**Activities:** Barnyard tours, horseback riding, cookouts, nature hikes, unique and challenging ropes course and climbing wall. Off-site tennis, golf, river rafting, mountain biking, sight-seeing.

**Amenities:** Large, shaded porch with "hidden hammocks" for relaxing, catfish pond for fishing, rock fireplaces, gift shop, conference center. Handicap accessible.

**Special Programs:** Earthshine goes out of its way to entertain and teach young children as well as curious adults. As an environmental-education center, the facility hosts upward of 2,000 school-aged kids each year, providing programs focused on earth science and history. Destination: 1840 is a living-history experience that puts kids in touch with early pioneer life; the Success program teaches self-accomplishment and team interaction through the High Ropes Course; Earth Explorers is a science program that capitalizes on a mystical trip in which children encounter odd mythical creatures. If interested, be sure to ask more about these fascinating educational programs. Baby-sitting available for young children.

**Rates:** $$ Full American Plan. Bed-and-breakfast rates also available. Reduced rates for kids and toddlers. Some activities are charged additionally.

**Credit Cards:** VISA, MasterCard, Discover

**Season:** Year-round

**Getting There:** Nearest airport, Asheville (35 miles). Lodge is located in Transylvania County off Highway 64, 11 miles west of Brevard.

**What's Nearby:** River rafting, golf, Pisgah National Forest.

# ASPEN RIDGE RESORT

## Bly, Oregon

Aspen Ridge Resort offers vacationers the chance to visit and participate in a real working ranch while enjoying the refined creature comforts of a genuine resort.

Located in the mountains of central Oregon, the ranch began life in the 1850s. In 1992, plans to create a resort destination in which well-heeled visitors could take an active hand in daily ranch work came to fruition. Presently, hosts Steve and Karen Simmons welcome guests from throughout the world who are drawn to this unique and wondrous place.

Aspen Ridge Resort boasts 14,000 acres of broad pastures and thick stands of evergreen trees surrounded by the Fremont National Forest. It is an ideal place to raise cattle, and the ranch maintains a full-scale cow/calf operation with close to 1,000 head of commercial cattle. Activities tend to follow the ebb and flow of the ranching seasons; spring is particularly busy as cattle are shipped from the range in California and calving season begins. Guests may ride herd on the new arrivals, helping with branding, and "working" and doctoring cattle. Fences are mended, and the ranch is put back into tip-top operational shape.

Summer work often involves moving cattle to new pastures, weaning the older calves, and overseeing newborns, which begin arriving in August and continue to hit the ground through October. Guests are assured of plenty of opportunities to ride.

Fall is a good time to take in the Annual Lake County Fair and Rodeo, view the fall colors, and do some trout fishing. You may also be called on to help with gathering, separating and shipping the cattle as they are prepared for market. In November, the final gather takes place, and the cattle return to winter pasture in California.

Don't think, however, that it is all work and no play at Aspen Ridge. If playing cowboy loses its romance, you can break out your racquet and play tennis on the excellent hard courts. Mountain biking is another favorite pastime as is wilderness hiking. Guests who like to fish can choose from many excellent and unspoiled fishing holes and streams.

Come winter, the cattle work is done. Guests strap on cross-country skis and explore thousands of acres in silent reverie. Those up for more raucous fun can head out on snowmobiles. Holidays are special times at the ranch, redolent of the spirit of the season.

Evening entertainment is homespun: Listen to the coyotes sing, watch the stars, or settle in with a good book. Occasionally, the ranch hosts a cowboy poet or balladeer, and guests are always welcome to demonstrate their own unique talents.

If you've always wanted to play at being a cowboy but are a little reticent about the primitive conditions that tend to characterize working ranches, you no longer have an excuse not to pull on your boots, pull down your hat, and saddle up your horse. This is the genuine item, but one with the genteel appointments that make it a great place to break in a "gunsel" used to the more urbane comforts of life in the big city.

## Aspen Ridge Resort

P.O. Box 2
Bly, OR 97622
Phone: (800) 393-3323; (541) 884-8685
Fax: (541) 884-8685
E-mail: aspenridge@silverstar.com
Web site: www.aspenrr.com

**Owners/Managers:** Steve and Karen Simmons

**Accommodations:** Capacity, 40. A rustic log lodge with modern appointments and 4 commodious guest rooms form the centerpiece of the resort. Guests may also choose from 5 luxurious 1,200-square-foot cabins that house up to 6 people, or 2 large log-cabin homes suitable for larger families and groups. Cabins and houses include large kitchens, woodstoves, and bathrooms.

**Meals:** 3 meals are served daily in the ranch-house restaurant. Guests choose from standard menu items. Enjoy hearty country breakfasts, sandwiches, soups, and salads, and dinners ranging from barbecued beef and ribs to river trout and chicken prepared in numerous fashions. Fresh-made desserts and baked breads. Cocktails and appetizers served in the Buffalo Saloon, open daily. Just passing through? The restaurant is also open to the general public.

**Activities:** Cattle work and horseback riding are the central activities here; take part in the actual workings of a true western cattle operation. Arena competitions include cutting, team roping, and fun games on horseback. Tennis, hiking, mountain biking, fishing, swimming. In winter, cross-country skiing and snowmobiling.

**Amenities:** Tennis courts, elegant lodge with antique furnishing, expansive guest quarters and cabins, cocktail lounge, swimming lake. A very civilized approach to a working-ranch vacation.

**Special Programs:** Ask about the fall rodeo in Lake County and special holiday celebrations on Thanksgiving, Christmas, and New Year's.

**Rates:** $$–$$$ European Plan. Riding, dining, and fishing charged separately.

**Credit Cards:** None. Personal checks accepted.

**Season:** Closed in March.

**Getting There:** Aspen Ridge Resort is located 18 miles southeast of Bly, off Highway 140.

**What's Nearby:** This is a secluded mountain property.

# BAR M RANCH AT BINGHAM HOT SPRINGS

Adams, Oregon

Although most people think of the Pacific Northwest as a rainy land of thick evergreen forests, the eastern portions of Oregon and Washington are actually high-desert regions, with wide-open spaces, and well-spaced stands of ponderosa pine peppering the rolling hills. It's in this environ that you'll encounter the Bar M Ranch at Bingham Springs, located in the Blue Mountains of eastern Oregon. The Bar M composes 2,500 acres bisected by the Umatilla River, named for the local Native Americans who populate the region to this day.

Large grassland pastures provide perfect grazing for horses, and the Bar M takes great pride in their fat but fit riding string. Guests are encouraged to "partner up" with their horses, which are assigned for the week. Learn the basics of grooming and saddling; then head out on the trail with your new best friend!

The Bar M was first settled around the time of the American Civil War, and the original ranch house (built in 1864) provides the perfect testament to this ranch's long history. Updated to comfortably accommodate guests, the ranch house serves as the main dining area and is the place where guests tend to congregate and share laughter and good times after a day on the trail. A huge front porch and an indoor stone fireplace invite guests to kick back and relax.

Weather permitting, guests are offered the opportunity to take part in an overnight campout, just as the cowboys of old did more than a century ago. Most guests agree that sleeping out under the stars and hearing the wranglers spin yarns is a memorable event.

For more than a century, folks have come to Bingham Hot Springs to soak in the mineral springs. You'll get to enjoy this spa-style luxury in the ranch's 40-by-60 foot pool, a great way to sooth sore muscles after a day of strenuous activity.

A favorite side trip is to visit the frontier town of Pendleton, home of the famous

## PENDLETON ROUND UP

One of the most famous rodeos in America, the Pendleton Round Up began as an informal riding contest on the streets of town. Businessmen quickly realized that a festival would provide a great tourist draw, and the Round Up was born. Folks traveled from as far as Chicago and Seattle to see the earliest shows, which drew upward of 30,000 visitors.

At present, the Round Up continues to pull visitors from throughout the country and, indeed, the world. Held on a huge grass field on the Round Up grounds, the rodeo is as wild as the Old West ever was. In keeping with the heritage of the region, Native Americans from various tribes come to town to perform dances and ceremonies; many pitch tepees in the Indian Village. The event features daily parades, colorful costumes, a carnival midway, and nonstop entertainment.

Pendleton Round Up and the Pendleton Woolen Mills. While there, be sure to take the underground tour, an adventure that will take you through nearly a half-mile of underground tunnels that facilitated commerce among the local businesses and also served as home to thousands of Chinese immigrants in the early days of settlement.

Back at the ranch, there are plenty of activities. Informal recreational games, including schoolyard favorites such as tetherball and volleyball, along with staples such as horseshoes, croquet, and badminton, invite spirited competition. You can also fish for trout in the Umatilla, participate in arena games on horseback, or go for a peaceful hike in the woods.

For guests who prefer leisurely fun to rigid schedules, the Bar M Ranch is a great choice.

### Bar M Ranch at Bingham Hot Springs
58840 Bar M Lane
Adams, OR 97810
Phone: (888) 824–3381; (541) 566–3381
Fax: (541) 566–0100
E-mail: barmranch@eoni.com
Web site: www.virtualcities.com/ons/or/u/oruc501.htm

**Accommodations:** Capacity, 45. Accommodations vary from 8 guest rooms with shared baths in the Main Ranch House to 2 private cabins suitable for families. Homestead Lodge has 2-room suites, with a queen-sized bed in the master bedroom and twin beds in the second sleeping room; also, a 3-room unit with queen, two twins, and a double bed and private bath. Brookside Cabin has 3 rooms, a queen bed and 3 twin beds, bathroom, and small refrigerator.

**Meals:** Country cooking emphasizes home-cooked ranch staples (beef, chicken, etc.), the occasional Mexican meal, fresh-baked breads and jams, fresh garden vegetables, and desserts. Weekly outdoor barbecue cookouts. BYOB.

**Activities:** Horseback riding is the main formal activity. The ranch has 45 saddle horses, ensuring that each guest has his or her own mount for the week. Overnight campout and lunch rides available. Riding instruction in the arena. Bingham Hot Springs is a favorite place to soak and relax. Fishing in the Umatilla River (equipment available). Private stocked fishing pond for kids. Dozens of recreational games such as Ping-Pong, tetherball, volleyball, basketball. Excursions to nearby Pendleton. Self-propelled boating on ranch pond. Evening campfires, sing-alongs, storytelling, barbecues, and barn dances in a real log barn.

**Amenities:** Hot-springs pool; main lodge with comfortable lounging furniture; coin-op laundry, ice machine, room refrigerators. No daily maid service.

**Special Programs:** Prefer children 6 and older; no formal children's program. Kids participate alongside their parents.

**Rates:** $$ Full American Plan.

**Credit Cards:** VISA, MasterCard. Traveler's and personal checks accepted.

**Season:** Year-round

**Getting There:** Bar M Ranch is 31 miles east of Pendleton, Oregon, and 45 miles south of Walla Walla, Washington. Horizon Airlines serves Kennewick/Tri-Cities, Pendleton, and Walla Walla Airports. Round-trip ground transportation from Pendleton airport available.

**What's Nearby:** Pendleton, home of the Pendleton Woolen Mills and the famous Pendleton Round Up Rodeo. Be sure to take the fun and fascinating Pendleton Underground Tour.

# THE PONDEROSA RANCH

Seneca, Oregon

Realizing that the urge to "play cowboy" runs deep in many guest-ranch vacationers, we've included several working ranches in this book. The Ponderosa Ranch is one of them, a true "big outfit" cattle ranch where guests ride side by side with real cowboys and take an active part in authentic ranch work. There is no artifice to this place. You won't move cattle unless they need to be moved, as nothing is "manufactured" simply to captivate guests.

Calving commences in May, offering a fantastic opportunity to see the wonder of the birthing process. Things are busy, as the cows must be prepared for their return to the high country. Hot-iron branding is the order of the day, and the buckaroos here do it the old-school way: no branding tables, just ropes, horses, and a hot fire.

In June, the cattle are pushed into the high country, where fresh grass is plentiful. Expect some long days in the saddle! July and August require constant attention to the herd, and you'll get to help scatter cattle and move them among the summer ranges. By September, a chill comes into the evening air, making the horses lively and anxious to work. Cows are gathered, run into corrals, and vaccinated and doctored if necessary. Calves are weaned, giving able riders the chance to do some exciting "cutting" in the corral.

This is the real deal, but don't get the idea that it will be all work and no play. The Ponderosa is a comfy place, with a huge main lodge and individual cabins with double beds, full bathrooms, and porches to relax in when the day's activities are complete. You can get some stick time shooting pool, catch a John Wayne classic on the VCR, sip a well-deserved cocktail at the bar, or soak your aching muscles in the Jacuzzi. You may be a cowboy, but who ever said cowboys don't enjoy a little luxury?

Of course, you can opt out of the day's chores and take a day off to go fishing, hiking, swimming, or spend a quiet morning with your camera trying to capture the perfect image of an elk grazing (the ranch maintains its own private herd of the majestic animals). There's lots of native wildlife to discover here, including pronghorn antelope, bald eagles, deer, coyotes, migratory waterfowl, and the occasional black bear.

This is a big-shouldered ranch, with an astounding 120,000 acres of property to explore. You can expect to spend six or eight hours a day in the saddle, so be sure that riding is something that you really want to spend time doing. This is also not the place for young children; a minimal age of eighteen is required.

You'll be hard-pressed to find a better cowboy experience anywhere among those described in this book, or for that matter, anywhere in the West. So pull on your boots, place your hat down low on your head, and get ready to ride, pardner!

**The Ponderosa Ranch**

P.O. Box 190
Seneca, OR 97873
Phone: (541) 542–2403
Fax: (541) 542–2713
E-mail: ride@ponderosa-ranch.com
Web site: www.ponderosa-ranch.com

**Owners/Managers:** Izzy and Nancy Oren

**Accommodations:** Capacity, 48. 8 total units. Guests stay in triplex cabins; each unit includes a bedroom with 2 double beds and full bathrooms. Units include separate entrances, front porches, wood floors, but no television or telephones. Cabins have wonderful western decor and feature attractive quarter-sawn log construction.

**Meals:** Meals are served in the main lodge, as well as out on the trail. Expect hearty western fare, served family style.

**Activities:** Cattle work is the focus of your vacation, although guests can always opt out and "take a day off." Fishing in the creeks or local rivers, seasonal big-game hunting, recreational games.

**Amenities:** Despite being a true working ranch, the Ponderosa is surprisingly comfortable. Guests can enjoy a Jacuzzi hot-tub bath, bar, gift shop, and a commodious main lodge with a reading/game room and covered veranda.

**Special Programs:** No children. Guests must be 18 years or older. Photo seminar welcomes shutterbugs with a desire to create authentic cowboy pictures or simply to shoot the amazing western landscape of eastern Oregon's high desert. Two veteran photographers lead participants in class and field experiences designed to enhance one's photographic skills and yield a scrapbook full of fantastic and unique ranching images.

**Rates:** $$$ Full American Plan.

**Credit Cards:** VISA, MasterCard

**Season:** May to mid-October for cattle programs

**Getting There:** Located 240 miles west of Boise, Idaho, 320 miles southeast of Portland. Nearest airport, Burns, Oregon. You must drive to the ranch from Portland, Boise, or Redmond airports (170 miles) or arrange for a private air taxi to the ranch airstrip.

**What's Nearby:** Nothing; this is a remote ranch property.

# ROCK SPRINGS GUEST RANCH

## Bend, Oregon

Rock Springs Guest Ranch was the dream of retired schoolteacher Donna Gill, who wanted to provide an outdoor classroom, of a sort, where parents and their children could share in a healthy, active, outdoor vacation. An extraordinary woman and world traveler, Gill owned and operated two other ranch properties, a girls' camp and the Indian Ford, before discovering her own Eden in the mountains of central Oregon.

Bend was a natural choice, given its outstanding scenery, fresh mountain air, and proximity to Oregon's main population center, Portland, a city renowned for its active and environmentally conscious citizenry.

Presently, Donna's nephew John and his wife, Eva, continue the Rock Springs Ranch tradition. One of the best features of Rock Springs is its children's program, which accommodates kids from age three up to age twelve. An outgrowth of Donna Gill's years of work with children, the program utilizes full-time youth counselors to oversee the kids. Counselors participate alongside the children in activities ranging from horseback riding, swimming, team sports, and nature walks to arts and crafts and storytelling. A talent show put on by the kids for the adults is one of the highlights of the week, along with a kid's campout and a Mexican piñata party. As the ranch owners like to say, at Rock Springs, kids are guests, not merely the children of guests. Undoubtedly, this will be one of the most remembered vacations of your young children's lives.

While your kids are having a blast, you can find dozens of things to stimulate mind and body. Horseback riding, of course, is a summertime specialty. Trail rides offer scenic vistas of the giant volcanoes of the Cascade Range, some of the most spectacular peaks in the Lower 48. Small groups of six riders ensure the flexibility to stop and take lots of pictures.

The ranch also offers somewhat genteel suburban sports such as tennis (on two courts) or a round of golf with John Gill, who welcomes the opportunity to tee it up with guests at the Awbrey Glen Golf and Country Club, a private championship course and one of Oregon's premier golf-resort destinations.

The nearby Metolius and Deschutes Rivers provide anglers with world-class fly-fishing waters, or you can opt for the more serene shores of several large and well-stocked lakes. A local guide service can be employed to help you scout out the best waters and the proper lures and flies for the predominant species and the time of season.

After a day of activities, relax with a massage by a licensed massage therapist and get ready for a gourmet dinner featuring wild game, followed by more wild games, in the form of Casino Night. While the kids take part in evening activities with the counselors, adults get a chance to demonstrate their skill at cards or roulette. It's a favorite evening, even if you don't get to keep the money.

In keeping with Donna Gill's educational intents, guests are invited to take nature hikes with a naturalist guide who will elucidate the native flora and fauna of Oregon's mountain region. Learn about the lives of Native Americans whose culture was shaped by the verdant landscape, and the abundant wildlife of this particularly bountiful region of North America.

## Rock Springs Guest Ranch

64201 Tyler Road
Bend, OR 97701
Phone: (800) 225–3833; (541) 382–1957
E-mail: info@rocksprings.com
Web site: www.rocksprings.com

**Owners/Managers:** John and Eva Gill

**Accommodations:** Capacity, 50. Cabins and condo suites with 2 and 3 bedrooms. Cabins include private entrances, sundeck, and bathrooms adjoining each bedroom. The Owl's Nest and Killdeer Cabins, originally living quarters in old mining camps, were renovated for guests' comfort. Most cabins feature fireplaces, refrigerators, and wet bars.

**Meals:** Meals are served buffet style; a wide range of selections at each meal guarantees you won't tire of the offerings. Typically, guests may choose from select beef such as prime rib, native seafood specialties such as Pacific salmon, along with vegetarian entrees. Special diets accommodated. Fresh fruit, cookies, and lemonade always available in the main lodge to tide guests over between meals. Beer and wine service.

**Activities:** Guests can take advantage of dozens of lakes and streams near Bend, a popular fly-fishing destination. Be sure to bring a pole and tackle box. Horseback riding is done in small groups, assuring personal instruction and lots of flexibility. You'll enjoy excellent views of the Cascade Mountains. Weekly luncheon rides are also scheduled.

Hiking with a naturalist guide, tennis on the ranch's courts, guided canoeing trips. Nearby golf and white-water rafting. Be sure to go spelunking in the Central Oregon Lava Tubes and make time to visit the High Desert Museum, where Native American culture is mixed with natural history and animal exhibits—a truly inspired museum!

**Amenities:** Whirlpool, swimming pond, game room, licensed massage therapist, on-site photographer, conference facilities.

**Special Programs:** Exceptional kids' program for children ages 3 to 12.

**Rates:** $$$–$$$$ Full American Plan. Reduced children's and infants rates. Off-season discounts.

**Credit Cards:** VISA, MasterCard, Diners Club, Discover, American Express

**Season:** Late June through August, Thanksgiving. Corporate retreats, conferences, and retreats scheduled throughout the off-season.

**Getting There:** Located 9 miles east of Bend, Oregon, approximately 3 hours' drive from Portland.

**What's Nearby:** Golf on 2-dozen championship courses in and around Bend; High Desert Museum, a nationally acclaimed natural-history museum; the town of Bend, with shopping and dining; Oregon Lava Tubes, a fascinating set of volcanic blow holes that can be explored with a local tour company.

# RRR RANCH

## Keystone, South Dakota

As a young man, Theodore Roosevelt left New York to go west, living a vigorous outdoor life on a family ranch in the Dakotas. The experience, which transformed him from a sickly city boy to a robust man, shaped the course of his life and his advocacy for "wild places."

Fortunately, South Dakota maintains those same restorative charms to this day. The Triple R Ranch is located within the 27,766-acre Norbeck Wildlife Preserve and just a few miles from the expansive Black Elk Wilderness Area, giving guests the chance to experience wilderness in its pristine majesty. Guests spend most days much as Roosevelt did, in the saddle, pursuing wild game (with a camera) and fishing in local waterways. And, of course, guests are always delighted to see Teddy himself at the national treasure, Mt. Rushmore, as well as to check on the progress of the huge sculpture of Crazy Horse that is being carved nearby. Plan as well on a visit to Custer State Park, home to large herds of native bison (the preferred name for buffalo).

Summers are comfortably cool and relaxed, thanks to the ranch's mile-high elevation. The air here is marvelously clean, with a hint of pine scent from the abundant forests that populate the land here.

Daily rides will take you to abandoned mining towns, interesting and odd geological sites (including the famed Outlaw Cave), and scenic overviews. Breakfast rides are a favorite way to get acquainted before hitting the trail; in the evening, you'll thrill to the sight of the clear night sky, where you'll see more stars than you ever thought possible.

If you enjoyed the Kevin Costner film *Dances with Wolves,* you might like to know that many scenes from the film were made not far from the Triple R. You may tag along on an excursion to one of these sites.

Uniquely, the ranch owners, Jack and Cherrylee Bradt, have gone out of their way to make their property wheelchair-friendly, truly making this a place that the entire family can enjoy. Guests with special needs are happily accommodated at the Triple R.

Special programs include a cattle roundup and an evening "cowboy dinner," where you'll enjoy homespun meals much like those enjoyed by the cowboys who moved cattle into these parts a century and a half ago. The cowboy supper is followed by a rousing show of cowboy poetry and singing.

If your vacation designs include taking in the fabulous monuments of the Rapid City area, the wonderful wildlife of this truly wild state, and plenty of time in the saddle, the Triple R is your place. It's hard to imagine a place with so many fascinating things to see and do.

## RRR Ranch

P.O. Box 124
Keystone, SD 57751-0124
Phone: (888) RRRANCH (777–2624); (605)
   666–4605
E-mail: rrrranch@sd.value.net
Web site: www.rrrranch.com

**Owners/Managers:** Jack and Cherrylee Bradt

**Accommodations:** Capacity, 10. Guests stay in simple cabins, each with private bath. Additional accommodations for 2 in the ranch house.

**Meals:** Home cooking based on simple but robust ranch meals. Typical evening fare includes ranch-raised beefsteaks, barbecued ribs, and chicken. Meals served family style. BYOB.

**Activities:** Horseback riding and more horseback riding. Swimming in the outdoor pond, fishing, breakfast rides, barbecues, and lots of excursions, including all-day riding trips to Spokane Ghost Town, visits to the bison herds at Custer State Park, the Crazy Horse Memorial Monument, and an evening trip to see the lighting of Mt. Rushmore. Evening parties, cowboy sing-alongs and shows, wagon rides, talent shows.

**Amenities:** Simplicity characterizes the ranch. Rooms are simple but adequate and comfortable; special provisions for wheelchair-bound guests.

**Special Programs:** No kids' programs. The ranch is best enjoyed by mature children aged 7 and up.

**Rates:** $$ Full American Plan. Nonrider rates, daily rates available.

**Credit Cards:** VISA, MasterCard. Personal checks accepted.

**Season:** Year-round

**Getting There:** Triple R Ranch is located 25 miles from Rapid City off Highway 16A. Closest airport in Rapid City, 25 miles.

**What's Nearby:** Custer State Park, Mt. Rushmore, Crazy Horse Monument, gaming in Deadwood.

# CIBOLO CREEK RANCH
## Shafter, Texas

If you want to travel back to the Old West, this is the place. Cibolo Creek Ranch is a fascinating historical monument, an actual time machine back to the way the West was more that 150 years ago. Painstakingly restored in the late1980s to its original splendor (right down to the square-headed nails) by owner John Poindexter, Cibolo Creek began receiving guests in 1993.

Cibolo Creek is so wonderfully authentic that it has been a favorite location for fashion photographers. On any given day, you may find yourself sharing the porch with a vacationing Hollywood star or an in-demand supermodel. Just don't gawk; Cibolo Creek endeavors to cloak guests in comfortable serenity and relative obscurity, which is achievable in this remote area of west Texas, where neighbors often drive an hour or more just to visit.

The Cibolo Creek Ranch is not, strictly speaking, a dude ranch, but rather a working cattle ranch that raises registered Texas longhorn cattle for rodeos and "collectors." Although cattle work isn't typically part of the guest experience, you may inquire about working alongside the ranch vaque-ros. Groups of ten or more can also arrange a special overnight chuckwagon camping trip, a special occasion you'll remember for the rest of your life.

Located 20 miles north of the Mexico border, Cibolo Creek is heavily influenced by the fluid border culture that has existed since before Texas was even admitted into the Union. Much of the architecture and furnishings borrow generously from Mexico. Rooms are furnished with authentic Mexican and Spanish antiques. You'll feel as though you've been transported to a foreign land and culture, while still maintaining a comfortable toehold in the United States.

As a world-class resort, Cibolo Creek pampers its guests. In addition to a standard list of activities (horseback riding, cattle drives, spa services, hiking, fishing, etc.), the ranch will also customize your vacation to meet your unique desires. If you want to make an extended trip into the rugged and little-explored backcountry of the 300,000-acre Big Bend Park, that can be arranged. Interested in a historical tour of Fort Davis or Fort Leaton? A tour of the Big Bend Region's colorful towns? Or a trip to the

## CIBOLO CREEK AND THE FASCINATING HISTORY OF WEST TEXAS

Milton Faver is known as the Mystery Man of the Big Bend. Local lore holds that Faver fled to this little-populated land after fighting a duel in which he killed his opponent. Faver married a Mexican woman and initiated a cross-border trading business, which prospered hugely, thanks to trade contracts with nearby Fort Davis.

Faver built el Fortin del Cibolo (the Fort of the Buffalo) as a personal estate, later adding two more fortresslike homes on his vast property. His fortresses withstood the attacks of native Comanches and Apaches and helped to protect his loyal employees during dangerous times. An early pioneer of the Texas cattle drives, Faver was a broad-shouldered and important figure in the early history of the Big Bend region of Texas.

famous Chinati Hot Springs? Perhaps a rafting trip on the Rio Grande? Whatever your desire, the staff will work hard to fulfill it.

Cibolo Creek is first-class in every sense of the word. You'll revel in the Old West while enjoying all the privileges and perquisites of a wealthy cattle baron. If luxurious relaxation coupled with challenging activities and exceptional fine dining in a fascinating and authentic historical setting fires your imagination, you won't find a better place anywhere.

### Cibolo Creek Ranch

P.O. Box 44
Shafter, TX 79850
Phone: (915) 229–3737
Fax: (915) 229–3653
E-mail: reservations@cibolocreekranch.com
Web site: www.cibolocreekranch.com

**Owner/Manager:** John Poindexter

**Accommodations:** Guest capacity, 120-plus at 3 separate facilities (El Cibolo, Hacienda La Cienega, La Morita). Inquire about accommodations and availability. Double beds, queen-sized beds, king-sized beds, and suites with fireplaces, verandas, whirlpool bath, and double showers. The restored forts at 3 separate sites on the ranch carefully adhere to historical accuracy to conform to the architectural style of the late 1800s. Adobe walls, cottonwood beams, and period antiques typify all guest rooms and buildings on the ranch. Traditional Mexican architecture and appointments such as spacious verandas, Saltillo tile floors, tin retablos, and vintage-style lamps. Rooms have full baths with resort-level appointments, fireplaces in the rooms, down comforters and hand-stitched quilts on the beds.

**Meals:** Cibolo Creek's award-winning menus have been featured in magazines that include *Travel & Leisure, Food & Wine,* and *Gourmet.* Exceptional nouveau-Southwest cuisine and Mexican regional specialties include buffalo rib-eye steaks from Katy, Texas; venison, antelope, and wild boar from Ingram, corn tortillas from south of the Rio Grande; seafood; and pecans from Fort Stockton. Sea bass Veracruz-style and grilled honey-and-chile-glazed pheasant are just a hint of what delights await. Special needs accommodated with advance notice.

**Activities:** Standard ranch activities and off-site tours augmented by custom-tailored itineraries based on individual requirements and desires. Horseback riding, cattle work, visits to various ranch attractions and historic sites, excursions to and within Big Bend National Park and Big Bend Ranch State Park, river rafting, evening trip to McDonald Observatory, Chinati Hot Springs trip, vehicle ranch tours, wildlife viewing, cowboy singing by the fireside, educational lectures, shopping in the Mexican border region, and much more. Be sure to take in the unusual Marfa lights, a natural but unexplainable phenomena of nearby Marfa, Texas (authorities speculate that the lights are caused by static electricity or natural gas upwellings). Exceptional wine cellar and south-of-the border beers.

**Amenities:** This is a full-fledged luxury resort; expect comfy down pillows, rich soaps and bathroom amenities, thick towels, and wonderful appointments throughout the ranch. Spa, available massage therapist, poolside dining or formal dinner service, historical and contemporary library, game room with video and music libraries, and much, much more.

**Special Programs:** No formal children's programs. Best for mature children ages 8 and over. Nannies welcome.

**Rates:** $$$$–$$$$$ A la carte activities with moderate prices. Guests may choose to reserve a room, 1 of the 3 forts, or the entire ranch for large parties. Prices vary widely according to accommodations. No minimum stay.

**Credit Cards:** VISA, MasterCard, American Express, Discover, Diners Club

**Season:** Year-round

**Getting There:** Midland Airport, 212 miles; El Paso, 224 miles; Alpine, Texas, 60 miles. Paved, lighted private airstrip located on the ranch.

**What's Nearby:** Fort Davis National Monument, Fort Leaton, Big Bend National Park, Big Bend Ranch State Park, ghost town of Shafter; Marfa, shopping in Mexico border villages.

# DIXIE DUDE RANCH

Bandera, Texas

Bandera is known as The Cowboy Capital of the World, and once you've stayed at the Dixie Dude Ranch, you'll know why. The Dixie is not simply a dude ranch but rather a working cattle outfit that welcomes dudes. A fine distinction, yes, but an important one, particularly for guests who desire to become immersed in authentic cowboy culture.

Founded in 1901 by William Wallace Whitley, the ranch has been passed down through five generations. The Dixie began welcoming guests in 1927, giving the folks here decades to hone their hospitality to a razor-sharp edge. There's a nice folksiness to the Dixie that will make you feel less like a paying guest and more like a visiting city cousin.

The Dixie is situated on 720 acres in the Texas Hill Country. For those unfamiliar with Texas geography, the area is not the dry desert many imagine but rather a lush, green landscape with abundant water, gentle rolling hills, and stands of live oak and mesquite. It's an enchanting landscape favored by many Texans (who often prefer to explore their huge state rather than take their chances among "the Yankees," a name bestowed on virtually anyone not born in the Lone Star Republic).

The Dixie is tantalizingly close to San Antonio, home to the Alamo and a wonderful mixture of Hispanic and Anglo culture. Plan an extra day to tour the city, and be sure to visit the authentic El Mercado and have lunch along San Antonio's beautiful River Walk. Your sight-seeing won't end there, however: Bandera offers the fascinating Frontier Times Museum, there's the Cowboy Artists of America Museum in Kerrville (also a favorite spot for music festivals), Sea World and Fiesta Texas in San Antonio, and seasonal rodeos at many of the nearby towns. Be sure to confer with the ranch activity planner for schedules and events prior to booking your trip.

Back at the ranch there's a broad list of activities. Lots of folks enjoy hunting for fossils and arrowheads, which crop up with regularity but require hawklike eyes to identify. Planned activities include swimming, hayrides, campfire sing-alongs, dancing, and, of course, daily horseback riding (Sundays excepted). Year-round fishing is offered in San Julian Creek and Medina Lake.

The Dixie also has plenty of outdoor recreation facilities, including hoops, a volleyball court, shuffleboard, and tetherball. An added bonus, loved especially by kids is inner tubing in the Medina River, not far from the ranch.

In the evening, the Old West comes alive, as cowboy entertainers frequent the spread. Take in a rodeo, enjoy a hayride, sing along to old singin' cowboy standards, and enjoy a trick roper plying his trade. Every night is different, but always captivating and fun.

Texans enjoy a loud, rollicking good time, and the Dixie reflects that spirit. If you are looking for plenty of activities, lots of opportunities for interesting sight-seeing, a good horse program, and plenty of evening entertainment, the Dixie will exceed your expectations.

## Dixie Dude Ranch

P.O. Box 548
Bandera, TX 78003
Phone: (800) 375–YALL (9255); (830)
    796–4481
E-mail: cccdixie@hctc.net
Web site: www.dixieduderanch.com

**Owners/Managers:** Clay and Diane Conoly

**Accommodations:** Capacity, 75. 20 total units. Guests can choose from duplex cabins, cottages, lodge rooms, and the 2-story bunkhouse. All accommodations feature private baths, air conditioning, vented heat. Some include fireplaces. Family rooms with 2 or more beds, as well as rooms for singles or couples.

**Meals:** Served family style and buffet style. Expect Texas cuisine, heavy on beef specialties such as barbecue brisket, as well as pork ribs, fried chicken, all with the expected side dishes. Cowboy breakfast served out on the trail as a special event. No bar; BYOB.

**Activities:** Horseback riding at a slow-to-moderate pace. Swimming, hayrides, campfire sing-alongs, dances, and dozens of recreational games and activities. Catch-and-release fishing, hiking, nature trails. Plan on off-ranch excursions to the lovely Hill Country towns and cities.

**Amenities:** Swimming pool, children's playground and wading pool, shooting range at Bandera Gun Club, seasonal rodeos on-site and in neighboring towns, conference center with 140-person capacity.

**Special Programs:** No formal children's program. Kids take part alongside parents and are the parents' responsibility. Baby-sitting available.

**Rates:** $–$$ Full American Plan. Daily and weekly rates. Reduced children's rates, group rates; kids under 2 stay free.

**Credit Cards:** VISA, MasterCard, American Express, Discover

**Season:** Year-round

**Getting There:** Located 55 miles northwest of San Antonio off Highway 173, south of Bandera. Shuttle service available at San Antonio International Airport.

**What's Nearby:** San Antonio (approximately 1 hour); Bandera, The Cowboy Capital of the World with its Frontier Times Museum; waterpark attractions in New Braunfels and San Antonio; Lost Maples State Park in Vanderpool; nearby golf and tennis.

# FLYING L GUEST RANCH

## Bandera, Texas

When it comes to family vacations, it's sometimes hard to get everyone on the same page. Dad wants to go golfing, but Mom wants to spend time outdoors riding horses. And the kids want to go to an amusement park and play in the water. At the Flying L Guest Ranch, it's possible to do it all—and then some.

A premier resort destination in the central-Texas Hill Country, the Flying L not only boasts of an outstanding guest-ranch property but also a 72-hole championship golf course. Nearby San Antonio features several world-class amusement parks and zoos, along with restaurants, shops, historical sites, and fine dining. And the kids won't get bored on the ranch, as the list of activities for children and adults alike is enough fill up any vacation schedule and leave you with an incomplete "to do" list.

Ideal for singles, couples, extended families, and corporate or church retreats, the Flying L is truly all things to all people. A wide variety of accommodations enables the ranch to custom-fit everyone's needs. Furthermore, the activities schedule is flexible, allowing guests to have as active or leisurely vacation as they like. Let's look at some of the activities the Flying L has to offer.

A whole host of recreational facilities awaits. There are volleyball courts and soccer fields, a softball diamond, shuffleboard, table tennis, swimming in the Texas-sized pool, and fishing in either nearby San Julian Creek or Medina Lake. You can also take a mountain-bike ride, a nature hike, or learn the intricacies of cattle roping in the arena. Guests wishing to improve their equitation can opt for private riding lessons, either in the arena or on the backcountry trails in the Hill Country State Natural Area. There are also numerous opportunities for excursions to surrounding Hill Country towns and attractions, so plan for a day or two to see the sights.

Lodging here leans toward resort accommodations rather than traditional and rustic ranch digs. The modern rooms are maintained daily; the suite-style villas include one or two bedrooms and a living room/dining area, plus amenities such as cable TV, refrigerators, full bathrooms, and coffee service. More luxurious suites are also available, as are less-opulent lodging in the bunkhouse, a facility designed to accommodate large groups. With thirty beds, nine bedrooms, and a shared lounge area, the bunkhouse is perfect for group or extended family retreats.

Golfers, especially, will appreciate the Flying L. One of only a handful of ranch resorts offering on-site golfing, the Flying L has its own championship 72-par, 18-hole course, pro shop, driving range, putting green, snack bar, and PGA-certified professional instruction. The challenging courses meander over rolling hills, with plenty of water hazards and native and introduced trees. Still hungry for more golf? The Flying L can arrange for additional tee times at the Woodlake Golf Course in San Antonio.

Other attributes that make Flying L a first-class destination include exceptional meals based on Texas and Southwestern recipes, nightly entertainment, and a climate that is temperate and enjoyable year-round. If you're looking to fit a number of vacations into one location, you won't find many resorts offering the variety and quality that characterizes the Flying L.

**Flying L Guest Ranch**
P.O. Box 1959
Bandera, TX 78003
Phone: (800) 292–5134; (830) 460–3001
Fax: (830) 796–8455
E-mail: sales@flyingl.com
Web site: www.flyingl.com

**Manager:** No manager info.

**Accommodations:** Capacity, 140. Guests may choose from suite-style villas with 1 or 2 bedrooms, deluxe suites, or, for groups, the bunkhouse, ideal for extended families, youth groups, or church groups of up to 30 people. Villas include cable TV, sitting room, refrigerator, microwave oven, coffeepot and coffee service, wood-burning stoves, full baths, and wood-burning fireplaces. More spacious deluxe suites include these amenities plus whirlpools and private patio decks.

**Meals:** Menu varies from Southwestern specialties to Mexican dishes to good ol' Texas barbecues (served in a grand buffet fashion outdoors). Special menu items for young cowpokes.

**Activities:** Horseback riding for guests ages 6 and up; separate supervised riding for children 3 to 6. Golf on the ranch's 18-hole championship course; swimming in a heated outdoor pool; tubing at nearby river (extra); 2 lighted tennis courts; recreation area including shuffleboard, table tennis, horseshoes, practice roping, volleyball, soccer, basketball. Mountain biking. Fishing in Julian Creek and Medina Lake. Evening entertainment, local excursion trips.

**Amenities:** Golf-course pro shop, driving range, and putting green; cable TV, wood-burning fireplace and refrigerator in all private rooms; hot tub and private whirlpool baths; daily maid service.

**Special Programs:** Supervised children's program for kids ages 3 to 12 (seasonal); activities include pony rides, arts and crafts, fishing, recreational games. Baby-sitting available.

**Rates:** $–$$$ Modified American Plan (lunch served separately at additional cost). Reduced children's rates. Prices include run of the ranch, morning and evening meals, horseback riding, nightly entertainment, supervised children's program. Reduced greens fees for golf. Some off-site activities charged additionally.

**Credit Cards:** VISA, MasterCard, American Express, Discover

**Season:** Year-round

**Getting There:** 45 miles southwest of San Antonio.

**What's Nearby:** San Antonio (approximately 1 hour) with theme parks, shopping, fine dining, historical sites, museums and internationally acclaimed zoo. Hill Country rodeos held throughout spring, summer, and fall; nearby town of Bandera, The Cowboy Capital of the World. Inquire about sight-seeing excursions.

# GARRETT CREEK RANCH

## Paradise, Texas

We've intentionally provided a great deal of variety in this book, including nontraditional ranches and geographically distinct ranches. Garrett Creek Ranch is different in that it is not, strictly speaking, a "vacation" guest ranch, but rather a ranch conference facility. Realizing that a minority of our readers will be looking for a ranch facility to hold conferences and retreats, we've added this property due to its high standards of service to corporate groups and organizations looking for a unique ranch getaway.

Located a mere 45 miles from Dallas/Fort Worth International Airport, the ranch is nonetheless far from the hustle and bustle of urban life. Boots, dungarees, and straw hats take the place of suits and power ties as proper business attire. Take a break during the day's schedule of events, activities, and meetings to watch cowboys herding cattle past the main lodge or bale hay in the fields. This is a real working ranch, with 460 acres of undulating pastureland. The pastoral environment encourages guests to free their thinking and helps to put conference attendees on a friendly, democratic footing. The staff goes out of its way to meet groups' needs, providing exceptional facilities, support materials, catering, whatever you might require.

Rooms are designed for the ease and comfort of business visitors. All rooms feature digital alarm clocks, hair dryers, coffeemakers and coffee service, lighted makeup mirrors, and complimentary newspapers and soft drinks in the lobby. There are no telephone surcharges and no gratuities required.

When your meetings are over, you and your conference attendees can choose from a broad palette of recreational activities: swimming in the outdoor pool, relaxing in one of two hot tubs, hiking on more than 23 acres crisscrossed with trails, or jogging on the ParCourse Fitness trail. There are lots of fun-filled outdoor games ideal for team building: volleyball, basketball, and horseshoes, for instance. Golfers can work on their swing on the driving range.

In the main building, indoor recreation is the order of the day. Play Ping-Pong, cards, or board games with fellow conference mates.

Exceptional facilities and service have earned the Garrett Creek Ranch numerous awards, including the Meeting News' Planner's Choice Award, Sales and Marketing Management's Executive Choice Award, and *D Magazine*'s selection as the "Best Place for a Corporate Retreat."

Groups large and small rave about the Garrett Creek Ranch experience. "Thank you so much for all your help in arranging our team building session. Garrett Creek offered the perfect setting for just such a meeting. The facilities, accommodations, and food were excellent. Also, the challenge course was a perfect tie-in to our theme of 'team building'," said a Mobil meeting planner. "Everything at Garrett Creek was first class, from the excellent food, efficient maid service, beautiful individually decorated rooms, great hot tub and campfire, and all the delicious snacks and drinks provided for our teams," adds another from Southwest Airlines.

Because 80 percent of Garrett Creek's Ranch business comes from referrals, it's clear that, when it comes to business, they know what it takes to do it right.

**Garrett Creek Ranch**
270 Private Road 3475
Paradise, TX 75073
Phone: (940) 433–2055
Fax: (940) 433–8767
E-mail: info@gcrnet.com
Web site: www.gcrnet.com

**Owner/Manager:** Leslie Schultz

**Accommodations:** Conference capacity, 100. 30 total housing units, including guest rooms, executive suites, and 5 modernized turn-of-the-twentieth-century guest cabins. A western town, Paradise Junction, includes 16 guest rooms; 6 log cabins add an additional 26 rooms, and there are 3 guest rooms in the main lodge building. Rooms include many amenities, including facilities to enable telecommunications and Internet connections.

**Meals:** 3 dining areas located in the main lodge. Arrangements can be made for meals at the pool pavilion, in The Shed facility adjacent to the main dining hall, or in the airy sunroom, ideal for smaller groups looking for a more private and intimate dining space. 3 meals served daily for overnight groups; meeting planners confer with ranch staff to set dining menus.

**Activities:** Team building via the Challenge Course; horseback riding, swimming in outdoor pool, hiking, fitness trail, indoor and outdoor recreational games.

**Amenities:** Conference facilities include 3 separate meeting rooms in the main building, 2 additional meeting rooms in adjacent buildings, a saloon and parlor in Paradise Junction for meetings, user-friendly audio/visual equipment, a "breakout" area for session breaks, special meeting environments such as outdoor patios and gazebos.

**Special Programs:** Garrett Creek Ranch works with nonprofit organizations in the North Texas region by providing meeting grants. Grants include complimentary board meeting (up to 20 attendees), meals, breaks, overnight guest rooms, meeting room, audiovisual equipment, and sessions with a professional meeting planner. A limited number of grants, available only to North Texas nonprofits, are awarded each year. Inquire for grant request and requirements.

**Rates:** $$$ Full American Plan. Meeting Package price includes overnight guest rooms, 3 meals per 24-hour period, meeting room, meeting-room supplies, continuous beverage service, basic but up-to-date audiovisual equipment (ask if you have special A/V needs), professional conference planning, and on-premise recreational facilities. Additional: transportation, alcoholic-beverage service, special audiovisual needs, state and local taxes, use or facilitation of Challenge Course.

**Credit Cards:** Inquire for payment details and arrangements.

**Season:** Year-round

**Getting There:** Garrett Creek Ranch is located northwest of Fort Worth off State Highway 114. Commercial airline service to Dallas/Fort Worth International. Ground transportation available through independent limousine company. Guests arriving in private cars should request specific driving directions.

**What's Nearby:** Dallas, a buttoned-down business town (be sure to visit Deep Elum, the city's music-and-arts district) and funky Fort Worth, with its wonderful old, historic stockyards and western heritage and art museums.

# HART & HIND FITNESS RANCH

## Rio Frio, Texas

I love everything about this ranch: the basic idea behind it (fitness in a beautiful setting), its location (in the heart of the Texas Hill Country), and its simplicity.

Owner Kit Detering took the California concept of a country spa/resort, and gave it a Texas twist: Strip away the froufrou frills and replace them with the down-home friendliness and simple flair that is Texas. The result: a delightful retreat where you can enjoy healthful food, exercise, and solitude in a laid-back, unpretentious ranch setting. Brilliant!

Detering chose the name "Hart & Hind" from the Old English names for buck and doe. The name is perfect, for this is a place equally comfortable for men and women. Furthermore, it is populated with native wildlife that includes white-tailed deer. And finally, the name suggests the dedication to the rejuvenation of body and soul that is the essence of a vacation here.

Detering originally had designs for a women's-only retreat, but during her first year of operation, the women guests repeatedly said that this would be the perfect place for their husbands or boyfriends. A writer for *Travel & Leisure* described it best when she wrote, "It's the stuff of boyhood John Wayne dreams —ten-gallon hats, cattle, wide open spaces." Wisely, Detering changed her plans, and now the ranch serves both males and females.

Each guest meets with Angela King, the in-residence fitness director, who helps develop an individual program of activities designed for health and relaxation. Don't worry, you won't be sent off to the gym to toil and sweat. King, in fact, believes that fitness is best achieved through enjoyable exercise. "You don't have to do it in a gym full of people showing off. You can get a good workout in the privacy of your own home or even right outside your front door," says King, who coordinated fitness programs at major health clubs in Dallas and New York before jumping at the chance to work for Hart & Hind.

Guests receive an evaluation on their health, diet, and exercise. A wide variety of activities allows each guests to find exercise that makes them happiest: yoga, hiking, horseback riding, kickboxing, power walks, jogging, and meditation and stretching classes are just a sampling of the myriad possibilities.

When your vacation is through, you will be sent off with a personalized workout schedule and resistance bands for total body strengthening. King will even follow up with calls to see how you are doing!

Don't think that dining here is an exercise in deprivation and bland diets. The cuisine is highly seasonal ranch fare (or one might call it nouveau-ranch) that includes wild game from Broken Arrow Ranch, peaches from Fredricksburg, vibrant greens from South Texas, honey from nearby Uvalde, and fat pecans from the ranch's own groves. Breads and desserts are made on-site under the eye of chef Paula Disbrowe, a renowned former travel and food writer who developed her cooking skills during extended stays in Spain, southern France, and the Tuscany region of Italy.

Hart & Hind is truly a special ranch destination. If a vacation that combines fitness and overall well-being appeals to you, there is no doubt that this is your kind of place.

## Hart & Hind Fitness Ranch

Buffalo Creek Road
Rio Frio, TX 78879
Phone: (866) 868–1264 (toll-free)
E-mail: info@hartandhind.com
Web site: www.hartandhind.com

**Owner/Manager:** Kit Detering

**Accommodations:** Capacity, 12. Guests are housed in 3 native limestone cottages, complete with living areas that include overstuffed couches and King Ranch rockers, fully stocked kitchens, and screened porches. Hill Country Rustic style with a Ralph Lauren designer flair.

**Meals:** 3 healthful meals served daily. Chef Paula Disbrowe's star cuisine serves "modern cowboy fare" with a Mediterranean flavor. Acclaimed baker David Normal creates artisan breads in the ranch's antique brick oven. Enjoy a breakfast of Migas (a Hill Country favorite, made of sautéed corn tortillas, fresh vegetables, and ranch-grown eggs) or poached eggs over fresh-laurel polenta; a "cowboy lunchbox," eaten high on a hill overlooking the ranch; and enjoy a dinner of low-calorie, high-flavor fare such as chicken tostadas, tart lime-cabbage slaw, tender chicken breast, and pickled chipotles atop a crispy corn tortilla shell. Delicious!

**Activities:** Horseback riding, fitness classes, swimming and "aqua exercise," hiking, and one-on-one fitness and diet planning. With a small number of guests, the emphasis is on personal attention and fulfilling personal experiences. Guests are treated to 2 massages during their visit, as well as a hot-tub bath to sooth tired muscles. Classes in yoga, kickboxing, meditation, and low-impact, high-results aerobic exercise. Cooking demonstrations; sports and other outdoor activities.

**Amenities:** Comfortable lounging chairs overlooking the ranch's geese pond; indoor fitness-class facilities; luxurious and tasteful ranch furnishings in rooms and common areas; hot-tub bath.

**Special Programs:** This ranch is primarily a place for adults interested in relaxation and fitness. Individual fitness counseling and nutritional counseling are a central part of the ranch program.

**Rates:** $$$ Full American Plan. Rates are all-inclusive and range from 3-night to full-week, 6-night stays. T-shirts, sweatsuits, shorts, and robes are provided daily for each guest. No "hidden costs." Airport transfers from San Antonio Airport, all meals, 2 massage-therapy sessions, fitness classes, aqua exercise, cooking demonstrations, and all fees and gratuities are included.

**Credit Cards:** VISA, MasterCard, American Express

**Season:** January to June, September through November (excluding Thanksgiving)

**Getting There:** Commercial flights into San Antonio or private flight into Uvalde, where a Hart & Hind representative will meet you. Driving: west of San Antonio on Highway 90, 70 miles to Sabinal, north on 127 for 20 miles to Concan, north on U.S. 83 for 10 miles to Rio Frio. Driving time/distance from San Antonio: 1½ hours/100 miles.

**What's Nearby:** Lost Maples State Park in Vanderpool, floating the Frio River in Rio Frio, the Wild Hog Festival in Sabinal, the Frio Bat Cave in Rio Frio, Cody's Hat Shop and the Gitano Tortilla Factory in Uvalde, Main Street Antiques in Utopia.

# LAZY HILLS GUEST RANCH
### Ingram, Texas

Since 1959, the Steinruck family has been welcoming guests from throughout the world to Lazy Hills Guest Ranch, the family's 750-acre spread in the lovely Hill Country of central Texas.

Lazy Hills is appealing for many reasons: It is moderately priced, offers a wide variety of recreational activities, and is located in an area of Texas that many consider to be blessed with the finest climate in the state. The oppressive heat and humidity of east Texas isn't a problem here, nor is the furnacelike dry heat of the western reaches of this massive state. Rainfall is plentiful, and that results in a verdant green landscape of mesquite trees, cedar, and lush native grasses. The Kerrville-Ingram area is a favorite year-round destination of vacationing Texans, and there are lots of intriguing and entertaining sights to see and things to do. All in all, there is no finer place in Texas for an extended visit.

Lazy Hills is a traditional guest ranch with a conventional approach to activities. Hayrides, morning breakfast rides, outdoor barbecues, and campfires are the main events around which socializing takes place. Horseback riding is the central daytime activity, with guided hour-long rides that take guests to scenic overviews and spring-fed creeks.

Fishing is another favorite pastime. Three ponds await fishermen: two stocked with bass and a third that is filled with fat catfish. Guests, however, don't have to "swim with the fish." A 40-by-80-foot heated pool awaits adults and teens, while small fry can take a dip in the kids' wading pool. If the day's activities leave you saddle sore, you can also partake of a hot tub located in the pool area.

Day or night tennis matches are made possible on lighted courts; if you aren't an avid tennis player, you can borrow equipment from the ranch office. Kids will be amply entertained, as the ranch maintains an organized kids' program for children as young as age two. Activities run the gamut from storytelling to nature hikes, songs, arts and crafts, and indoor and outdoor games. There's also a big playground. Kids also join their parents for special family-fun activities such as relay races and family competitions, bonfires, hayride cookouts, and the Friday night buffet and fireworks display.

In the evening, guests are also welcome to join a rousing game of volleyball, take a sunset hike, or sing songs around the evening campfire. There are also scheduled events such as bingo and scavenger hunts.

Beyond the ranch boundaries, guests can enjoy a variety of local entertainment spectacles including weekend rodeos and rodeo dances in nearby Crider and a popular outdoor theater performance. There are also art museums, musical festivals, and many small towns with exceptional antiques shops and boutiques with that unique Texas flair. Where else will you find an armadillo lamp?

Lazy Hills is a good value in a traditional ranch vacation. You won't find rich gourmet cuisine here, and there are no yoga classes or spas. Just good ol' down-home hospitality and plenty of fun. If that's the type of vacation that sparks your imagination, book a trip to Lazy Hills. You may find yourself among the many people who return here time and again.

## Lazy Hills Guest Ranch

P.O. Box G
Ingram, TX 78025
Phone: (800) 880–0632; (830) 367–5600
Fax: (830) 367–5667
E-mail: lhills@ktc.com
Web site: www.lazyhills.com

**Owners/Managers:** The Steinruck Family

**Accommodations:** Capacity, 100. 26 total units. Guest rooms are furnished with twin or queen beds and will sleep 4 to 6. Rooms have electric heat, air conditioning, and full bathrooms with showers. There are pleasant porches, and some rooms include wood-burning fireplaces. Daily maid service.

**Meals:** Outstanding food and service characterize Lazy Hills. 3 ample home-style meals are served each day except Sunday, where brunch is served in lieu of lunch. Picnic lunches made by request. Special diets accommodated. Dinner entrees include Mexican specialties, chicken-fried steak, barbecue staples, and hot-dogs and hamburgers served poolside.

**Activities:** Daily trail riding with 4 scheduled rides each day; hayrides, breakfast rides, and luncheons on the trail. Olympic-sized swimming pool and children's wading pond; fishing, hiking, recreational games such as shuffleboard and horseshoes, basketball, and volleyball.

**Amenities:** Covered porch decks, hot tub, tennis courts, game room with billiard table, kids' playground and treehouse. RV hookups available. No phones or TVs in guest rooms but available in the main lodge.

**Special Programs:** Excellent kids' programs with activity counselors. Morning and afternoon activities. Baby-sitting available.

**Rates:** $–$$ Modified American Plan. All-inclusive except for horseback riding. Horseback riding is $15 per ride but free for guests staying 7 or more nights.

**Credit Cards:** VISA, MasterCard, Discover

**Season:** Year-round

**Getting There:** Car rentals available at San Antonio International and Kerrville. Limousine service from Kerrville available at additional charge. Airport transfer from San Anonio via Greyhound bus to Kerrville, where a limousine service can be employed to take you to the ranch. Ranch is located 70 miles from the San Antonio International Airport, 115 miles from the state capital, Austin.

**What's Nearby:** Golf at nearby courses. Kerrville, a favorite weekend destination of vacationing Texans, Cowboy Artists of America Museum; LBJ Ranch on the Pedernales River; Fiesta Texas and Sea World in San Antonio.

# THE REID RANCH

## Salt Lake City, Utah

The Reid family, Mervin and Ethna, ventured into the Uintah Mountains of Utah looking for a getaway that would provide them with a quiet retreat. When they came upon a remote property recommended by a friend, they knew they had found their place.

Over the years, the Reids have transformed the undeveloped property into a high-desert Shangri-la, perfect for conducting Ethna's seminars for the Exemplary Center for Reading Instruction, which endeavors to improve the teaching techniques of educators. When not conducting these important seminars, the Reids open their ranch to groups and family reunions, providing the perfect site for religious instruction, team building, and recreation for extended family groups. If you are looking for a place to host a large group, one that offers plenty of recreational opportunities, solitude, and meeting space, the Reid Ranch could be the ideal haven.

The Reid Ranch is situated at 7,800 feet in the mountains just east of Salt Lake City. This area is resplendent in native wildlife, including deer, elk, moose, bear, beaver, porcupines, and the occasional skunk. It is also a place of great historic folklore. Butch Cassidy and the Sundance Kid were said to hide out in these parts, and Mormon patriarch Brigham Young financed his early settlement in part with revenues from the productive Rhodes Mine, traces of which can still be explored. Fruitland is another intriguing historic artifact: More than a century ago, a land developer lured naive settlers to Utah County with pictures of lovely groves of fruit trees and promises of productive farmland, but when the settlers arrived, all they found was sage, cedar, and hard red rock!

Still, the bounty of this land for those who stayed was in the beauty of this semi-arid desert and in the fascinating geology of Utah's spectacular mountains. Said one visitor from South Dakota, the Reid Ranch and its environs compose "one of the seven wonders of the world."

There's plenty to do here, from horseback riding to swimming in either of two heated swimming pools. Guests take part in a variety of outdoor recreational games, including soccer, basketball, volleyball, and tennis. You can practice your archery skills, fish in a stocked pond, or just relax at the ranch spa. The lake provides a rare opportunity to spend a romantic afternoon in a rowboat or canoe. Paddleboats also provide a leisurely lake tour.

Meals are simple but savory. Don't expect gourmet cooking, just good down-home western ranch staples such as steaks and baked potatoes, barbecued chicken and baked beans, and piles of pancakes and ranch eggs for breakfast.

The main appeal of the Reid Ranch is as a group retreat, ideal for plenty of communal bonding. Because the emphasis is on catering to groups, the Reids can accommodate your schedule and goals rather than pigeonholing you into a rigid schedule.

## The Reid Ranch

3310 South, 2700 East
Salt Lake City, UT 84109
Phone: (801) 486–5083; (800) 468–3274
E-mail: greid@reidranch.com
Web site: www.reidranch.com

**Owners/Managers:** Drs. Mervin and Ethna Reid

**Accommodations:** Capacity, 60+. Groups of 60 or more can reserve the entire ranch. Guests can choose from a number of accommodations ranging from dormitory-style lodging to individual guest suites in the lodge to a private cabin and guest house (both ideal for families). There's even a provision for group campouts. Individual rooms have private baths and beds varying from twins to queen sizes. Dormitory-style accommodations in the bunkhouse feature bunk beds and single-sex, locker-room style shower facilities.

**Meals:** 3 meals served daily; a sample menu includes breakfast of ranch eggs, potatoes, toast, and fruit juice; lunch of barbecued chicken, baked beans, potato salad, rolls, and watermelon; dinner of baked ham in pineapple sauce, rice pilaf, carrots and peas, pasta salad, and rolls.

**Activities:** Daily horseback riding, swimming in 1 of 2 pools, archery, beach volleyball, basketball, tennis, softball, fishing, hiking, boating, and evening campfires.

**Amenities:** Conference facilities, spa, lighted sports court, sauna, Reid Ranch Trading Post.

**Special Programs:** This ranch caters exclusively to groups, including supervised youth groups, corporate groups, religious groups, and extended families. No special children's programs.

**Rates:** $ Full American Plan. As a group-retreat location, the Reid Ranch is designed for communal living and activities. Teen groups, especially, adapt well to the dormitory-style bunkhouse, whereas families may prefer the more private and commodious guest house and cabin or individual rooms in the main lodge. Outdoor camping also accommodated for as low as $30 per day, all inclusive of activities and dining. A real bargain for groups!

**Credit Cards:** Personal and company checks preferred.

**Season:** 3 seasons: Inquire about early spring and fall dates. Due to seminars, large segments of the summer months are unavailable. Most groups book reservations a year or more in advance.

**Getting There:** Nearest commercial airport, Salt Lake City (approximately 1 hour's drive). Ground transportation to and from the ranch at additional per-person charge. Reid Ranch is located in Uintah Mountains east of Salt Lake City, off I–40 at the Fruitland exit.

**What's Nearby:** Red Creek Reservoir, an excellent spot for cutthroat trout fishing; Salt Lake City, the Mormon-dominated cultural center of Utah; various resort towns, including Park City; Great Salt Lake, Arches National Monument, Zion National Park.

# HIDDEN VALLEY RANCH

## Cle Elum, Washington

The folks at Hidden Valley claim that it is "Washington's oldest and finest guest ranch." We concur. Located in the Cascade Mountains just 90 miles east of Seattle, Hidden Valley's history goes back well over one hundred years, when a homestead was established here in the foothills of the Wenatchee Mountains. In 1947, Hollywood film star Tom Whited purchased the land from its original owners. Whited, a friend of such true cowboy stars and rodeo performers Yakima Cannutt, Slim Pickens, and William O. Douglas, was also a talented horseman and cowboy. He transformed the ranch into a cowboy haven and opened its doors as a guest ranch in 1947—and so it has remained to this day.

The feel of this place is definitely "old school." Rooms are decorated with antique saddles, historic photos, and horse tack, and each is unique. Most have porches giving guests a scenic overlook over the valley, one of the most productive farmlands in America. Modern comforts haven't been forsaken, however. You'll have your own private bath and gas heat. Some of the rooms feature gas-log stoves; others have antique woodstoves. Furnishings are simple but welcoming, with heavy blankets on the double or queen-sized beds, and there are sitting rooms and chairs for reading and lounging.

Riding makes up the backbone of activities here. You'll have a number of daily riding options to pick from, with as many as four different rides scheduled each day. Guest are welcome to bring their own horses, so long as they are current on vaccinations.

Ride as little or as often as you please; packages are designed for riders and non-riders alike. In addition to instructional rides, breakfast rides, and scenic trail rides, guests can enjoy fishing in local creeks and ponds, hiking, wildlife observation, recreational games, swimming in a heated pool, tennis and volleyball. Those who wish to take a mountain-biking tour, river-rafting trip, or fly-fishing excursion can arrange to do so through outside outfitters.

Evening barbecues from the chuck-wagon are a favorite means of socializing. You can also expect informal entertainment in the form of storytelling and musical performances around the ranch's piano.

Hidden Valley's proximity to Seattle also invites a day in the Emerald City, so take time to plan an extra day if you haven't visited this lovely place. Take in a Mariners' baseball game, visit the Pike Place Market, or tour the underground around the charming Pioneer Square area.

On Labor Day weekend, Hidden Valley Ranch bustles with activity as wranglers and guests alike make plans to attend the Ellensburg Rodeo, an exciting local event that attracts top cowboys from throughout the country.

## Hidden Valley Ranch

3942 Hidden Valley Road
Cle Elum, WA 98922
Phone: (800) 5–COWBOY (800–526–9269);
  (509) 857–2322
Fax: (509) 857–2130
E-mail: info@hvranch.com
Web site: www.hvranch.com

**Owners/Managers:** The Coe Family: Bruce, Kim, James, and Hannah

**Accommodations:** Capacity, 40. Guests stay in 1-, 2-bedroom cabins, along with 2 4-plex cabins. Most have porches and valley views. Rooms are heated and have private baths and antique woodstoves or gas fireplaces.

**Meals:** Guests are served family style, with fresh-baked breads and pastries. Typical dinner entrees include bourbon-basted pork chops, barbecued beef and chicken, and Cajun deep-fried turkey. Light entrees, vegetarian dinners, and special diets also served by request. No bar; BYOB.

**Activities:** The ranch's horse program is the central activity; special attention paid to instruction. Swimming in the heated outdoor pool, fishing, hiking, breakfast rides and evening barbecues, tennis, volleyball, and basketball. Expect an informal approach to recreation based upon guests' desires. Off-site rafting, mountain biking, and guided fly fishing available.

**Amenities:** 10-person hot-tub bath; tennis courts; authentic chuckwagon; conference facilities; large main lodge with recreational facilities and large, comfy outdoor hammocks on the porch.

**Special Programs:** Kid Korral for children ages 3 to 10. New kids' program includes daily activities, arts and crafts, picnics, and short hikes. Leave the kids in the Korral and enjoy your day, or take them along with you on activities.

**Rates:** $$ Full American Plan. Guests may also opt for lower-cost packages without horseback riding. Slow-season rates, weekday rates, reduced rates for children. 2-night minimum stay during the busy season.

**Credit Cards:** VISA, MasterCard

**Season:** Year-round

**Getting There:** Cle Elum is approximately 90 miles from Seattle. Nearest commercial airport, Ellenburg or Yakima. Numerous flights to Seattle-Tacoma Airport. Rental car advised if flying to Sea-Tac. Ranch is located 8 miles northeast of Cle Elum off Highway 970.

**What's Nearby:** Guests may want to plan an extra day or two to visit Seattle and its wonderful museums, restaurants, and tourist attractions.

# ABSAROKA RANCH

## Dubois, Wyoming

Wyoming's Absaroka Range is one of the most spectacular and unspoiled wilderness areas in the Lower 48. Many would argue that this region, less developed by far than the Jackson Hole Valley, although sharing many of the same scenic qualities, is even better for its relative seclusion.

The Absaroka Ranch is a gem of a property, located in the foothills of the Absarokas, overlooking the Dunoir Valley. At 8,000 feet, the ranch offers commanding views of the broad park and pastureland below and the peaks at its back. Wildlife abounds in this region, and your chances are always good of encountering elk, moose, bighorn sheep, eagles, beaver, and the occasional bear. In spring, the mountains explode in a colorful palette of wildflowers, and in summer, the region is green, lush, and pleasantly warm without being too hot—a welcome retreat for people from the sweltering East and Southwest. Fall is dedicated to the changing of the leaves, followed by hunting. The ranch works in tandem with Absaroka Outfitters, owned and operated by the Betts family, who also own the ranch. Guests interested in fall big-game hunting should contact the family to plan a special hunt with their licensed and very experienced guides.

This is a small guest ranch, accommodating a mere eighteen guests at a time. Its small size allows for personalized service and a sense of shared adventure with owners Budd and Emi Betts and their family. You'll never feel as though you are being herded from one activity to the next here.

The Absaroka will appeal most to persons seeking a traditional guest ranch. The emphasis here is on horseback riding, fishing, and nature appreciation. Individuals looking for spas and a deep list of activities will be disappointed, but for those who want to put in plenty of saddle time, the Absaroka employs expert wranglers with an excellent knowledge of and appreciation for the Wyoming high country. The ranch is ideally situated for fly fishing; trout species include brown, cutthroat, brook, and rainbow trout. Guided fishing trips to the best, crystal-clear fishing waters of the Dubois area can be easily arranged.

As an outfitter, the Betts family knows the backcountry and welcomes people to explore the wilds on overnight and extended pack trips. This is probably the best opportunity to see lots of wildlife, and you'll enjoy the camaraderie of the campfire. With horses to carry your load, you won't want for any comforts, and you'll sleep soundly in spacious tents pitched in flower-bespeckled subalpine meadows. A memorable trip if ever there was one!

Guests who prefer solid walls will appreciate the rustic but comfortable cabins. Each cabin has two bedrooms and an adjoining bath, ideal for families with teens, and is individually heated. Though there is no formal children's program, the ranch is very family oriented, and its owners will go out of their way to make sure that kids enjoy their stay. A recreation room, children's games, horseback riding, and fun contests on horseback assure that kids won't get bored during their stay.

The Absaroka Ranch is a good choice if you are looking for a peaceful getaway that offers outstanding scenery, good food, good fishing, and personalized care with a family that loves this part of the world and loves sharing it with guests.

**Absaroka Ranch**

P.O. Box 929
Dubois, WY 82513
Phone: (307) 455–2275
Web site: www.dteworld.com/absaroka

**Owners/Managers:** The Betts Family

**Accommodations:** Capacity 18. 4 total units. Duplex cabins are rustic but comfortable, and ideal for families. Each individually heated cabin has 2 bedrooms with adjoining bath and carpeting. All offer mountain views.

**Meals:** Meals, served in the main dining hall, are of excellent quality, freshness, and variety. Served family style with complimentary evening wine service; otherwise, BYOB.

**Activities:** Horseback riding is the main activity, with several rides of varying lengths available throughout the day. For a backcountry camping experience, inquire about overnight and extended pack trips. Guided fishing (mainly fly fishing) and guided nature hikes available.

**Amenities:** Covered porches, main lodge with dining area, recreation room with table games, board games, a foosball table, and jukebox.

**Special Programs:** No formal kids' programs, although children are welcome. Baby-sitting available on special request.

**Rates:** $$$ Full American Plan. Group, family, and children's rates available. Reduced rates for return guests at certain times of the season.

**Credit Cards:** None. Personal checks accepted.

**Season:** Mid-June to mid-September

**Getting There:** On U.S. Highway 26/287, 10 miles west of Dubois and 45 miles east of Grand Teton National Park. Daily airline service from Denver International and Salt Lake City to Jackson Hole Airport. Limited air service also available to Riverton, Wyoming. Shuttle service to ranch at additional charge.

**What's Nearby:** Jackson Hole, Grand Teton National Park, Yellowstone National Park, and town of Dubois, a friendly western town well worth the visit.

# BILL CODY RANCH

Cody, Wyoming

Wild Bill Cody was an astute businessman who understood and knew how to capitalize on the allure of the West. Cody, Wyoming, is a lot like Wild Bill. Of the many towns in "the Cowboy State," Cody seems best suited to capitalize on its frontier heritage. From its nightly rodeos to its old-time fiddlers' jams, Cody is a bubbling Dutch oven of Wyoming culture—a place where the Old West never got old.

Cody boasts not one, but two gateways to Yellowstone National Park. The town also serves as the hub for several loop-tour drives that access five different Scenic Byways. Poised midway between the park's east entrance and Cody, is the Bill Cody Ranch. Fortuitously situated in one of the most scenically awe-inspiring areas in North America, the ranch has been a favorite stop for westward-faring tourists since its opening in 1925. Short of, perhaps, Niagara Falls or the Grand Canyon, you won't find a more appealing site than the towering Sawtooth mountains of this sparsely populated state.

And talk about authenticity—the ranch was at one time owned by a direct descendant of Buffalo Bill himself.

At present, hosts John and Jamie Parsons ride herd on all the ranch details, maintaining a high level of quality and personal attention that has made this one of the best traditional guest ranches in the state. Whether your desire is to fill every minute with excitement or you simply want to kick back on the porch and relax, the Parsons will help to create a personalized itinerary that suits you and your family's desires. Flexibility is the key here. There's no minimum stay or, for that matter, a maximum stay. Come for a day, a week, or a month if you like.

Besides the obvious appeal of sightseeing in Cody and Yellowstone, there's plenty to do on the ranch. Horseback riding, naturally. Rides depart at all hours of the day, depending on rider's desires. The wranglers will surprise you with a meal cooked over an open fire or with yarns about local mountain-man and cowboy lore. Groups are limited to about ten riders, ensuring personal instruction if you desire it. Overnight pack trips take you even farther into the wonderful wilderness of the 2.5-million-acre Shoshone National Forest.

Guests also enjoy guided fishing in some of the best waters the West has to offer. Those wishing to raft those same waterways can make arrangements to do so, or just sit by the river with a good book!

Evening entertainment tends toward the informal. One night, a cowboy singer may stop by; on another you'll be treated to a lavish barbecues, or you can simply join your family around the campfire. You'll want to take in the Cody Nite Rodeo, an institution in these parts, and you'll also want to stop in at the Buffalo Bill Historical Center, one of the finest historical and western art collections in the country.

## Bill Cody Ranch

2604 Yellowstone Highway.
Cody, WY 82414
Phone: (800) 615–2934; (307) 587–6271
Fax: (307) 587–6272
E-mail: billcody@billcodyranch.com
Web site: www.billcodyranch.com

**Managers:** John and Jamie Parsons

**Accommodations:** Capacity, 65. 14 units. Guests stay in 1- and 2-bedroom cabins with private baths. Comfortable western furnishings and shaded porches.

**Meals:** Meals are served in the main lodge, a restaurant and bar open to the public. Expect ranch-style meals of steak, river trout, and chicken with homemade bread, soups, and salads. Wednesday and Saturday barbecues by the creek. Day lunches available for activities.

**Activities:** Horseback riding is the main activity. Rides go out most hours of the day, with overnight and extended pack trips also available. Guided fishing in area lakes and rivers. Fun family activities and nightly entertainment.

**Amenities:** Hot tub, restaurant.

**Special Programs:** Various packages allow guests to choose on-site activities, pack trips, and combination riding/fishing excursions. No formal children's program, although babysitting is available by arrangement.

**Rates:** $$–$$$ Nightly lodging rates with a la carte activities and dining or all-inclusive American Plan packages. Prices vary accordingly.

**Credit Cards:** VISA, MasterCard, Discover

**Season:** May–September

**Getting There:** Located midway between Cody, Wyoming, and the east entrance of Yellowstone National Park on the Yellowstone Highway. Commercial airport in Cody, Wyoming.

**What's Nearby:** Cody, a charming western town with myriad tourist activities, including the Buffalo Bill Historical Museum; Yellowstone National Park, 26 miles west.

# BITTERROOT RANCH

## Dubois, Wyoming

Bitterroot is a rider's ranch, run by able horsemen. Rather than simply being a passenger on the trail, you'll really learn to work with and understand your equine partner. Arguably, the ranch offers one of the most advanced trail-riding programs in the country, and the day-to-day riding is augmented by annual riding clinics conducted by some of America's top clinicians. If you are an experienced rider or a novice with a desire to greatly advance your equestrian skills, the Bitterroot is the ideal environment.

The Bitterroot borders the 2.5-million-acre Shoshone National Forest, which in turn abuts Yellowstone National Park. Riders can explore mile upon mile of trails, including the broad plains of the Wind River Indian reservation. The ranch maintains a herd of 130 saddle horses, ranging from ranch-bred Arabians, as well as quarter horses, to Appaloosas and mustangs. This large herd permits a horse-to-rider ratio of about three to one, which means you'll give out long before the horses do! The ranch maintains its own breeding program and has initiated the training of its Arabian horses; among their breeding stock is a Crabbet-bred stallion judged champion foal at the 1985 British Nationals.

Your week begins with an arena demonstration of riding techniques, followed by an evaluation of guests' abilities (a much better criteria for assigning mounts than simply asking guests about their experience). Guides lead riders on short, two- to three-hour rides. Guests may choose from western or English tack, and riding helmets are available and encouraged.

On Tuesday and Thursday, you'll have the opportunity to be videotaped, a helpful way to improve your fundamental riding skills. On Friday, guests compete in a team cattle-sorting event, a great introduction to cattle work. On Saturday, guests take part in an all-day picnic ride. In July and August, you may take part in cattle gathering and herding, which resumes in September for fall guests.

The Bitterroot is owned and run by Bayard and Mel Fox, fascinating individuals with extensive globe-trotting backgrounds. Bayard is a Yale University graduate who spent years in Europe, the Middle East, and the South Pacific. Mel grew up on a farm at the foot of Mount Kilimanjaro and worked with wildlife in the famous Kenya National Park. Given their multilingual skills and multicultural backgrounds, you should not be surprised that many of the guests are European or that the cocktail conversation sparkles with fascinating adventures and wry commentary on the world.

Bayard is a particularly avid fisherman, and when the conversation lags, you can always engage him in a discussion of the local waters. Excellent fly-fishing opportunities abound, both on the ranch and in nearby lakes and streams. The East Fork of the Wind River cuts through the ranch, offering roughly a mile of private fishing access. Above the ranch base, the river cuts through a deep gorge that is difficult to access, but well worth the effort if you desire a place where fishing pressure is almost nonexistent and big, strong cutthroat flourish. There are also several small, stocked ponds on the ranch, and numerous fishing holes are accessible via hiking or horseback. Bayard usually goes fishing with guests two or three times a week.

## Bitterroot Ranch

1480 East Fork Road
Dubois, WY 82513
Phone: (800) 545–0019; (307) 455–3363
Fax: (307) 455–2354
E-mail: BitterrootRanch@wyoming.com
Web site: www.bitterrootranch.com

**Owners/Managers:** Bayard and Mel Fox

**Accommodations:** The ranch can accommodate up to 30 people in 12 charming cabins, each with private bathrooms, wood-burning stoves, and electric heat. Cabins are situated on either side of a trout-filled stream for maximum seclusion. Guests gather in the main lodge for meals and relaxing evenings.

**Meals:** A special effort is made with cuisine. Salads come fresh from the garden, ranch-raised beef and lamb are served, and bread is baked in the kitchen. Wine is offered at cocktail gatherings and dinner.

**Activities:** Horseback riding is the primary emphasis; videotaping of riding lessons is available. Special activities include early summer and fall cattle drives, riding clinics with renowned clinicians, and overnight pack trips. Guests looking to spend a lot of time in the backcountry should inquire about extended pack trips into the Yellowstone and Shoshone National Forest. Bayard Fox is an avid fisherman and leads guests on frequent fly-fishing trips.

**Amenities:** Hot tub, video analysis of riding skills, large lodge with stone fireplace, pool table, piano, and extensive video library for guests' enjoyment.

**Special Programs:** No children's programs, although children are welcome.

**Rates:** $$–$$$ Full American Plan. Lower weekly nonrider rate available. Reduced rates for children under 16; pack trips at added cost. Minimum stay: half week (3 days riding, 4 nights lodging); one week stay runs Sunday to Sunday.

**Credit Cards:** VISA, MasterCard, Discover. Personal checks and traveler's checks accepted.

**Season:** May 25–September 30

**Getting There:** 26 miles northeast of Dubois, 80 miles west of Riverton. Airport transfer available from Riverton or Jackson, Wyoming (100 miles east) at added cost.

**What's Nearby:** Dubois.

# BROOKS LAKE LODGE

## Dubois, Wyoming

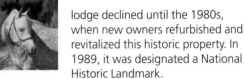

Individuals who appreciate the finer things in life will certainly enjoy Brooks Lake Lodge, a premier destination where rustic charm and luxurious elegance go hand in hand. Chosen among America's ten best adventure lodges by *Outside* magazine in 2002, this high-end lodge offers peaceful serenity, superb amenities, and an exceptional staff dedicated to pampering guests.

David Brooks, writing in *Travel & Leisure* magazine, summarized Brooks Lake Lodge well when he described it as "a high-end wilderness experience that marries the refinements of civilization with a reverence for nature."

That reverence for nature is a big part of the Brooks Lake Lodge lore. The lake was first discovered by Bryant B. Brooks in 1889. At the time, the namesake discoverer remarked, "Among the pines glistened a lake . . . what a sight! Where I sat on my horse stretched a broad, peaceful valley. I stood closer that day to nature's heart than ever before."

Brooks Lake Lodge has a long history, steeped in the tradition of the great western lodges that first welcomed guests at the turn of the nineteenth century. Built in the 1920s to serve as a stopover for visitors to Yellowstone, Brooks Lake Lodge (then the Diamond G Ranch) quickly expanded to serve as a vacation-destination dude ranch. Easterners often stayed for weeks or months at a time. Built of logs in the Craftsman style popular during that era, the lodge declined until the 1980s, when new owners refurbished and revitalized this historic property. In 1989, it was designated a National Historic Landmark.

Located in the Shoshone National Forest not far from Yellowstone Park, the lodge is surrounded by the Pinnacle Mountains and the Continental Divide. Brooks Lake, ensconced in the valley, dominates the view north, with nearby Brooks Mountain providing yet another inspiring image.

Guests may choose from a variety of activities best suited to this subalpine environment. Horseback riders are matched carefully to mounts that suit their abilities. A favorite excursion is riding to some of the area lakes and streams to fly fish or simply engage in nature photography. On the trail, you are likely to encounter elk, deer, moose, bighorn sheep, and bald eagles, and at high elevations, the adorable whistling marmot.

Brooks Lake offers a more leisurely fishing experience. Borrow a canoe and paddle out for a few hours of peaceful trolling. And you need not worry that the kids are having a good time; the ranch employs counselors who cook up a full day of fun indoor activities and outdoor adventures.

In the evening, guests congregate in the Tea Room to enjoy conversation and ever-changing entertainment. Local musicians, artists, and craftspeople, as well as special speakers, drop by to delight and enlighten guests.

## Brooks Lake Lodge

458 Brooks Lake Road
Dubois, WY 82513
Phone: (307) 455–2121
E-mail: brookslake@wyoming.com
Web site: www.brookslake.com

**Manager:** Jinifer Ables

**Accommodations:** Capacity, 36. 6 lodge rooms, 1 "premier" lodge suite, 6 newly remodeled deluxe cabins, 2 family cabins. All have private baths. Cabins have sitting areas, wood-burning stoves, and electric heat; 2 new cabins have 2 bathrooms, 2 bedrooms, sitting room, loft, and private porch.

**Meals:** Breakfasts of fresh fruits, home-baked breads, malted waffles; lunch of soups, sandwiches, and pasta dishes; high tea in late afternoon; formal evening dining featuring a 3-course meal of local specialties prepared in gourmet fashion.

**Activities:** Fly fishing and lure fishing in Brooks Lake, as well as area streams and lakes with professional guide (equipment provided); horseback riding suited to rider experience and preferences; guided wilderness hiking; overnight and extended pack trips at additional cost; evening entertainment. Winter cross-country skiing on tracked trails, snowmobiling, snowshoeing, dogsledding, ice fishing.

**Amenities:** New! Full-service, 3,000-square-foot spa with workout room, dry sauna, 10-by-17-foot outdoor Jacuzzi, 2 treatment rooms. Game/card room; opulent lodge with guest rooms and common areas, furnished with antiques, paintings, and sculptures by Wyoming artists; full bar; comfortable outdoor furniture and shaded porches; recreational equipment and fishing tackle available.

**Special Programs:** Children's coordinator and children's program with guided and supervised daytime activities such as hiking, canoe trips, horseback riding, arts and crafts. Evening activities, too. Children 7 and older may ride horses.

**Rates:** $$$$ Full American Plan. Off-season, children's rates; reduced winter rates. 3-day minimum stay in summer.

**Credit Cards:** VISA, MasterCard, American Express

**Season:** Summer, mid-June to September; winter: late December to mid-April

**Getting There:** The area is served by major airlines to the Jackson Hole, Riverton, and Idaho Falls airports. If driving to the lodge from Jackson Hole, proceed north on Route 191/26/89; at Moran, turn east on Route 26/287. If driving to the lodge from Dubois, Lander, or Riverton, follow Route 26/287 west. From both east and west, there is a USFS Recreational Area sign for Brooks Lake. There you will turn onto Brooks Lake Road. The lodge is 5 miles away.

**What's Nearby:** Jackson Hole, approximately 60 miles west; Dubois, approximately 23 miles east; Yellowstone National Park, approximately 65 miles northwest; Grand Teton National Park, approximately 40 miles west.

# CM RANCH

## Dubois, Wyoming

Dubois and its surrounding environs might be called the epicenter of dude ranching in Wyoming, and perhaps even North America. There are scores of dude ranches in this area, all touting the scenic splendors and isolation that makes this part of Wyoming extra special.

The CM Ranch is one of the oldest and most venerated guest ranches here. The property first opened in 1927, and it is listed with the National Register of Historic Places. In its way, the CM set the standard for dude ranches and continues to define just what a great dude ranch can and should be.

Situated in a peaceful, secluded valley at the mouth of Jakey's Fork Canyon in the Wind River Range, the ranch shares a border with the Shoshone National Forest and the Fitzpatrick Wilderness Area, permitting guests access to a seemingly endless network of trails and some exceptional fishing waters. (Incidentally, the CM also owns 4 miles of stream on Jakey's Fork, giving guests the chance to fish for native and introduced trout species on a managed and low-pressure waterway.)

During the day you can ride, swim, picnic, participate in activities, or just relax with a book. Evenings are occupied with square dances and cookouts, softball games, horseshoes, and volleyball on the lawn. Every week, a local photographer presents a slide show, and there's an evening dedicated to cowboy poetry and music.

The CM strives to provide an environment for families but also welcomes singles and couples. Here, nobody will feel like the odd man out; a broad mix of clients and the friendly staff (experienced horse instructors and college students, mainly) ensures that you will find suitable people to share in your adventures. And if the idea of vacationing with kids doesn't appeal to you, the ranch hosts adults-only weeklong sessions in early fall.

The look of the ranch is old school, with actual chinked-wall log buildings down at the corrals. The logs for the ranch buildings were cut up in the valley and hauled to the present site by teams of horses and wagons. The scathed pine logs give the interiors a warmth that's hard to beat, and the various lodging houses and guest rooms have been tastefully updated to suit modern standards of comfort. Guest houses, for instance, include large modern kitchens, washers and dryers, and electric heat.

Guests looking to rough it, however, can opt for an extended pack trip into the Wind River Mountains. After reaching the base camp at Moon Bay, riders can take forays into the Fitzpatrick Wilderness, enjoying the high-alpine scenery of Simpson and Alice Lakes, or take a journey to the Continental Divide to see Gannett Peak, the highest mountain in Wyoming, and Three Rivers Mountain, where rainwater splits and divides to form the headwaters of the Columbia, Missouri, and Colorado Rivers.

One of the most fascinating aspects of the CM is the bands of striated rock that make up its broad valley geology. The strata of rock here are a virtual storybook of the earth, displaying three billion years of development. Here, one can see leaf imprints, along with shell and dinosaur fossil deposits amid the cake-layer-like formations—an extraordinary place for casual geologists or anyone with a curious and inquisitive nature.

This is a great old-time ranch with modern appointments and a wonderful staff. It's no wonder that it has been a favorite for more than seventy-five years.

## CM Ranch

P.O. Box 127
Dubois, WY 82513
Phone: (800) 455–0271; (307) 455–2331
Fax: (307) 455–3984
E-mail: ranch@cmranch.com
Web site: www.cmranch.com

**Managers:** Mike and Kass Harrell

**Accommodations:** Capacity, 60. Well-built older cabins with modern appointments line the Jakey's Fork stream that runs through the property. Above the main ranch are more modern log houses well suited to larger families and groups. Cabins have 1, 2, and 3 bedrooms with old-timey log furniture, wood-burning stoves, and large porches. The larger houses will accommodate up to 6 guests: These have 2 or 3 bedrooms and a living room; 2 feature fireplaces, and the third, Hardie House, has a woodstove.

**Meals:** Guests dine together in the main lodge. Made-to-order breakfasts and feature such items as homemade granola and fresh fruits, omelets, sourdough pancakes, and fresh-baked breads. Lunch is served buffet style and mainly taken on the shaded outdoor porch. Dinner, served family style, includes savory fare such as game hens and poached salmon. Vegetarian dishes are available, and special diets can be accommodated with advance notice.

**Activities:** CM's horse-riding program emphasizes exhilarating trail rides with small groups (average size, 6 persons). Weekly all-day picnic rides to Whiskey Mountain, home of the largest herd of bighorn sheep in North America. Fly fishing on private stream as well as gold-medal waters near the ranch and high-mountain lakes. Catch-and-release encouraged. Swimming in heated outdoor pool.

Hiking. Evening dances, slide shows by area photographer, outdoor games such as softball, volleyball, and more. Cowboy entertainers. Weekly arena gymkhana game on horseback; breakfast and picnic rides.

**Amenities:** Outdoor heated pool; well-appointed cabin homes available with indoor kitchens, stone fireplace or woodstove. Recreation room ideal for reading and games, Ping-Pong table, small library, and geology study room.

**Special Programs:** Supervised riding for kids 5 and older. The ranch strives to create a variety of activities for children and teens, including explorations of Native American petroglyphs, visits to a local fish hatchery, lawn games, Ping-Pong tournaments, and overnight campouts. Pack trips offered as part of the ranch vacation package or as a separate vacation. Inquire for pack-trip-only rates.

**Rates:** $$–$$$ Full American Plan. Reduced rates for nonriders and children. All-inclusive except for fishing-guide services and fishing-tackle rental.

**Credit Cards:** VISA, MasterCard. Personal checks preferred.

**Season:** Mid-June–September

**Getting There:** The area is served by major airlines to the Jackson Hole, Riverton, and Idaho Falls airports. Inquire for specific directions to the ranch.

**What's Nearby:** Yellowstone National Park, Grand Teton National Park, Jackson Hole, Whiskey Mountain (home to the largest herd of bighorn sheep in North America), float trips on the Snake River. Dubois, a small western town, includes 2 museums devoted to regional history.

# DOUBLE DIAMOND X RANCH

Cody, Wyoming

"Our son Tim's comment summed it up for us. 'Better than Disney World!'" That comment, from visitors to the Double Diamond X Ranch, is the best guest-ranch recommendation imaginable. Its author went on to say, "Our stay . . . was exceptional. The scenery was much more impressive than your brochure suggests. The food was great. The entertainment was varied and first-rate. But what made our stay so enjoyable was the people."

A more welcoming place might be difficult to find. The Double Diamond X is a traditional western guest ranch nestled amid a lovely and compelling backdrop of Rocky Mountain peaks. A mere 34 miles southwest of Cody, Wyoming, it serves as the perfect portal to Yellowstone National Park or as a complete destination in and of itself.

One of the niftiest things about this ranch is its special programs. The Double Diamond X has one of the most complete kids' programs in the dude business. The whole idea behind it is to give kids their own "western experience." Days are structured around themes: horse science and safety, cowboys and Indians, Wyoming wildlife, and The Old Trail Town. Activities and field trips, arts and crafts, and music and storytelling all support the day's theme. It is wonderfully entertaining for kids, and they'll scarcely know their days are also educational (the counselors won't tell them if you don't).

For the adventurous, there are backcountry pack trips. If you've ever wanted to explore the mountains on horseback and camp under the stars, you might seriously want to consider spending a few nights of your vacation with the Double Diamond X mountain guides. These very popular trips take guests up into the wild Absaroka Mountains, the Bridger-Teton National Forest, and the Washakie Wilderness. Without the burden of carrying your own gear, you'll be free to really see and enjoy the stunningly majestic mountains, the delicate alpine wildflowers, and the cascading waters of snowmelt streams. If your luck is good (and it surely will be), you should encounter a profusion of wildlife that might include deer, elk, birds of prey, and perhaps even something more exotic, like Rocky Mountain bighorn sheep.

Of course, you may instead prefer a comfortable stay at the ranch. The Double Diamond X, though not opulent, is certainly homey, warm, and quite relaxing. Guests stay in quaint log cabins or the two-story Trail House, a kind of cowboy rural inn. The main lodge houses a vast living room with a fireplace, library, gift shop, kitchen, and dining room. It's where guests like to mingle and socialize and is the center of the evening's entertainment. A broad, shaded veranda with comfortable rocking chairs provides a nice place to relax in between daytime or evening activities. Each of the guest cabins and the Trail House also accommodate quality "porch time."

Perhaps you'd prefer to relax beside the heated indoor pool? This popular attraction has been recently upgraded with the addition of a hot tub, great for soaking saddle-sore muscles.

Although it would be hard to single out any one thing that sets the Double Diamond X apart from the rest, it is easy to say that the folks here strive to do everything just a little better. It's that dedication to service and the staff's genuine friendliness that makes this ranch an outstanding place.

## Double Diamond X Ranch

3453 Southfork Road
Cody, WY 82414
Phone: (800) 833–RANCH; (307) 527–6276
Fax: (307) 587–2708
E-mail: ddx@cody.wtp.net
Web site: www.ddxranch.com

**Owners/Managers:** Patsy and Russ Fraser

**Accommodations:** Capacity, 38. 6 total units. Guests stay in 5 log cabins or the Trail House Lodge, a 2-story cabin with 7 guest rooms and 1 deluxe suite. All cabins feature sleep 4 to 7 individuals in 2 bedrooms, each with 1 or 2 baths. Trail House rooms and the suite have private baths. There are 2 handicapped-equipped rooms, one is a cabin, the other is in the Trail House. Covered porches with rockers are located in the Main Lodge, individual cabins, and The Trail House.

**Meals:** An eclectic and varied mix of western and nouveau American regional cuisines, along with an extensive children's menu. Beverage and snack station available between meals. BYOB.

**Activities:** Daily horseback riding. Never-evers can rely on great instruction, extra care in riding safety, and a horse well suited to one's abilities. 2 daily rides, plus all-day rides and overnight trips. Swimming in an indoor pool. Fishing in local rivers and lakes (try your hand at fly casting). Hiking, wildlife observation, photography. River-rafting trips and Yellow-stone Park visits available. Evening entertainment includes cowboy singers and poets, storytellers, and dancing—something new and different every night! Informally, there are classic western movies, table tennis, pool and foosball in the rec room, or just plain relaxing on comfortable rockers indoors or out.

**Amenities:** Indoor heated pool with new hot tub; main lodge with gift shop, sitting room, library, and broad veranda. Handicapped-accessible.

**Special Programs:** One of the best children's programs in the dude-ranch business. Broad variety of activities for toddlers and children to 12 years old; daily themes provide a basis for fun and education. Baby-sitters and nannies welcome.

**Rates:** $$$ Full American Plan. Children's rates, off-season rates.

**Credit Cards:** VISA, MasterCard

**Season:** Summer session, mid-June to late-October. Inquire about winter dates and rates.

**Getting There:** Located 34 miles southwest of Cody on Southfork Road. Nearest airport is in Cody and is serviced by United Airlines Express out of Denver, Colorado.

**What's Nearby:** Yellowstone National Park, western town of Cody with museums, shopping, famous Cody Nite Rodeo, and the Buffalo Bill Cody Historical Center.

# EATONS' RANCH

Wolf, Wyoming

It all began here. Well, sort of. In 1879, the Eaton brothers—Howard, Willis and Alden—established a horse-and-cattle ranch in Medora, South Dakota, and almost immediately began to welcome their friends from the East. Some stayed all summer. Eventually, the visitors began underwriting the costs of their visits, and the dude-ranch industry was born.

One of the "dudes" was a neighboring ranch owner, Teddy Roosevelt. Roosevelt extolled the virtues of life out West, and the Eatons' place grew as more and more people flocked to the area. In 1904, the brothers decided to move their outfit to Wyoming, a state with greater scenic grandeur and more varied terrain for horseback riding. They found the ideal setting along Wolf Creek, not far from Sheridan.

Eatons' Ranch, which has remained in the family's hands for a century, is now operated by the brothers' third-, fourth- and fifth-generation descendants. And, not coincidentally, many of the people who come here are the third-, fourth- and fifth-generation descendants of people who sought out the Eatons' western hospitality decades ago.

The ranch is a good-sized outfit capable of hosting 125 guests in fifty-one individual cabins. It's also home to a sizable herd of horses (about 200), providing everyone with a fresh mount. You'll need one to explore the roughly 7,000 acres of riding land, enough so you'll scarcely have to cross your old tracks the entire week. If that's not enough, you can head up into the Bighorn Mountains west of the ranch. The Eatons take an active interest in their community, hosting a number of popular celebrations in nearby Sheridan throughout summer. These events include a roping tournament, the Eatons' Ranch Cup, a cowboy/dude golf tournament, a "Calcutta" cowboy auction, and team-roping contest. If that's not enough, there are also several rodeos and the wonderful Don King Days Celebration (a roping, bronc riding, and polo tournament held at the Big Horn Equestrian Center), which is a social highlight attended by Sheridans each September. You'll scarcely be able to plan your vacation without overlapping a true Western celebration in which the Eatons have a hand!

Back at the ranch, you'll find more than enough activities to satisfy your interests. Drop your fishing line in Wolf Creek, take a hike, spend some time quietly observing native deer, elk, and bighorn sheep, golf on one of several local courses, or simply relax by the heated outdoor pool. You won't have to worry about the kids, as a whole day's worth of activities await them at Howard Hall (although babysitters, available at extra charge, are encouraged for the very youngest children). Activities range from arts and crafts to scavenger hunts to afternoons at the pool. There are also horseback rides for The Mosquito Fleet, kids ages six and older, along with nature hikes, movies, and marshmallow roasts.

For the adults, the Eatons host a weekly cocktail party, as well as bingo nights, country-western dancing, and an exciting team-roping competition for local cowboys held throughout summer. That, and the aforementioned rodeo and western events in town, will seldom leave you time to rest and reflect, but if you are so inclined, the ranch maintains a modest library for book readers.

## Eatons' Ranch

Wolf, WY 82844
Phone: (800) 210–1049; (307) 655–9285
Fax: (307) 655–9269
E-mail: jeffway@eatonsranch.com
Web site: www.eatonsranch.com

**Owners/Managers:** The Eaton Family

**Accommodations:** Interestingly, many of the cabins here were built by pioneering guests, and the structures were usually named for their builders. Talk about a working vacation! In some cases, these cabins still have actual iceboxes, which are still cooled by huge blocks of ice delivered aboard a vintage Model A pickup. Of course, they also have modern comforts, including private bathrooms. This ranch may be old, but you won't have to live entirely in the nineteenth century!

**Meals:** Meals served in ranch dining room. Western dining includes made-to-order breakfasts with eggs, meats, etc., plus healthful alternatives such as fruits, cereals, muffins. Lunch varies from buffets to barbecue cookouts. Dinner includes 2 nightly entrees, with choices of beef, poultry, fish, and pasta. Saturday-night barbecue by the creek. Special dietary needs accommodated with advance notice.

**Activities:** Horseback riding is the mainstay here; Eatons' is one of the few dude ranches that allow solo riding, once a guest has demonstrated proficiency. Twice-daily rides, pack trips, picnic rides, and arena instruction available. Fishing in Wolf Creek, swimming in the heated pool. Game room, hiking, nature observation, trips to Sheridan (extra cost), special events.

**Amenities:** Coin-op laundry, ranch store, coffee shop.

**Special Programs:** Children's programs with supervised activities. Arts and crafts, scavenger hunts, pool parties, planned kids' rides. Babysitting at additional cost.

**Rates:** $$–$$$ Full American Plan. Reduced rates for children, nanny rates. Rates vary according to room availability. Applicable rates will be clearly stated at the time of your booking.

**Credit Cards:** VISA, MasterCard, Discover

**Season:** June–October

**Getting There:** The Sheridan Airport is served by United Express Airlines out of Denver. Shuttle to ranch at no added charge. Other airports: Billings, Montana (2 hours), Casper, Wyoming (2½ hours).

**What's Nearby:** Yellowstone Park, ½-day drive; Little Big Horn National Monument, Fort Kearny, Tongue River Canyon, Whitney Gallery of Western Art, Buffalo Bill Museum in Cody.

# FLYING A RANCH

## Pinedale, Wyoming

We all love kids, right? Well, sometimes we'd also love an escape from their frenetic energy, too. If kids (either yours or someone else's) aren't part of your vacation plans, you might want to check into the Flying A Ranch, an adults-only guest ranch located in the beautiful Wyoming mountains just south of famous Jackson Hole.

Nestled in the Gros Ventre and Wind River Ranges, the Flying A offers an elegant guest-ranch vacation for discerning adults and older teens (at least sixteen years of age). To give you just a taste, guests are housed in six luxurious log cabins, each completely renovated with designer decors and modern luxury conveniences such as kitchenettes complete with coffeemakers, wine goblets, and cooking ware. The floors are solid oak, the furniture is made from hand-hewn pine, and the flannel sheets, overstuffed pillows, and luxurious bed coverings are sumptuous and cozy. You'll think you walked right into an L.L. Bean catalog!

The ranch sits in the middle of a grassy park, giving guests a wonderful view in every direction. You'll be able to enjoy glorious sunrises and sunsets, with views of woodland animals and grazing horses filling up the hours in between.

The ranch doesn't operate on rigid schedules. You can fill every minute of your day or work at elevating relaxation to a fine art. For riding enthusiasts, the Flying A offers shorter half-day rides or more rigorous full-day outings. Each guest is assigned his or her own horse for the duration of their stay, so you won't spend each day adjusting to a new mount. By week's end,

you may not want to part with your new friend.

If you'd like a change of pace, the ranch also offers guided hikes and mountain-biking tours in the Bridger-Teton National Forest, which surrounds the ranch. And by all means, pick up a pole and spend a morning or afternoon fishing. The ranch provides equipment and fly-fishing lessons for both beginning and experienced anglers. (Owner Keith Hansen is an avid fly fisherman and is happy to share his passion with guests.)

In addition to these common guest-ranch activities, one may also take a mountain bike for a ride, go on a guided nature hike, play volleyball, horseshoes, or join fellow guests in a game of cards. The ranch staff also can help plan and facilitate day trips to Green River, Waterdog Lake, Grand Teton National Park, or Jackson Hole. There's also the popular Mountain Man Rendezvous, held on the second weekend in July, and the Mountain Man Museum in Pinedale.

Befitting an adults-only ranch, the cuisine here appeals to mature tastes. The menu encompasses everything from western staples such as grilled steaks to south-of-the-border specialties to Italian pastas. Lunch is more than a simple sandwich; it's a healthful and hearty meal. And the morning ranch breakfasts will get your motor running.

The Flying A is a great alternative to the typical family ranch and truly a place to get away from it all, including those beloved but noisy kids.

## Flying A Ranch

771 Flying A Ranch Road
Pinedale, WY 82941
Phone: (800) 678–6542; (307) 367–2385
Fax: (605) 336–8731
E-mail: flyingaranch@wyoming.com

**Owners/Managers:** Debbie and Keith Hansen

**Accommodations:** Capacity, 14. 6 cabins. Cabins feature living rooms, fireplaces, private baths, kitchenettes, and decks with mountain views. All are furnished with handmade pinewood furniture, designer bedding and window coverings, and solid oakwood floors.

**Meals:** All meals served in the main dining room. Before-dinner appetizers served in the ranch saloon. Expect excellently prepared meals featuring ranch and continental cuisine. Be sure to take home a copy of *From the High Country of Wyoming,* the Flying A Ranch cookbook, featuring 350 favorite recipes served on the ranch. Some favorites include Kraut Top Chops, Spinach Lasagna, Oriental Chicken Casserole, and the humorously named Fowl Thing.

**Activities:** Unlimited horseback riding, evening hayride, mountain biking, hiking, swimming, fly fishing, guided hikes, volleyball games, horseshoes, local excursions to favorite sites in and around Jackson Hole.

**Amenities:** Hot tub, luxurious guest cabins, fly-fishing equipment, private covered porches, elegant main lodge and dining room, guest saloon.

**Special Programs:** Adults-only guest ranch (unless your party "rents" the entire ranch).

**Rates:** $$$ Full American Plan. Prices vary according to cabin. Off-site activities not included.

**Credit Cards:** No credit cards. Cash, personal checks, and traveler's checks only.

**Season:** Mid-June to early October

**Getting There:** Nearest airport, Jackson Hole. Transportation to and from the ranch at additional charge. Inquire for specific directions to the ranch, a 1½ hour drive.

**What's Nearby:** Jackson Hole, Grand Teton National Park, Yellowstone National Park.

# GOOSEWING RANCH

## Jackson Hole, Wyoming

As the gateway to the Yellowstone and Grand Teton Parks, Jackson Hole, Wyoming, is the epicenter of guest-ranch vacationing in North America. If one acknowledges that this is the area that sets the standard, then the Goosewing Ranch sets the gold standard.

This is an exceptional place. A working ranch reborn as an isolated retreat deep in the Gros Ventre River Valley, the Goosewing marks the entry to a protected, pristine wilderness. The valley is host to spectacular game: elk, moose, mountain sheep, antelope, bear, eagles, geese, cranes, and more. The Gros Ventre River cuts through the ranch, providing habitat to native cutthroat trout and an excellent opportunity for fishermen.

The Goosewing is a four-season vacation ranch, nearly as popular and appealing among winter guests as summer vacationers. Skiers enjoy the proximity to world-famous Jackson Hole Winter Resort, as well as the on-site cross-country and snowshoeing trails. Snowmobiling adds another element of winter fun, with guided tours through Yellowstone National Park and the backcountry surrounding the ranch.

Come spring, the Rockies come alive with fields of wildflowers, gushing streams, and fresh, green growth across the meadows. This is an especially good time to visit for photographers, bird-watchers, and amateur naturalists. Be sure to inquire about special-guest lectures and seminars conducted on the ranch.

Summer, of course, is vacation time for families. Typically, guests choose from a variety of activities that include horseback riding, fishing, nature hikes, bike riding, swimming, and trips to Jackson to sample its quaint shops. A favorite day trip involves a ride to Sportsman Ridge, where one can visit the cabins and corrals of the mountain men who used this as a base camp for their explorations. Young children often stay "back at the ranch," mastering their skills as riders and future rodeo cowboys (at week's end, they put on their own rodeo exhibition for the adults).

Should you have a special desire to see a rodeo, visit Jackson, take a rafting or float trip, an overnight pack trip, or a photography class with a professional, the ranch activity manager will be happy to help you make special arrangements.

Goosewing Ranch is small and relatively isolated, even by Jackson Hole standards. With a capacity of about thirty, one becomes instantly familiar with other guests and the small staff. The cabins are wonderful, with a distinct western feel and decor. The Mountain Man Cabin, for instance, is a lovely log-cabin design, with a decor of heavy pine-log furniture and the trophy pelts of a variety of game species native to the area. The Cowboy Cabin, with its decorative ropes and old leather tack, has the feel of a real cowboy bunkhouse, although, admittedly, one that is far cleaner and well-kept than ones where most buckaroos have ever slept!

Of the myriad ranches in the Jackson area, this is one the author is particularly fond of. Its combination of a wonderfully secluded location, tasteful decor, exceptional dining, reasonable and affordable prices, and a wide choice of seasonal activities make it a great choice for an unforgettable vacation.

## Goosewing Ranch

P.O. Box 4084
Jackson Hole, WY 83001
Phone: (888) 733–5251; (307) 733–5251
Fax: (307) 733–1405
E-mail: info@goosewingranch.com
Web site: www.goosewingranch.com

**Owner**: François Corrand

**Manager:** Michael Cooley

**Accommodations:** Capacity, 30. 8 cabins and 1 larger "family lodge," many of them themed (Cowboy Cabin, Trapper Canyon, Fishing Cabin, etc.). Log interiors with heavy pine furniture and western decor and artifacts. Daily maid service, private bathrooms, laundry facilities available.

**Meals:** An eclectic seasonal menu typifies dining at the Goosewing. Cookouts, trail lunches, wine cellar and bar (additional). Special diets accommodated with advance notice.

**Activities:** Horseback riding, mountain biking, fishing, sight-seeing visits to Jackson, swimming, horseshoes, Yellowstone Park tours, cattle drives, rafting and float trips, wagon rides, overnight campouts, photography. Winter snowmobiling, snowshoeing, alpine skiing, cross-country skiing.

**Amenities:** Hot tub, billiard room, swimming pool, large lodge with massive stone fireplace, plush guest robes and linens, airport transportation.

**Special Programs:** Children's program with riding lessons, nature walks, visiting naturalists, and a variety of supervised activities. Weekly kid's rodeo presented for parents and guests.

**Rates:** $$–$$$ Full American Plan. Reduced off-season rates, children's rates, package rates. Inquire about winter snowmobile package rates, shorter and longer stays.

**Credit Cards:** VISA, MasterCard, American Express (3 percent added charge for credit cards). Traveler's checks, personal checks, and cash accepted.

**Season:** Summer: June 1 to October 5; winter: December 15 to March 31

**Getting There:** Located 1 hour from Jackson Hole Airport. Connecting flights to Jackson through Denver International and Salt Lake City Airport. Airport shuttle available; call for specific driving directions.

**What's Nearby:** Jackson, Grand Teton National Park, Yellowstone National Park, Jackson Hole Ski Area, Grand Targhee Ski Resort.

# GROS VENTRE RIVER RANCH

## Moose, Wyoming

When he was president, Bill Clinton was enchanted with the Jackson Hole region of Wyoming. It's not hard to understand why. The area has a rich history dating back to its earliest days as a fur-trapping region all the way up to its present-day status as a world-renowned vacation destination. With its unsurpassed scenic beauty, winter skiing, exceptional dining, world-class shopping, and President Clinton's favorite diversion, golf, Jackson is truly a premier place to experience the West.

Needless to say, there are a lot of exceptional guest ranches in the Jackson Hole. Gros Ventre River Ranch is among the best of the best. The ranch is a mere 18 miles south of Jackson, 45 miles south of Yellowstone National Park. Its proximity to the Grand Teton mountains means that guests enjoy exquisite mountain views regardless of whether they are out on the trail, hip-deep in a fishing stream, or just kicking back and watching the sunrise from their cabin porch.

There is a simple beauty to this ranch. For example, the cabins and guest lodges, which include traditional log interiors and exteriors set off with rustic pine furniture, are pleasingly arranged amid stands of aspen and pine trees. Secluded, yet close to the action of the Main Lodge and situated so as to afford guests stunning mountain views and the Gros Ventre River.

Don't expect to lounge around a luxurious pool or get a facial and sauna in a spa. This is, first and foremost, a riding ranch. Remember, simplicity is the key here. If water is your thing, you can take a bracing dip in the river or relax in the privacy and relative luxury of your private bath.

That said, this ranch is very comfortable and accommodating. Dining takes place in the beautiful log-cabin-style Main Lodge, where guests are welcome to browse about the collection of western art and sculpture prior to meals. The dining is top-drawer, featuring entrees such as prime rib, rack of lamb, grilled chicken, and mountain trout. Breads and desserts are home-baked, and vegetables and fruits are fresh and wonderfully prepared.

Guests will enjoy riding through exceptionally scenic sections of the Teton National Forest and designated wilderness areas. Groups are arranged by riding skill and limited to eight riders per guide. Riders who wish to meander easily through fields of wildflowers, stopping often for photo opportunities, will find other riders of similar interests. Those who prefer a fast-paced, ground-covering ride are as easily accommodated.

Fishing is a big draw at Gros Ventre. The ranch has excellent Orvis fishing tackle on hand for guests, and there is great fishing in its own stocked ponds and on the Gros Ventre River. Guests wishing to visit some exceptional local waters (including the Snake River) may also coordinate with a ranch activity director to take part in off-ranch guided fishing excursions.

Gros Ventre, of course, serves as the ideal base camp for forays into Jackson (you'll want to visit the town square, with its elk-antler arches and its wonderful art shops) as well as the Yellowstone. A weekly rodeo held in Jackson is a favorite activity for ranch guests and something you won't want to miss. And golfers, don't forget to take along your clubs; the Jackson Hole Golf and Tennis Club is just 14 miles away. You may even find yourself sharing the course with a certain famous Arkansas politician.

## Gros Ventre River Ranch

P.O. Box 151
Moose, WY 83012
Phone: (307) 733–4138
Fax: (307) 733–4272
E-mail: info@grosventreriverranch.com
Web site: www.grosventreriverranch.com

**Managers:** Carol and Tina Weber

**Accommodations:** Capacity, 40. Guests are housed in duplex-style log cabins and larger duplex guest houses. All rooms are carpeted, electrically heated, and have private baths and porches. Cabins are rented by the "half," with each half consisting of a private bedroom and bath, with either a king bed or two twins. Log lodges are more like suites, with a bedroom, private bath, and living room, wood-burning stove, kitchenette, and a private deck with a view of the Tetons. Families of 4 or more can rent an entire log lodge, or it can easily be shared by 2 couples.

**Meals:** 3 meals served each day, with complimentary wine service with dinner. Meals range from rack of lamb to fresh mountain trout to prime rib. All meals feature home-baked breads and desserts. Evening barbecue cookouts to break up the evening routine. Box lunches available to guests taking off-site excursions.

**Activities:** Excellent horse-riding program, with a herd of close to 100 ensuring a good match and a fresh mount for each guest. Helmets, boots, and hats available for riders. Rides take place in the Grand Teton National Forest. Fishing in stocked ponds, local streams; off-site guided fishing available. Hiking and nature observation with guest naturalist. Canoeing. Mountain biking. Trips to Jackson, Yellowstone. Golf, tennis, and weekly rodeo competition.

**Amenities:** Beautiful log-cabin lodge with recreation room (pool and table tennis), large guest lounge with western art and sculpture, low guest-to-guide ratio, cabin porches, laundry facilities, airport shuttle.

**Special Programs:** No children's programs, although children are welcome. Riders must be at least 7 years old (arena pony rides for young children). Special activities for kids include scavenger hunts, recreational games, movie night, and special kid-sized fishing equipment. No day care or babysitters, although some staff may take babysitting assignments during their off hours.

**Rates:** $$–$$$ Full American Plan. Children's rates, off-peak rates. Rates include lodging, all meals, riding, use of ranch facilities, and airport transfers from Jackson Hole.

**Credit Cards:** None. Cash, personal checks, and traveler's checks welcome.

**Season:** May 25–October 12

**Getting There:** 18 miles outside Jackson; closest airport in Jackson. Airport transfers available. Inquire for driving directions.

**What's Nearby:** Jackson, Wyoming; Yellowstone National Park.

# HEART SIX RANCH

## Moran, Wyoming

The Heart Six began in the late 1800s as a trapping hideout for Dick "Beavertooth" Neil. Local lore holds that Beavertooth would don his snowshoes and walk backward over great distances to throw nosy game wardens off his trail. At present, Beavertooth Neill's original cabin makes up part of the main dining room at this Jackson Hole institution, the Heart Six.

The Heart Six dates from the early 1900s, a time of major settlement in the Jackson Hole region, coinciding with the creation of Yellowstone National Park. At one time, a stagecoach ran past the ranch, enabling folks to go on up to Yellowstone to see its amazing sights. Now the stage is gone, but folks still enjoy the Heart Six as a keyhole to the Yellowstone, away from the congestion and the madding crowds.

The ranch is owned by the Harris family, who purchased the property in the 1980s. It was and remains their dream to create a place where guests enjoy this beautiful slice of North America and vacation amid the lore and legends of the Old West.

At daybreak, you'll be aroused by the sound of wranglers gathering the saddle-horse remuda and the smell of breakfast cooking in the lodge. Standing on your porch, you can see the sun coloring the majestic Grand Teton, which rises to the formidable altitude of 13,770 feet—a sight you will not forget.

Getting your day underway involves choosing from a grand array of activities. You can, of course, explore the ranch and the Bridger-Teton National Forest on horseback. The ranch takes great pride in its horse herd, which includes twenty horses adopted from the Bureau of Land Management's wild-horse-adoption program. That's right, you may be paired off with a genuine mustang! (It's okay; they've been tamed for guests and enjoy your company).

You may wish to float the famous cataracts of the Snake River or fish along the meandering banks of the Buffalo River, which cuts through the ranch. A tour of Yellowstone will certainly be on your agenda, if not immediately, then at some time during your stay, so be sure to take a camera.

As the afternoon winds down, you can find a quiet place to read or if you are still feeling energetic, take a ride on a mountain bike or a hike on the numerous trails. And after dinner, you will enjoy the activities and evening entertainment taking place on the ranch.

As a change of pace, you may also choose to take part in an overnight pack trip, spending a night underneath the stars much as ol' Beavertooth surely did many times during his forays into trapping country. The lure of the high country is strong, what with its beautiful wildflowers in spring and early summer and cool summer afternoons perfect for riding and hiking. After a few days in the hills, you may be ready for a good scrub-down, a clean, fresh shirt and jeans, and a trip to Jackson for the weekly rodeo, a favorite of tourists and locals alike. Stop in the many western boutiques for a new pair of riding boots (yours may be scuffy due to all the riding) and a genuine cowboy hat.

It's tough to beat the natural beauty and the charm of the Jackson Hole region of Wyoming, and at the Heart Six, you'll become an instant part of this historic region of "The Cowboy State."

## Heart Six Ranch

P.O. Box 70
16985 Buffalo Valley Road
Moran, WY 83013
Phone: (888) 543–2477; (307) 543–2477
Fax: (307) 543–0918
E-mail: info@heartsix.com
Web site: www.heartsix.com

**Owners/Managers:** Brian and Millie Harris

**Accommodations:** Capacity, 50. Guests stay in modern but rustically fashioned cabins. Cabins vary from 1 to 3 bedrooms. All have electric or gas heat; many have woodstoves as well.

**Meals:** 3 hearty ranch meals served daily. Standard dinner fare includes steak, seafood, chicken, homemade pies and cakes, and a variety of American dishes. BYOB.

**Activities:** Summer activity focuses on horseback riding, hiking, mountain biking, canoeing, and river-float trips. Horseback rides take place in the morning and afternoon, with all-day rides also available. For a true wilderness experience, ask about extended pack trips into the Bridger-Teton National Forest and the Teton Wilderness. Trips vary from 3 to 10 days and offer excellent opportunities for wildlife observation and high-country fly fishing and lake casting. In winter, the Heart Six Ranch offers a wide variety of guided snowmobile tours, ranging from 1 day trips to 2-, 3-, and 5-day custom-package tours. Explore Yellowstone National Park or powder bust along the Continental Divide Trail. Combination packages are available, with 1 or 2 days in Yellowstone and the Continental Divide and a day off from snow machining to experience Jackson and the National Elk Refuge and Wildlife Museum. Winter guests may also enjoy cross-country skiing, snowshoeing, and downhill skiing at the world-renowned Jackson Hole Winter Resort.

**Amenities:** Spacious main lodge with stunning mountain views; laundry services.

**Special Programs:** Supervised children's activities for kids 3 and older. Younger children are their parents' responsibility. Baby-sitting at additional cost, when available.

**Rates:** $$–$$$ Full American Plan. Children 3 to 6, half price; no charge for kids 2 and under.

**Credit Cards:** VISA, MasterCard

**Season:** Year-round

**Getting There:** Nearest airport, Jackson, 35 miles. Ranch is northeast of Jackson on Highway 26. Transportation available from Jackson.

**What's Nearby:** Jackson, with museums, nightlife, restaurants, and shopping; Yellowstone National Park.

# HF BAR RANCH

## Saddlestring, Wyoming

Among the oldest guest ranches in America, the HF Bar Ranch has served generations of "westerning" vacationers. Founded in 1902 by physician Frank O. "Skipper" Horton, the ranch still reflects his philosophy that a vacation should test unused muscles and stimulate the mind.

"A vacation doesn't mean slumping," Horton liked to say. Couch potatoes, take note. A visit to this wonderful historic ranch will present plenty of physical challenges and lots of opportunities to experience new things. Never fired a shotgun? The HF Bar employs certified sporting-clay instructors to teach you gun safety and help you achieve proficiency on any range. Never ridden a horse? The staff of cowboys and cowgirls will pick out a gentle mount, match you to the proper saddle, and help in your progression from gunsel to seasoned hand (expert riders will also be suited to responsive mounts). And if you want to truly "get away from it all," you can partake of an extended stay in Willow Park, where you'll sleep beneath the stars, enjoy meals cooked over an open fire, and enjoy the peaceful serenity of this outstanding high-mountain camp, just like the mountain men of days past.

There is a delightful blend of the old and the new at the HF Bar. Moms and dads can work out with yoga or fitness instructors (including kickboxing and cardio power or strength training), and kids will certainly enjoy plenty of fun times in the heated outdoor pool. You can also take a mountain-bike tour or try the challenge course—a group activity requiring teamwork and the overcoming of physical and mental challenges.

Of course, you can also opt for more traditional guest-ranch activities, including fly fishing (guides available at added cost),

hiking, hayrides, and cookouts. One definite advantage of this sprawling, 9,000-acre working ranch is that it encompasses 15 miles of private fishing water along Rock Creek, ensuring that you'll be casting in lightly taxed waters, where catch-and-release is the order of the day. There's even a fly-fishing shop on-site.

Since you'll probably discover muscles you never knew you had, the ranch provides many soothing options to get you feeling relaxed again. A certified massage therapist is available, as well as a traditional "sweat lodge," where you can take a rejuvenating sauna bath. Afterward, settle in for a movie with the kids (the ranch maintains an extensive video library) or gear up for a wide range of evening entertainment.

Built in the heyday of early guest ranches out West, the HF Bar has a pleasing rustic feel and look that belies its modern appointments. Each cabin is unique and unusual, a reflection of their having been built to meet the growing needs of the facility and of its guests. You'll want to inquire about availability and types of accommodations, as guest houses vary considerably. Chances are, there is one ideal for you, your friends, or family members. You won't find telephones and televisions in the cabins, however: HF Bar is committed to socializing, away from the beckoning of modern communications. (Bring a cell or use the ranch phone if need be.)

With a century of service to guests, the HF Bar draws upon a deep well of experience when it comes to making folks happy. The ambience combines the best of the ranch's traditions while adding nice modern touches to make sure that every guest's needs are met. It's the perfect place for an active and engaging vacation.

## HF Bar Ranch

1301 Rock Creek Road
Saddlestring, WY 82840
Phone: (307) 684–2487
Fax: (307) 684–7144
E-mail: hfbar@wyoming.com
Web site: www.hfbar.com

**Owner/Manager:** Margi Schroth

**Accommodations:** Capacity, 95; 26 individual cabins. Guests are lodged in cottages with a living room, open fireplace, private bath, and outdoor porch. Cabins vary widely in size, from 1 to 7 bedrooms and 1 to 2 bathrooms.

**Meals:** Guest meals are served 3 times daily to the call of a clanging dinner bell. All food is prepared fresh, with home-baked breads and dessert items. Complimentary morning coffee or tea in your cabin as well as the main lodge. Expect hearty, filling fare. Outdoor cookouts feature a huge, river-rock grille. Children's menus and a morning Kiddy Breakfast Bar to satisfy young appetites. Special diets accommodated on request.

**Activities:** Excellent horse program with more than 180 horses, ensuring the correct mount for each rider. Daily rides in the morning and afternoon plus all-day "long rides." Riding lessons available upon request. Guided and unguided fishing (inquire about guided trips with HF Bar's sister company, Rock Creek Anglers). On-site Orvis fishing shop. Remote pack trips to Willow Park, a particularly fine fishing and hiking location (mid-June to early September). Shooting range with expert instruction (additional charge). Hiking, mountain biking, "challenge course," swimming pool, exercise classes and yoga classes, bird hunting.

**Amenities:** Heated pool, exercise and fitness studio, fishing shop, massage therapy, sweat lodge.

**Special Programs:** Children's program includes nature hikes, Frisbee golf, scavenger hunts, overnight camping trips, face painting, visits to the petting zoo, arts and crafts, and more. A children's director coordinates daily activities.

**Rates:** $$–$$$ Full American Plan. Children under 5 free; special nanny rates. In addition to living accommodations and meals, rates include use of a saddle horse and all ranch facilities. The only extra expenses normally incurred are for personal laundry, beverages, purchases in the Ranch Store, sporting-clay shooting, and instruction or fishing services from Rock Creek Anglers. Occasionally, special-event preparation fees may be charged.

**Credit Cards:** No credit cards accepted. Cash, traveler's checks, or personal checks only.

**Season:** Mid-June to mid-September

**Getting There:** Located 35 miles south of Sheridan.

**What's Nearby:** Sheridan, King's Saddlery Western Museum.

# HIGH ISLAND RANCH AND CATTLE CO.

## Hamilton Dome, Wyoming

Anyone who saw the film *City Slickers* has probably dreamed of mounting up and riding herd on cattle through the wild, lonesome country of Wyoming. Well, here's your chance to fulfill that dream.

The High Island is a genuine working cattle ranch that sprawls over 130,000 acres of central Wyoming. The country here varies from 4,000 to 9,000 feet, offering every type of weather condition one can imagine. Seasonal cattle drives through these high-desert plains and on up into the Rockies (or back again, as the season dictates) give hardy hands the chance to experience life on the range, circa 1880. Spend a week enjoying the largely unchanged countryside on horseback, trailing cattle 40 miles. Just don't anger the trail boss, or you may be riding drag and choking on dust! Hungry trail herders will gather around an authentic chuckwagon to feast on genuine western trail meals and enjoy the cowboys sharing stories around the evening campfire.

If that's a little too "cowboy" for you, you can also opt to stay at the ranch headquarters, where riding, fishing, and exploration are the order of the day. Sign on as a hand, and you can take part in the daily work of a real cattle ranch: mending fences, carrying salt blocks up into high-mountain pastures for the grazing cattle, branding calves, and doctoring cows. (Of course, as a paying guest, you'll be allowed to sneak off and enjoy more recreational pursuits if that's your desire.)

Guests who like horses will be pleased to learn that there are no set riding hours at High Island. You'll feel like the ranch owner, free to ride and explore to your heart's content. The trail boss will be happy to assign you a mount, based on your riding experience and your fitness level. Ride a lot or ride just a little; it's entirely up to you. And when you feel it's time to rest, you can kick back your boots in the rustic common room at Rock Creek camp, located at an altitude of 9,000 feet (be sure to bring plenty of warm clothes, as the temperature drops fast in the evening). At day's end, you can choose to sleep under the stars, in a tent, or in the comfort of the high-camps' cabins. Come morning, you'll be fresh and ready for a fishing excursion on Rock Creek, which abounds with mountain trout. Rock Creek Lodge features propane heat, a dining area, guest rooms, canvas wall tents, tepees, and a private cabin.

Guests also can avail themselves of ranch home life at the Main Lodge on Cotton Creek. Here, guests stay in a comfortable lodge with eight private rooms heated with log woodstoves.

Although many guest ranches profess to offer the cowboy experience, you'll look far and wide to find a place that offers the real deal. If you want to ride for long hours, trail cattle herds into the high country, enjoy authentic chuckwagon meals, and bed down under the stars with the sound of coyotes calling in the distance, this is the ideal place to do so. High Island is the real deal.

## High Island Ranch and Cattle Co.

346 Amoretti, Suite 10
Thermopolis, WY 82443
Phone: (307) 867–2374 (summer); (307) 864–5389 (winter)
E-mail: info@highislandranch.com
Web site: www.highislandranch.com

**Owners/Managers:** Frank and Karen Robbins

**Accommodations:** Capacity, 25. The lodge at Cotton Creek features 12 guest rooms, a common room, dining room, and gift shop, as well as canvas wall tents, private log cabins. Guests share men's and women's shower rooms. The high lodge on Rock Creek has 8 private rooms, canvas wall tents, and 2 tepees. Men's and women's shower houses and outhouses. Guests must provide their own sleeping bags and bathroom necessities.

**Meals:** Trail herders on seasonal cattle drives dine al fresco at the authentic chuckwagon, which is pulled from camp to camp by a team of draft horses. Enjoy Dutch-oven meals, fresh-baked goods, fresh fruits and vegetables, and genuine cowboy coffee. At the 2 lodges, standard western meals are served. Guests are asked to refrain from smoking and alcohol.

**Activities:** Most of the ranch activities focus on the real work of a cattle ranch; season activities include trail herding (approximately 3 days on the trail), roundups, calving, doctoring cattle, mending fences, branding, and more. There are no set schedules except during the cattle drives; guests may ride and participate in activities as their desires dictate. To get the most of the vacation, however, you'll want to spend a considerable time in the saddle alongside the "hired hands." This is an excellent opportunity for adults and mature children who want to experience western life as it was more than a century ago.

**Amenities:** 2 separate lodges, the Main Lodge and the Rock Creek Camp, serve as the base areas for guest activities. Trail herders spend the week in moving camps, trailing cattle over 45 miles of terrain. Be prepared for difficult environmental conditions and long days in the saddle!

**Special Programs:** Annual branding week, in which guests take part in marking and doctoring cattle; special family-riding weeks; cattle-herding weeks. Children 16 and older may take part in cattle drives; children under 12 are welcome to take part in cattle-roundup weeks. Families with younger children should inquire about special family weeks designed to accommodate the young folk.

**Rates:** $$$ Full American Plan.

**Credit Cards:** VISA, MasterCard

**Season:** Late May to September. Inquire for specific dates for roundup, cattle drives, and family weeks.

**Getting There:** The ranch is located 75 miles south of Cody, Wyoming. Inquire for specific directions.

**What's Nearby:** The Washakie Needles, an intriguing geologic formation; Legend Rock Petroglyphs; Buffalo Bill Museum and weekly rodeos in Cody, Wyoming, approximately 35 miles.

# LAZY L & B RANCH

## Dubois, Wyoming

It would be nearly impossible to find more interesting and varied riding terrain than what's available at the Lazy L & B Ranch. The property is surrounded by three distinct mountain ranges—the Absaroka, Wind River, and Owl Creek Mountains—and is bordered by the 50,000-acre National Elk Refuge, national forest, and the Wind River Indian Reservation. Guests explore everything from lush river bottoms to the sparse plateaus and "Badlands" formations of the Indian Reservation to forested mountain trails leading to wide-open, high-alpine meadows and breathtaking mountain vistas.

A rider's paradise? Indeed. But there's more to the Lazy L & B than just exceptional scenery. This is a family-run outfit, where hospitality is the word of the day. Owners Bob and Lee Naylon have more than a quarter century of experience in the western-hospitality field, and the couple takes a very hands-on approach to guest ranching. Whether you come with family, friends, or by yourself, you'll fit in comfortably and be "gathered up" by the Naylons and their staff.

Like most traditional guest ranches, the emphasis here is on riding, fishing, and hiking. The ranch accommodates fishermen with several stocked ponds and access to numerous rivers, namely the East Fork, Wiggins Fork, Bear Creek, and Wind River. You can also take an icy-cold dip in the river after a hot day on the trail; if you prefer a little warmer waters, try the solar-heated pool or luxuriate in the Jacuzzi, not far from the river's banks.

Children aren't left out of the action here. There's a supervised kid's riding program for those over age four that includes equestrian safety and basic riding instruction. Kids also participate in a wide variety of recreational games and arts and crafts, and they can help feed the horses or visit with the farmyard animals. On several evenings during the week, the children join the ranch wranglers at the cookouts or at the dining table, giving parents a little "quiet time" alone.

The main lodge has an inviting fireplace where guests can relax and enjoy a good book from the library or meet for parlor games or formal entertainment such as cowboy-poetry performances or cowboy singing.

Visitors looking for a wilderness adventure may wish to inquire about the Bear Basin Wilderness Camp, the center of the ranch's pack-trip program. From this base camp high in the Washakie Wilderness, guests are able to explore timbered canyons and high-mountain passes (as high as 11,000 feet in elevation). Camps are limited to eight guests, so the feeling is intimate.

You'll sleep in large and comfortable tents outfitted with wood-burning stoves, cots, and sleeping pads. But if you wish, you can always sleep under the stars, like the mountain men of old. Guests can book these wilderness trips as an inclusive vacation or add the trips onto their stay at the main ranch. In addition, there are special fall big-game hunting trips and fishing camps. Ask about bow hunting, as the ranch takes great pride in its guides' abilities at calling in the elk.

This is a small, friendly place that offers one of the finest horse programs in the guest-ranch business. If you are looking forward to plenty of riding with excellent mounts and very capable guides who share your passion for seeing varied and compelling wilderness areas, this could be for you.

## Lazy L & B Ranch

1072 East Fork Road
Dubois, WY 82513
Phone: (800) 453–9488; (307) 455–2839
Fax: (307) 455–2849
E-mail: lazylb@aol.com
Web site: www.lazylb.com

**Owners/Managers:** Bob and Lee Naylon

**Accommodations:** Capacity, 35. Guests are housed in individual cabins tucked amid cottonwood trees along the banks of a river. Cabins are furnished in traditional western decor and include refrigerators, private bath or shower, electric heat, and porches, some with mountain views.

**Meals:** Western ranch-style meals featuring homemade breads and desserts, buffet breakfasts, tailgate lunches, sit-down dinners, and outdoor barbecues.

**Activities:** The Lazy L & B features an excellent riding program emphasizing small, guided groups. Guests are paired with horses for the week, and if you get along, you'll form a bond with your personal mount; if not, you can always switch. There are fast horses for riders who like to go fast, slow horses for those who like to go slow, and, as Bob likes to say, "For those who don't like to ride, we have horses that don't like to be ridden." Fishing, recre-ational games, mountain biking, swimming in the river or in a heated pool, hiking, and rifle shooting. Evening entertainment featuring western performers, hayrides for children, barbecues, and trips to Dubois for evening dances.

**Amenities:** Pool, Jacuzzi, library in main lodge, shooting range, remote wilderness camp.

**Special Programs:** Children's program features riding lessons, games, arts and crafts, special dining sessions with ranch wranglers, hayrides, petting zoo, and a special barbecue. Inquire about Bear Basin Wilderness Camp pack-trip vacations and seasonal hunting trips.

**Rates:** $$$ Full American Plan. Special children's rates. Nannies stay free when caring for 2 or more young children.

**Credit Cards:** VISA. Personal checks preferred.

**Season:** Late May–August

**Getting There:** Nearest airport, Jackson (approximately 70 miles). Driving directions available. Shuttle service, $100 per vehicle, each way.

**What's Nearby:** Dubois, Grand Teton and Yellowstone National Parks.

# LOST CREEK RANCH & SPA

## Moose, Wyoming

An upscale resort ranch for the discerning traveler: This about sums up Lost Creek, a small but opulent facility, located a mere stone's throw from historic Jackson, and the gateway to Yellowstone National Park. This Mobil Guide four-star facility has received rave reviews from numerous sources, including several major travel and dining magazines.

This popular luxury resort and spa books months, even years, in advance, so you'll have to plan well ahead if you hope to visit. But for those of you who manage to book a trip, the rewards are great. The ranch offers a cornucopia of activities, ranging from the normal guest ranch staples—horseback riding, hiking, and park tours—to the types of things found only in the world's finest spas: massages, sea-salt body scrubs, facials, yoga classes, and strength training.

The Spa at Lost Creek includes a heated swimming pool, an oversized hot tub, tennis courts, and a wide variety of spa treatments. In addition to the aforementioned services, guests can order from a spa menu that includes seaweed and mineral wraps, mud masks, salicyl baths, manicures and pedicures, aerobics classes, aromatherapy, weight-room workouts, and personal consultations with fitness trainers. (Spa treatments are billed separately from the general charges.)

The ranch lodge is sumptuous and luxurious, with lovely custom furniture, tasteful furnishings, and original artwork. The oversized, lovely guest cabins are fully appointed with modern conveniences befitting a luxury hotel. Double-room cabins include living rooms and gas fireplaces, and all cabins include refrigerators, coffee service, one or two full baths, a porch, daily maid service, and personal laundry service.

Meals are prepared to an extremely high standard. All meals are prepared from fresh, seasonal ingredients. Two delicious entrees are served with the evening meal, and

## VISITING JACKSON HOLE

On the arts front, the small town of Jackson has more than thirty galleries that display a vast array of artistry, from traditional western works to contemporary pieces. Photography and painting are among the most prevalent art forms, but sculpting, particularly bronze work, is also commonly seen in Jackson's many galleries.

The National Museum of Wildlife Art, founded in 1987, is home to the nation's premier public collection of fine art devoted to wildlife. Its vantage point on a butte overlooking the National Wildlife Refuge provides incredible views of the mountain known as Sleeping Indian, as well as wildlife in both winter and summer.

Each summer the Grand Teton Music Festival presents an eight-week season of orchestral and chamber music performed by the resident company of 200 professional musicians from many of the nation's finest orchestras. Special winter concerts are also scheduled. Concerts are held in the 740-seat Walk Festival Hall, which is acclaimed for its intimacy and superb acoustics. Walk Festival Hall is located in Teton Village, just 12 miles northwest of the town of Jackson.

note that wine service is also available.

As one might expect of such a top-drawer facility, Lost Creek welcomes an international clientele. The young staff members often come from foreign countries as well, helping to bridge any language gaps that may exist. In many ways, the cultural exchange is a big part of what makes Lost Creek an interesting destination. You'll convene your own United Nations at each evening's dining table!

## Lost Creek Ranch & Spa

P.O. Box 95
Moose, WY 83012
Phone: (307) 733–3435
Fax: (307) 733–1954
E-mail: ranch@lostcreek.com
Web site: www.lostcreek.com

**Managers:** Mike and Bev Halpin

**Accommodations:** Capacity, 50. 10 luxurious cabins; 1-bedroom or 2-bedroom/2-bath cabins with refrigerators, coffeemakers, gas heat. Larger cabins have living rooms, kitchenettes, and gas fireplaces. Nightly turndown service, twice-daily maid service, courtesy laundry service.

**Meals:** Expect gourmet preparation of all meals, fresh seasonal ingredients, fresh-baked goods, accommodation of special diets. Wine list, beer service. Separate children's seating, if desired.

**Activities:** Riding program with excellent instructors personalized to individual needs. Rides divided by riding ability and further divided into small groups of 8 or fewer. Other activities include guided or unguided hiking, swimming, tennis, float trips on the Snake River, shooting sports, Yellowstone Park and Grand Teton National Park. Nearby golf and guided fly-fishing trips.

**Amenities:** Full-service spa including facial treatments, manicures and pedicures, body treatments, fitness center, exercise classes, and more. Spa activities not covered in guest lodging price.

**Special Programs:** Supervised daily children's program for kids 6 to 13. Recreation room, activities, daily horseback riding, cookouts.

**Rates:** $$$$$ Modified American Plan. All meals and ranch activities, except spa activities, are included in the price. 1-week minimum. Off-season and group rates. Children under 5 are free.

**Credit Cards:** American Express. Personal checks accepted.

**Season:** Late-May–mid-October

**Getting There:** Courtesy pickup from Jackson Hole Airport. Rental car suggested for sightseeing trips.

**What's Nearby:** Yellowstone National Park, Grand Teton National Park, National Elk Refuge, town of Jackson.

# MOOSE HEAD RANCH

## Moose, Wyoming

With its spectacular view of the Tetons, Moose Head Ranch is a postcard-perfect place to "get away from it all." Even more so when one considers that the Moosehead is a privately owned property uniquely situated in the middle of Grand Teton National Park, which gives ranch visitors an unprecedented opportunity to explore the popular park and yet have a peaceful and secluded retreat from which to enjoy the adventure.

Said one many-time visitor, "The owners are always there and know everything there is to do in Wyoming, and it's a pleasant place to just read and watch the scenery . . . the cabins are rustic, but we love them; that's Wyoming to us."

Moose Head Ranch, which was homesteaded in 1923, passed into the hands of the Mettler Family in the late 1960s. At present, the ranch is run under the capable guidance of Louse Mettler-Davenport and her husband, Kit Davenport. Louise enjoys a hands-on approach with guests, visiting with them when they arrive to help plan out a fun-filled and exciting week's adventure.

There are a number of activities that you won't want to miss. Trips to Yellowstone, of course, are de rigueur, but Louise can also suggest various hot spots for visiting in nearby Jackson, scenic routes winding up into the Tetons, and a trip to the famous Elk grounds, where Boy Scouts in the Jackson area fund their entire year's program with the annual collection of elk horns shed by the resident herds.

Moose Head is a fine place for family vacations, as the approach taken here is very family oriented. Children and their parents spend most of their time together, riding or fishing or taking hikes. Riders looking for fast gallops through open meadows might want to look elsewhere, as the pace of riding here tends to be slow, unless everyone in the family is an accomplished horse rider. Even then, the emphasis is on nature appreciation and contemplation, not on mad, exciting dashes.

There is no specific children's program or separate mealtimes for kids. If you are like most busy modern families, you'll probably welcome the ample amount of shared time you'll get to spend with your kids.

Kit is an avid fisherman and is a patient and willing instructor. You'll be able to participate in fly fishing on the ranch, which has ponds stocked with fat, healthy trout, thanks to the ranch's catch-and-release philosophy. You may not take home a trophy fish, but you can take home the photos to prove your own particular "fish tale."

Nearby, you will find exceptional golf courses, tennis facilities, and white-water rafting. The Davenports and their capable staff can help you plan any number of adventures or cultural events. One you won't want to skip is the weekly rodeo held in Jackson, featuring area cowboys and even wranglers from many of the guest ranches throughout the region. Afterward, stop in at the Million Dollar Cowboy Bar, just off the main park in Jackson, and peer at the hundreds of silver dollars that were set into the unique bar. Get there early, and you may even get to sit in a genuine cowboy saddle. Right next door, you'll also find one of the best hamburger shops in Wyoming—and perhaps even the entire West!

## Moose Head Ranch

P.O. Box 214
Moose, WY 83012
Winter address:
3100 Welaunee Road
Tallahassee, FL 32308
Phone: (307) 733–3141 (summer); (850)
877–1431 (winter)
Fax: (307) 739–9097
Web site: www.wyomingdra.com/moosehead

**Owners/Managers:** Louise and Kit Davenport

**Accommodations:** Capacity, 40. Guests stay in 14 modern log cabins nestled among pine and cottonwood trees. The cabins lack room phones or TVs but are hardly Spartan. You will enjoy private baths, electric heat and in-cabin coffeemakers and refrigerators; you can also relax on your own porch.

**Meals:** 3 meals served daily. Breakfasts cooked to your order, picnic lunches and buffet lunch service, and gourmet evening meals featuring 2 daily entrees. BYOB.

**Activities:** Twice-daily horseback rides and all-day rides on weekdays. Hiking, fishing in the Snake River and in stocked ponds (equipment and flies available); tennis, golf, and river rafting off-site. Outdoor recreational games and parlor games available.

**Amenities:** Library, airport shuttle, in-room refrigerators and coffeemakers; beautiful grand lodge, with a huge porch resplendent in overflowing flower boxes and lounge furniture for relaxing.

**Special Programs:** No formal children's program, although children of any age are welcome.

**Rates:** $$$–$$$$ Full American Plan. Minimum 5-night stay. Special rates for children under age 6.

**Credit Cards:** No credit cards. Traveler's checks and personal checks or cash only.

**Season:** Mid-June to late August

**Getting There:** Nearest airport, Jackson (26 miles). Airport shuttle to ranch available.

**What's Nearby:** Jackson Hole Valley, National Elk Refuge, Yellowstone National Park.

# PARADISE GUEST RANCH

## Buffalo, Wyoming

You set up high expectations when you name a place Paradise, but in this case, this Wyoming guest ranch meets them.

The name wasn't simply chosen, but rather given to the ranch by visiting friends of founder Dr. Gordon Meldrum, whose father had homesteaded the ranch at the foothills of the Bighorn Mountains. Dr. Meldrum often invited friends to join him on the ranch, where riding and seasonal hunting were the order of the day. Many friends remarked that the beautiful mountain meadow where the original homestead was situated was "a paradise on earth." And, naturally, the name stuck.

Meldrum and his wife, Mabel Lee, formally opened the ranch to guests around 1905, with the property passing into Mabel's capable hands in 1911 upon the doctor's passing. She operated the ranch capably and successfully until 1927, when it was sold to the nearby Horton's HF Bar (also featured in this book).

Eventually, it was sold to a colorful cowboy character named "Wyoming" Jack O'Brien. O'Brien became well known in these parts as a cowboy entertainer among the dude ranches, and he eventually went on to make recordings and perform on radio shows. He saved enough salary to buy the ranch, then passed it off to an industrious woman, who followed in Mabel Lee Meldrum's pioneering spirit. Finally, the ranch was purchased in 1981 by Apache Oil, which went to great pains to restore the property to the pristine condition it now enjoys.

This is an informal ranch, with a whole host of traditional guest-ranch activities and features. Nestled in the heart of the Big Horn National Forest, the ranch provides an ideal place for riding, hiking, and fishing. A large swimming pool with comfy lounge furniture is a great respite from the dusty trail, one that might have been welcomed by Butch Cassidy and the Sundance Kid, who holed up not far from here (one of the finales of any visit is a hike into the red-rock canyons to explore their one-time hideaway).

This is an exceptional place for naturalists. Spring brings carpets of wildflowers, woodland birds, and a huge variety of wildlife, including elk, deer, coyotes, badger, beaver, fox, antelope, and birds of prey. Naturalist guides will help you find and identify the flora and fauna.

A rec hall is perfect for prone-to-be-bored kids, and dad or mom can shoot billiards or play Ping-Pong or board games. Need a cowboy hat? The original homestead now serves as a general store, where guests can pick up a few cowboy mementos. Active recreationists will find many outdoor games in which to compete. And the recently added fly shop is the place to fill holes in your tackle box.

Individuals looking for true outdoor adventure can sign up for backcountry pack trips into the Cloud Peak Wilderness. The Frying Pan Lake Camp is a 12-mile ride from the ranch, and the lake there provides a great place for fishing. (An enormous trout-rearing pond, fed by spectacular Rock Creek, assures that even the rank amateur won't get skunked.)

Incidentally, Paradise offers some intriguing special programs, including adults-only weeks and special women's-riding weeks that cater to individuals with out-of-the-mainstream vacations. Singles, couples, and adventurous women will find themselves as welcome as families at the Paradise Guest Ranch.

## Paradise Guest Ranch

P.O. Box 790
Buffalo, WY 82834
Phone: (307) 684–7876
Fax: (307) 684–9054
E-mail: fun@paradiseranch.com
Web site: www.paradiseranch.com

**Owners/Managers:** Jim and Leah Anderson

**Accommodations:** Capacity, 70. Guests stay in 18 luxurious 1-, 2- and 3-bedroom cabins equipped with fireplaces, kitchenettes, washers and dryers, and outdoor porches with meadow views.

**Meals:** Meals are served in the main dining hall, convenient to the lodging cabins. 3 meals served family style each day plus covered chuckwagon meals outdoors, cookouts, and "gourmet night." French Creek Saloon serves up cocktails, wine, and beers and also serves as a gathering point for talent shows, square dancing, and general socializing.

**Activities:** Horseback riding features small groups (8 or fewer) with capable riding instructors/guides. Numerous rides of varying length go out throughout the day, allowing you to ride briefly or at length. Families can ride as a group, or children can ride separately. Special lunch-on-the trail ride is a favorite. Some cattle-work and team-penning events held for guests. Swimming in a large, heated outdoor pool. Outdoor recreational games include volleyball, badminton, and horseshoes. Indoor rec room with billiards, Ping-Pong, and board games. Hiking and fly fishing are popular pastimes. Inquire about backcountry pack trips to Frying Pan Lake Camp.

**Amenities:** Heated pool, gift shop, fly-fishing shop, indoor Jacuzzi, deluxe rooms with many amenities not typical at most guest ranches.

**Special Programs:** Great children's program for kids of all ages. Special teen socials and overnight camping trips. Women's weeks feature extensive riding programs, ranch-cooking classes, wine-tasting parties, fishing, and more just for the gals. Backcountry pack trips also available.

**Rates:** $$–$$$ American Plan. Reduced rates for kids 12 and under; kids 2 and under stay free. Reduced off-season rates, discounted family week, special ladies' dates. Off-peak rates will save you considerable money.

**Credit Cards:** None. Personal checks, please.

**Season:** Late May–October

**Getting There:** Nearest airport in Sheridan, 45 miles north. Ranch is 16 miles west of Buffalo. Commuter flights from Denver to Sheridan. Transportation available from the Sheridan airport.

**What's Nearby:** Sheridan, a very western town with restaurants and shopping, museums, and rodeo events.

# THE RED ROCK RANCH

## Kelly, Wyoming

The Red Rock is a small, family-oriented ranch situated in a secluded valley of the spectacular Jackson Hole Valley. At the end of a long, winding road that follows the sinuous contours of the Gros Ventre River, the ranch is set back in a pleasant open meadow of the Gros Ventre Mountains, surrounded on all sides by the Bridger-Teton National Forest.

With a capacity of only twenty-five guests, the Red Rock Ranch gives one the feeling of participating in an intimate family retreat. Guests stay in quaint, clean, and comfortable cabins outfitted with traditional woodstoves. A large log-cabin style lodge is an inviting place to socialize or to simply relax, and great home-style meals are also served here.

Activities at the Red Rock are traditional. The horse program is at the center of most daily action, but guests may also take time out to fish and swim. A beautiful outdoor pool offers an inviting temptation to simply "take a day off" and read the newest hot summer novel. In the evening, barbecue meals along the banks of the river offer a pleasant diversion, and guests regularly join in sing-alongs of old western standards sung by a guitar-strumming cowboy entertainer. After supper, kids and adults alike can enjoy the recreation room, which features an antique Brunswick pool table built in 1892.

A traditional cattle ranch that was homesteaded in the 1890s, Red Rock Ranch is named for the colorful red cliffs and rock formations characteristic of this area. Since 1972, the ranch has been owned and operated by the MacKenzie family, who enjoy sharing their western life with the guests.

Although Red Rock is a family-friendly resort most of the season, the MacKenzies set aside certain weeks just for adults. If you are a couple without kids or simply need a break from the children, you may wish to explore that option.

A tidy ranch layout gives the ranch a pleasant and clean appearance and facilitates activities. The cabins are neat little log units with new rooms, sitting porches, a sitting room, refrigerator, and hitchin' racks. The names for each cabin are taken from Indian tribes, and the furnishings have an old-timey Western style.

Overflowing flower boxes give a nice, cheerful ambience to these very private lodgings. The cabins are arranged in a horseshoe configuration that surrounds the main lodge, where most of the after-hours activity takes place. It's a short walk to the pool area, which is the place to be after a hot day on the trail. Guests wanting to soak their saddle-sore bodies can take a dip in the eight-person hot tub, then follow that up with a refreshing cool-off in the pool.

Of course, the ranch's proximity to Jackson is the main reason guests come here. Day trips to the Yellowstone and to Jackson are de rigueur for first-time visitors, but seasoned returning guests often find that they'd rather spend every moment of their vacation on the ranch. It's such a peaceful and lovely place that this sentiment is an easy one to understand.

## The Red Rock Ranch

P.O. Box 38
Kelly, WY 83011
Phone: (307) 733–6288
Fax: (307) 733–6287
E-mail: redrockranch@onewest com
Web site: www.theredrockranch.com

**Owners/Managers:** The MacKenzie Family

**Accommodations:** Capacity, 25. Guests stay in individual log cabins named for North American Indian tribes. Cabins have 1 or 2 bedrooms, sitting room, porch, electric heat, a woodstove, and twin- and queen- or king-sized beds. A few have sofa sleepers for extra children. Daily maid service.

**Meals:** 3 daily meals, all carefully prepared by the ranch chefs. Separate children's dinner seating. Breakfast cookouts and end-of-week evening barbecue.

**Activities:** The horse program includes half-day and full-day rides through the scenic country that surrounds the ranch. On the day of arrival, guests are schooled in horse safety and handling before heading out on the trail. Weekly kids' gymkhana (games on horseback) in the arena. Fishing in area streams and local guided fishing, by arrangement. Outdoor recreational games, evening dances in the dance hall. Float trips on the Snake River may be arranged.

**Amenities:** Outdoor pool with large hot tub.

**Special Programs:** Children can be watched while parents ride and during the adult dinner hour. Youth wranglers will guide children on horseback rides and will oversee children during a midweek campout. Nannies are encouraged for guests with small children.

**Rates:** $$$ Full American Plan. Reduced rates for children under 12; children under 2 are free.

**Credit Cards:** None. Cash, traveler's checks, or personal checks only.

**Season:** June through September

**Getting There:** Nearest airport, Jackson Hole, approximately 30 miles. Airport pickup available at additional charge.

**What's Nearby:** Yellowstone National Park, Grand Teton National Park, Jackson.

# RIMROCK DUDE RANCH

## Cody, Wyoming

Since 1956, the family-owned-and-operated Rimrock Dude Ranch has provided a traditional guest-ranch experience to small groups of guests. Many return season after season, drawn by the ranch's scenic beauty and the friendly service of owners Gary and DeDe Fales. Among its guests have been American ski racer and Olympic champ Tommy Moe and President George Bush!

Of course, you don't have to be a celebrity to visit the Rimrock. In fact, the very reasonable, all-inclusive rates make this ranch a very good choice for families that have to stretch every vacation dollar.

With a rather small guest capacity (thirty), the daily program follows a fairly predictable yet accommodating schedule. Guests arrive on Sunday, easing into the "vacation mode" and meeting the ranch staff during the evening picnic dinner. On Monday, wranglers work with guests to find just the right horse for each person's skills and temperament, and saddles are fitted. An afternoon ride follows lunch, and the evening kicks off with cowboy entertainment around the campfire. Each day follows this sort of prescribed routine.

Highlights of the week include a trip to the Cody Nite Rodeo, a white-water rafting trip, and an all-day ride to Table Mountain (some guests opt for a less taxing half-day ride). On Friday, everyone heads to Yellowstone National Park to tour Yellowstone Lake and the Geyser Basins, to view the abundant wildlife, and, of course, to witness the eruption of Old Faithful Geyser. (Guests who've already toured the park may decide to visit nearby Cody or simply spend the day horseback riding.)

The week closes with a ranch rodeo with plenty of games on horseback, along with a sumptuous prime-rib dinner. Guests get a chance to entertain the staff during the concluding talent show.

The ranch is neat, quiet, and lovely, with authentic chinked log-cabin architecture and naturalistic landscaping that is very congruous with the native environment. The ranch swimming pool is a welcome amenity for parents with children. Individuals who like fishing can work the private pond—no license required. Serious anglers may hire a local guide and fish some of the fine trout waters for which northwest Wyoming is famous. The ranch's prime location in the Absaroka Mountains puts it midway between Cody, a frontier town founded by Buffalo Bill Cody, and the east entrance to Yellowstone National Park. You'll be afforded ample opportunity to visit both of these fascinating tourist destinations.

Guests wanting to travel off the beaten path should inquire about wilderness pack trips, a specialty of the Rimrock. A limited number of these special pack trips are scheduled each season. One takes guests from Cody to Jackson, Wyoming, along the scenic Shoshone River. After crossing over Crescent Pass, riders descend into Bridger-Teton National Forest to the headwaters of the Snake River. The eight-day trip ends 55 miles northeast of Jackson, and guests often stay in town to enjoy its many diversions before flying home.

The second pack adventure picks up where the first left off, crossing through Yellowstone country. There are plenty of opportunities for fishing on this adventure, which includes a stop at Two Oceans Pass, whose waters flow to the Pacific and Atlantic Oceans. You'll even see where a small stream strikes a rock and splits into two separate streams named, appropriately, Pacific Creek and Atlantic Creek.

**Rimrock Dude Ranch**
2728 Northfork Route
Cody, WY 82414
Phone: (307) 587–3970
Fax: (307) 527–5014
E-mail: fun@rimrockranch.com
Web site: www.rimrockranch.com

**Owners/Managers:** Gary and DeDe Fales

**Accommodations:** Capacity, 30. 9 log cabins from small (suitable for a couple) to large, ideal for big families. Cabins include private baths and daily maid service and are located along both sides of Canyon Creek, a small stream bisecting the property.

**Meals:** All meals served family style in the ranch dining room, except for frequent barbecues served throughout the week. Basic, hearty American dishes and typical ranch fare.

**Activities:** A fairly structured week, but with numerous options, will satisfy almost any visitor. Horseback riding, trailside cookouts, barbecues, trips to Cody Nite Rodeo, softball games, Yellowstone Park or Cody, Wyoming trip, fishing, river rafting, swimming, hiking, ranch rodeo event.

**Amenities:** Swimming pool, ranch shuttle service, kids' rec room.

**Special Programs:** Children's program while parents are riding and during dinner, if desired; children's horseback instruction and trail rides, children's gymkhana (games on horseback).

**Rates:** $$$ Full American Plan. Reduced rates for children, varying by age. Prices do not include taxes, gratuity, and park use fees.

**Credit Cards:** VISA, MasterCard. Personal checks.

**Season:** June through September

**Getting There:** Located midway between Cody, Wyoming, and the east entrance to Yellowstone National Park. Most guests fly into Cody. Ranch shuttle from airport available.

**What's Nearby:** Cody, founded by Buffalo Bill Cody, site of the Buffalo Bill Cody Historical Center; Cody Nite Rodeo. Also, Yellowstone National Park.

# R LAZY S RANCH

## Jackson Hole, Wyoming

A prime location virtually on the skirts of the Teton Mountains, just a stone's throw from internationally famous Jackson Hole Winter Resort, would be enough to attract many to the R Lazy S. But when you couple superlative location with a top-drawer staff (there are roughly two guests to every one staff member) and throw in a broad and flexible menu of activities, you have the recipe for an exceptional guest-ranch experience.

The 325-acre ranch abuts the south boundary of Grand Teton National Park, with the scenic Snake River to the east and the soaring Tetons to the west. During trail rides and hikes, you'll trek through pine and fir forests that give way to subalpine meadows lush with wild grasses and native wildflowers, finally arriving at craggy alpine basins. Once there, you may see whistling marmots greeting the rare visitor, and if you peer closely into the crystal-clear lakes, you might spy trout on the prowl for insects.

Sound too good to be true? Read on. Back at the ranch, the facilities are first-rate without being pretentious or stuffy. The guest cabins are individually distinctive, offering a variety of floor plans to accommodate families or groups of different sizes. All have full baths and are heated, and a few have sitting rooms or a living room with fireplace. After a quick washup following a day of activities, guests relax in the main lodge, where most meals are served. The lodge looks out over the Jackson Hole Valley, often described as one of the most scenic areas of the West. Be careful sitting by the huge stone fireplace in a big comfy chair—you might just nod off to sleep and miss the night's exceptional dinner!

We're quite keen on the mix of activities at the R Lazy S. The traditional guest-ranch activities are all there, but there are a few added extras that are equally inviting. Once a week, for instance, guests are invited to try waterskiing at a nearby lake (for persons not familiar with the West, waterskiing is something rare in these parched parts). You can also try your hand at rock climbing, a natural in these parts. There are two nearby championship golf courses ideal for duffers—golf balls are known to fly noticeably farther in the thin mountain air.

Of course, the town of Jackson offers numerous possibilities, from cultural events to county fairs to the popular weekly rodeo contest. You can also visit a myriad of western art galleries (there are close to thirty in this rather small town), and no visit would be complete without a stopover to see the Silver Dollar Bar at the historic Wort Hotel.

Although the ranch is generally family oriented, in fall during the height of fly-fishing season, the ranch becomes the providence of adults-only. Guests looking for a more mature experience and who have an interest in improving their fishing skills will want to inquire about the fall adults-only season.

Given its proximity to Yellowstone National Park, the Jackson area is the epicenter of the guest-ranch industry in North America. Given its long-standing tradition of serving guests, the R Lazy S stands as one of the finest of the area's many guest-ranch destinations. A long list of repeat customers is testament to the quality and attention to detail that characterize this fine establishment.

**R Lazy S Ranch**
P.O. Box 308
Teton Village, WY 83025
Phone: (307) 733–2655
Fax: (307) 734–1120
E-mail: info@rlazys.com
Web site: www.rlazys.com

**Owners/Managers:** Howard and Cara Stirn

**Accommodations:** Capacity, 45. Guests stay in 14 log cabins featuring 1, 2, or 3 bedrooms, some with sitting rooms or living rooms and fireplaces. All have 1 or 2 bathrooms. Teen dorm with bathroom accommodates 4, either boys or girls.

**Meals:** 3 meals served daily plus outdoor barbecue cookouts and trailside lunches. Western-style home cooking, served buffet style or family style. Separate seating for children and teens. BYOB.

**Activities:** Horseback program with arena instruction for riders of all abilities. More than 80 horses allow wranglers to custom-fit their guests. Pack trips available. Other activities include fly fishing with instructors or guided fly fishing (extra). Numerous rivers, lakes, and streams, on-site and off-site, from which to choose. Weekly fishing clinic for anglers. Float trips on the Snake River, off-site golf and tennis. Waterskiing weekly on Jackson Lake. Swimming hole and inner-tubing in nearby river. Warm-spring pools in the Jackson Hole Valley. Evening activities include talent shows, slide shows, dances, hayrides, recreational games such as softball and volleyball. Excursions to Jackson and the Yellowstone National Park (private car or rental encouraged).

**Amenities:** Superb lodge with valley and mountain views, a massive fireplace and a rec room. Teen "bunkhouse." Outdoor recreational games area; on-site laundry facilities.

**Special Programs:** Children 7 and older. Children's riding program in which kids ride separately from parents, if desired. Separate children's dining. Inquire about pack trips.

**Rates:** $$–$$$ Full American Plan. Minimum 1-week stay. Inquire about pack-trip rates and guided fishing trips.

**Credit Cards:** None. Personal checks preferred.

**Season:** Mid-June through September

**Getting There:** Located 1 mile from Teton Village, approximately 12 miles west of Jackson, Wyoming. Nearest airport: Jackson.

**What's Nearby:** Teton Village, Jackson; Yellowstone National Park.

# SAVERY CREEK THOROUGHBRED RANCH

## Savery, Wyoming

In this book, we've included a number of unique guest ranches that provide something a little bit out of the ordinary. Savery Creek Thoroughbred Ranch is one of those properties. Savery Creek is ideally suited to advanced-intermediate and expert riders who want to spend a large part of their vacation riding exceptional mounts and who really desire to advance their riding skills.

The ranch is owned and operated by Joyce Saer, an expert horse trainer who spent much of her early career training racehorses in Spain. She continues to be active in fox hunts, traveling to Europe and Colorado to ride.

Saer's family owns the adjacent Boyer YL Ranch, a historic property that is no longer used for guest ranching. Combining her interest in equitation with her family's history of guest ranching resulted in Saer's opening Savery Creek as a haven for dedicated horsemen and horsewomen.

Savery Creek Thoroughbred Ranch is pretty far off the beaten path of tourist destinations. Located north of the Colorado border, the region has remained largely as it was centuries ago, when the only residents were the nomadic bands of Indians who passed through while hunting bison, elk, and other game species. The ranch house is situated on the banks of Savery Creek, a free-flowing waterway where huge cottonwood trees provide cool, pleasant shade. You may wish to bring your fishing gear, as the creek and nearby Little Snake River are excellent sanctuaries for trout.

If you love horseback riding in a lovely prairie setting, you'll enjoy the fact that riders aren't limited in the time they spend on horseback. Ride the entire day, if that is your desire, and choose from either western or English tack (instruction in either discipline is available). Or play cowboy and join in the cattle work, helping to move cows between pastures.

In addition to riding trails, the ranch features a cross-country course through the woods. There is also a jumping course, with riding instruction available.

For a change of pace, guests can play tennis, badminton, or go for a hike. In the evening, informal entertainment, reading, and an early bedtime are the norm. Children may find the adventure a bit slow, unless they are enthusiastic horse fanciers who want to spend their vacation time in the saddle.

Only six guests stay at the ranch at a time, and many return year after year; therefore, reservations are at a premium. Guests stay in the main ranch house, in rooms that remind one more of a private home than a modern hotel. Antique furnishings decorate the rooms and common areas of the house. The largest room has its own full bath; the other two smaller rooms share a common bathroom.

Meals are plentiful, healthful, and highly personalized. Expect numerous opportunities for picnics and cookouts, as outdoor living is a big part of this guest-ranch experience.

## Savery Creek Thoroughbred Ranch

P.O. Box 24
Savery, WY 82332
Phone: (307) 383–7840
E-mail: info@savery-creek.com
Web site: www.savery-creek.com

**Owner/Manager:** Joyce Saer

**Accommodations:** Capacity, 6. Guests stay in a traditional ranch home, in 3 bedrooms. Largest room has a private bath; 2 smaller rooms share a common, contiguous bathroom. All with queen-sized beds.

**Meals:** Dinners are prepared to high standards. Typical dinner-menu items include leg of lamb or sherry chicken, fresh vegetables (often from the garden), and fresh fruits. Joyce avoids high-cholesterol and fattening foods. Wine served with dinner; BYOB.

**Activities:** This is a ranch for dedicated horsemen and -women with advanced skills who are looking to spend many hours in the saddle. Your reward: exceptional horses, many of them arena schooled for and shown in competition. Some cattle work for competent riders. Arena instruction in English, Western, jumping, and dressage. Western and English Tack. Jumping course and cross-country course. Fishing in nearby creek and the Little Snake River. Tennis.

**Amenities:** This is a basic ranch, more like a friend's home than a formal guest ranch. Persons looking for a broad variety of amenities and activities will be disappointed. Still, a comfortable and inviting home for guests who love riding.

**Special Programs:** None. Children are welcome but should be good riders with a strong desire to spend their time horseback.

**Rates:** $$ Full American Plan. Special family and children's rates.

**Credit Cards:** None. Personal or traveler's checks.

**Season:** Mid-June through October

**Getting There:** Most guests fly into Denver and drive by rental car, a 6-hour trip. Nearest town is Savery (9 miles south). Others may fly to Hayden, near Steamboat Springs, Colorado, approximately 2 hours. Ask for specific driving directions.

**What's Nearby:** Dixon, Wyoming, a small town that hosts numerous rodeo-related events; Steamboat Springs (2 hours), a wonderful year-round resort town; Baggs, one-time hideout of Butch Cassidy and the Sundance Kid; and The Red Desert, 700 square miles of red-sand desert with numerous archaeological sites and interesting geological formations.

# 7D RANCH

## Cody, Wyoming

Originally opened as the Dewey Riddle Ranch, for its original owner, the 7D gained its present name when it was purchased in the late 1950s by the Dominick Family: Dr. DeWitt "Doc" Dominick, his wife, Lee, and their five children. At present, the ranch is still owned and operated by the Dominicks, who have passed the operation down through successive generations.

From the original log cabins to the Molesworth furniture in the Main Lodge, this place exudes an old-timey vibe that will help connect you to the past. (For readers unfamiliar with the Molesworth name, Thomas Canada Molesworth was a Cody furniture maker whose work graced many of the best guest ranches, hotels, and private homes in the West.) Persons looking to visit a classic and timeless western guest ranch little changed since the heyday of the postwar 1950s western-vacation craze owe it to themselves to visit the 7D.

The folks at the 7D are horse lovers, and they will take extra care to instruct you and to fit you to a complementary horse. For guests who wish to really improve their riding skills, arena riding lessons are available—and encouraged—throughout your weeklong stay. Even the most expert rider is likely to gain some valuable new insights during his or her stay. An exhibition on horse training, given in the ranch's training-specific round pen, is fascinating, even to guests who haven't had much experience with horses.

Like many guest ranches in the Cody area, the 7D prides itself on offering great fishing. The Sunlight River cuts through the property, offering a great "first time" experience for novices who will find it easy to catch the small brook trout. Below Sunlight Falls, rainbow and cutthroat trout abound for fishermen willing to go a little bit afield to stalk these larger and more challenging species. Furthermore, the ranch staff includes a full-time fishing guide, who can demonstrate some of the better spots on nearby rivers and lakes throughout the region.

Guests wishing to hike can head out in virtually any direction and attain awe-inspiring vistas without completely exhausting themselves. But for those who crave a true peak experience, the ranch can help you to devise an all-day climb leading to one of the many summits surrounding the property.

In the evenings, the 7D schedules diverse and fun entertainment. There are lawn sports, slide shows, lectures on the wild species of the region, cowboy singers and storytellers, square dances, a Native American sweat lodge, campfires, and the thrilling Cody Nite Rodeo. You'd have to work hard at being bored!

In addition to its regular dude-ranch program, the ranch also offers wilderness pack trips and fall guided hunting trips. Special events, such as a summer plein-air painting seminar with Wyoming master artist Kay Meeks (held in the summer of 2002), add a different twist to a typical guest-ranch experience. Be sure to inquire about new "special" event weeks at the ranch.

All in all, this is a ranch with lots of family character and tradition. The Dominick family's excellent stewardship has helped to retain the vintage personality of the place and allows guests the chance to step back in time to a less-hurried time.

## 7D Ranch

P.O. Box 100
Cody, WY 82414
Phone: (307) 587–3997
Fax: (307) 587–9885
E-mail: 7Dranch@wyoming.com
Web site: www.7dranch.com

**Owners/Managers:** The Dominick Family

**Accommodations:** Capacity, 32. 11 cabins shaded in Aspen groves. Cabins vary in size from 1 to 4 bedrooms and feature woodstoves, full bathrooms, and charming western decor. Daily maid service and laundry facilities available.

**Meals:** Meals are served family style in the main dining hall. Food is of superb quality, including such staples as 7D ranch-raised beef, fresh-baked breads, and crisp salads with vegetables from the ranch garden. Weekly "cowboy breakfast" on the trail and outdoor barbecue are signature experiences of any 7D visit.

**Activities:** Horseback riding includes full- and half-day rides, limited to small groups of similar abilities. Excellent preride instruction. Great fishing, either in ranch ponds, the ranch river, or guided fly fishing (extra). River rafting, wildlife viewing, mountain biking, local sightseeing, cattle drives, overnight campouts.

Special backcountry pack trips from 2 to 7 days (inquire for details). Archery range, basketball court, horseshoes, roping lessons, and volleyball. Evening activities include expert speakers whose topics range from wild animals to geology; evening square dances, Indian sweat lodge, sing-alongs, campfires with marshmallow s'mores, and lawn games.

**Amenities:** General store, laundry facilities, youth rec room, skeet-shooting range.

**Special Programs:** Excellent children's program includes full-time counselors and riding instructors, hikes, and organized activities for kids ages 6 to 12. Backcountry pack-trip vacations, fall hunting trips, and special September adults-only weeks.

**Rates:** $$$ Full American Plan. Children's and off-season rates. Minimum 1-week stay.

**Credit Cards:** None. Personal and traveler's checks only.

**Season:** Mid-June through mid-September

**Getting There:** Nearest airport in Cody, 50 miles from the ranch, and in Billings, Montana. Ranch shuttle available.

**What's Nearby:** Cody, a charming western town founded by Buffalo Bill Cody. Be sure to explore the Buffalo Bill Cody Historic Center and Museum.

# TA GUEST RANCH

## Buffalo, Wyoming

When Earl and Barbara Madsen purchased the TA Ranch in 1991, their first thought was to continue operating it as a traditional cattle outfit. But as restoration of the Victorian-era ranch buildings progressed, they recognized that this property was simply too wonderful not to share it with others.

Presently, the TA stands among the finest traditional historic ranches in North America. You won't find swimming pools and a posh spa facility on the TA, just lovingly kept facilities and gracious hosts who enjoy providing a taste of the West as it was more than a century ago.

Each of the buildings has been faithfully restored to its 1800s-era origins, right down to the period wallpaper. The TA has fifteen sleeping rooms, which will accommodate up to thirty guests. Each guest room has a private bathroom, but no phones, televisions, or clock radios to disturb you. (You can, however, reconnect to the modern world with televisions, VCRs, and Internet access provided for the guests' use and enjoyment.)

This place overflows with local history. While at the TA, you can see the reminders of itinerant cowboys who carved their initials and names into the barn's old pinewood doors. If you examine the barn more closely, you'll also discover bullet holes from a gunfight that took place here in 1892! As the story goes, a group of cattle barons set out to control the Powder River area. Their intention was to hunt down the small, independent ranchers of the region and chase them out. Events didn't follow their plan, however. When word got out among Johnson County residents, the hunters became the hunted. The rapacious cattlemen were pinned down at the TA Ranch, where the gun battle ensued. (You can learn more about this intriguing tale during your visit.)

If you're looking for more outlaw history, the bank robbers Butch Cassidy and the Sundance Kid once hid out in this country, and you can take an off-ranch hike to their famous Hole-in-the-Wall, where they would escape the pesky Pinkerton detectives. This tour will also take you to an authentic buffalo jump and to a place where Indian artists drew pictographs on the rock walls. You'll have tales to tell your friends for months to come.

Folks who like to ride and are concerned about the pokey nose-to-tail trail rides common to many guest ranches will be pleased to learn that the TA follows a different path. Guests are taught the essentials of riding safety and etiquette and carefully matched to horses that suit their riding skills. You'll be able to ride across vast open meadows, through creeks, over canyon passes, and along ancient Indian trails—a liberating experience for both rider and horse. Guests interested in cattle work can pitch in alongside the wranglers to gather and move the herd, check fences, water holes, and salt licks.

Guests looking for alternate trail transportation can head out on a mountain bike (if you can't bring one, the staff can help get you mounted). Trails vary from mild to wild, with the beautiful Bighorn Mountains providing the perfect backdrop for an enervating ride.

What's intriguing about the TA Ranch is that the owners, Earl and Barbara Madsen, have taken great pains to retain its authenticity and history. They've even helped to create a foundation to provide for the research and illumination of the ranch's rich history and the history of the region. True western-history buffs, as well as just plain folk looking for an authentic western getaway, will appreciate all the work and care evident in all details of the TA Guest Ranch.

## TA Guest Ranch

P.O. Box 313
Buffalo, WY 82834
Phone: (800) 368–7398; (307) 684–5833
Fax: (307) 684–5663
E-mail: taranch@trib.com
Web site: www.taranch.com

**Owners/Managers:** Earl and Barbara Madsen

**Accommodations:** Capacity, 30. Guest rooms are integrated into several historic properties on the ranch. All buildings have been carefully renovated and are decorated with authentic antiques, as well as more modern furnishings such as kitchenettes with microwave ovens, coffeemakers, and refrigerators. Guests dine in the Cook House, a restored homesteader's cabin, which, in addition to the dining room, includes 2 bedrooms that make an ideal family suite.

**Meals:** Nouveau Western-style ranch cuisine. Breakfasts include oven-baked goods such as caramel-pecan rolls, banana-walnut muffins, and buttermilk biscuits with homemade jams. These are followed with egg dishes, breakfast burritos, ranch fries, breakfast cereals, and fresh fruits. Lunch is similarly robust, with sandwiches, salads, and desserts. Dinner is a truly special occasion. Menu items vary, but a typical weekly menu may include prime rib, Basque pasta, boneless pork chops, and country-fried chicken. You'll enjoy crisp garden salads, side dishes, and toothsome desserts.

**Activities:** Daily activities focus on horseback riding, hiking, mountain biking, fishing, and tours of nearby attractions. Golfing at 3 nearby championship courses. Local rodeos. Living-history presentations that bring to life the Native American culture and the Western history of this region of Wyoming. A variety of outdoor and indoor recreational games including horseshoes, volleyball, roping practices, and board games.

**Amenities:** This is an authentic historic property, where amenities such as pools and such would seem out of place. That said, it is like stepping back into the Old West, but with all the rough edges sanded off. A big main lodge with a wide porch invites guests to relax with a book from the ranch library. Wet bar for socializing and a study for quiet reading and relaxation.

**Special Programs:** No children's program. Rambunctious youngsters probably won't feel as at-home as more quiet children. Children are their parents' responsibility and should be at least 8 years old if they will be riding horses. Nannies encouraged for younger children.

**Rates:** $$$ Full American Plan. Rate includes room, 3 meals, snacks, horseback riding, and all ranch activities, as well a scenic day tour throughout the Powder River Basin, reservoir or stream fishing, and more. Stay a day, a week, or a month. Reduced rates for kids 11–15 and children 5–10; children under age 4 are free.

**Credit Cards:** VISA, MasterCard

**Season:** May through October

**Getting There:** Nearest airport in Sheridan, 45 miles. Ranch is located 13 miles south of Buffalo on Wyoming Highway. 196.

**What's Nearby:** Historical attractions include Custer Battlefield, the Oregon Trail, and the famous Hole-in-the-Wall hideout of Butch Cassidy's gang. Rodeo events in Buffalo, as well as shopping, dining, museums.

# T-CROSS RANCH

## Dubois, Wyoming

Once you cross under the main gate that greets newcomers to T-Cross Ranch, you'll have left the modern world behind and magically stepped back into the Old West. Ahead lies the rugged and preternaturally beautiful Absaroka Mountains, whose secrets you will soon begin to learn. The historic ranch buildings are nestled in a quiet, secluded meadow back-to-back with the Shoshone National Forest, part of the contiguous public lands that connect northwestern Wyoming to the Yellowstone National Park, the Grand Teton Wilderness, and tens of thousands of acres of forest lands.

The T-Cross Ranch was first homesteaded in the late 1800s by a fugitive from the Johnson County Cattle Wars. It opened as a dude ranch in 1920 and has served its customers proudly and graciously ever since that date. The buildings on the ranch were handcrafted from the native lodgepole pine, lending the perfect ambience to this mountain escape. Inside the guest cabins, the lodgepole furniture ties you to the outdoor theme, while Indian rugs and western artifacts serve to remind you (not that you could forget) that this is indeed the real West. Don't worry that you'll have to fuss with nineteenth-century outhouses or draw water from the horse corral; the plumbing is modern, with full showers and plenty of hot water.

The main lodge is likewise folksy and rustic, with lots of Wyoming cowboy charm. Far from austere, however, the lodge is wonderfully comfortable and cozy, with its massive stone fireplace and its spreading veranda. Guests tend to congregate here to socialize before and after the lavish meals, to swap fish stories, and to tell tales of their day's adventures.

And there will be plenty of stories to tell. Owner Ken Neal takes deserved pride in his horse herd. A lifelong horseman, he's got a good eye for a dude horse that will dutifully pack its passenger through the roughest mountain country as unstintingly as it will travel across a broad, grassy meadow. Each guest (beginning with kids as young as six) is assigned his or her own horse for the duration of the stay. Once properly mounted, guests can choose from half-day to full-day rides that wind through groves of aspen trees and pine and fir forests and that offer spectacular views of the Washaki Wilderness. Keep quiet and be attentive, and you'll likely encounter wildlife ranging from slow-moving porcupines to dashing coyotes. There's a fair share of elk, deer, and moose to see, too.

This is old-school, traditional guest ranching at its best. Owners Ken and Garey Neal grew up in this country, and both have spent their entire lives around horses and dudes. They know how to make both comfortable and will even help you and your equine partner understand each other and get along famously. At week's end, you may even want to take your horse home (but that would be a little selfish for the next guest, wouldn't it?).

In addition to riding, you will enjoy fishing in picturesque Horse Creek, where brook trout and mountain whitefish abound. An annual stocking program has also added rainbow and cutthroat trout to the species list, but you'll have to play catch-and-release, for the benefit of the other guests—not to mention the fish!

**T-Cross Ranch**
P.O. Box 638
Dubois, WY 82513
Phone: (307) 455–2206
Fax: (307) 455–2720
E-mail: info@tcross.com
Web site: www.tcross.com

**Owners/Managers:** Ken and Garey Neal

**Accommodations:** Capacity, 24. 8 cozy log cabins tucked into the pine trees. Cabins feature Indian rugs, handcrafted log furniture, down quilts, woodstoves or fireplaces, hot showers, and individual porches.

**Meals:** Hearty and filling ranch cuisine served family style. Cook will prepare your freshly caught trout. Breakfast, lunch, and dinner rides. BYOB happy hour every evening in the lodge.

**Activities:** Horseback-riding program with half- and full-day rides conducted at the walk, trot, lope, and canter as well as "the wild ride," for experienced horsemen. Arena instruction, gymkhanas, perhaps some cattle work. Inner tubing, hiking, horseshoes, rock climbing, rifle range, volleyball games, overnight campouts, lake and river fishing. Inquire about backcountry wilderness pack trips and guided fall hunting. Evening entertainment with local cowboy poets and musicians, square dances, campfires, and cookouts.

**Amenities:** Jacuzzi hot tub, gift shop, main lodge with grand stone fireplace, large porch, and western artifacts and memorabilia.

**Special Programs:** Children 6 and over ride, hike, and tube-float the river with youth counselors. Overnight tepee campouts for kids and Friday-morning kids' gymkhana (games on horseback).

**Rates:** $$$ Full American Plan. Rates prorated in the off-season (anytime but July and August) for shorter stays.

**Credit Cards:** None. Personal or traveler's checks only.

**Season:** Mid-June to late September

**Getting There:** Nearest airports are in Jackson and Riverton. The ranch can arrange ground transportation from either airport, or you may rent a car. Dubois has a private airport with a 5,000-foot blacktop runway for private and charter flights.

**What's Nearby:** Dubois.

# TRAIL CREEK RANCH

## Wilson, Wyoming

For some people, the idea of a structured guest-ranch vacation is a little, well, claustrophobic. For those who want to explore western Wyoming on their own time schedule, the Trail Creek Ranch, located just minutes from Jackson and within easy driving distance of Yellowstone National Park, is the perfect retreat.

A unique bed-and-breakfast located on a real working ranch, Trail Creek is situated in a lush valley, surrounded by groves of aspen, pine, and green meadows that support the resident horse herd. Its 280 acres offer ample elbow room, with plenty to explore right on the ranch. It's a great place to charge your batteries and enjoy a sumptuous country breakfast before heading out to explore all that the Jackson Hole region has to offer.

Great recreation is what the original owner, Elizabeth "Betty" Woolsey, had in mind when she purchased the property in 1942. The captain of the first U.S. women's Olympic ski team, Woolsey discovered the ranch's main lodge while skiing in the wonderful dry-powder snow that made this region so famous for skiing. The ranch proved equally appealing in summer, when cool weather and wonderful views made it a natural place for outdoor activities.

Woolsey passed away in 1997, but not before creating a conservation agreement that prevents the 280-acre ranch from development. Now the ranch is run by Muggs Schultz, an elderly woman who has been at the ranch for more than fifty years, and Alex, a young woman who has been with Trail Creek for most of her adult life and who is raising her family in this unique little slice of paradise.

A working dude ranch since 1946, Trail Creek has always enjoyed an international clientele, as well as Americans "in the know."

Guests congregate in the main lodge, with its comfortable living room and dining room. Mornings are spent over a leisurely breakfast featuring homemade pastries, fruits, and the wonderful creations of the resident chef. At the end of the day, guests return to enjoy the sunset on the large covered porch, and impromptu cocktail parties often arise (there's a bar, but you'll need to bring your own liquor, wine or beer).

For vacationers wishing to head directly for the hills to enjoy mountain biking, hiking, or some other local activity, sack lunches or romantic picnic baskets can be ordered. There's horseback riding on the ranch, as well, at added charge. This is an "a la carte" experience, more than an all-inclusive guest-ranch visit. The folks at Trail Creek Ranch will offer their assistance and advice in finding perfect activities to suit your vacation wishes and your activity level, whether that means guided fly fishing in a local river or shopping for new shoes in Jackson's posh shops!

You can, of course, also relax for the day on the ranch itself. There's plenty of native wildlife for early risers to observe, including moose, elk, coyotes, and birds. Wolves and bears have also been sighted, though they are not easy to come by—thank goodness!

The ranch also features a heated swimming pool with views of the pasture and the rustic barn. This is the kind of place independent explorers will love—their own special ranch retreat in the heart of Jackson Hole, one of the great recreational destinations in North America.

**Trail Creek Ranch**

P.O. Box 10
Wilson, WY 83014
Phone: (307) 733–2610
Fax: (307) 733–2610
E-mail: TrailCreekRanch@msn.com
Web site: www.jacksonholetrailcreekranch.
com

**Owner/Manager:** Muggs Schultz

**Accommodations:** Capacity, 25; 12 in winter. Guests stay in a number of cabins ranging from small units suitable for couples to large family-sized, multiroom cabins. Prices reflect accommodations rather than the number of guests. Winter guests enjoy 3 meals per day with their accommodations.

**Meals:** Breakfast of homemade pastries and baked goods, fruits, and hearty ranch breakfasts. Sack lunch or gourmet picnic lunches available by request and at added charge.

**Activities:** Horseback riding, hiking, mountain biking, swimming in the outdoor pool. The staff will assist you in making off-site plans that take advantage the myriad of activities in the Jackson Hole region.

**Amenities:** Lovely guest cabins, each with a unique design and appeal. The Suite, for example, has antique king- and twin-sized beds, wonderful artwork, full bath with tub, and a gracious Victorian feel. The Ritz is a 2-bedroom cabin with living room and fireplace, kitchenette, queen-sized bed in the master suite, twin beds in the loft, and extra sleeping space in the living room.

**Special Programs:** No children's program or scheduled activities, although young guests are welcome.

**Rates:** $$$ European Plan, bed-and-breakfast. 3-day minimum stay in summer.

**Credit Cards:** None. Personal or traveler's checks.

**Season:** June 15 to September 30. Winter accommodations (December to March) for 12.

**Getting There:** Located near Wilson, on the Teton Pass northwest of Jackson. Most guests fly into Jackson, Wyoming, or drive in private cars. Airline shuttle service to Jackson from Denver International Airport and Salt Lake City. Inquire for specific directions to the ranch. Rental car or private vehicle for local sight-seeing and activities are strongly recommended.

**What's Nearby:** Jackson Hole region, including the famous Jackson Hole Ski Area, Grand Teton National Park, Teton Village, and Jackson. Yellowstone National Park, Grand Targhee Winter Resort.

# TRIANGLE C RANCH

## Dubois, Wyoming

A first-class ranch in a spectacular setting with innovative programs and dozens of activities. What more could you want in a ranch vacation?

The Triangle C Ranch is a great place to "get away from it all" without forsaking creature comforts or being too far from the action. The main lodge is a big, gorgeous 8,000-square-foot log building with a wraparound pine deck and is backed by a huge rock escarpment that gives it a postcard aspect. Kick back in The Moose Room Lounge, where a towering log ceiling and a huge stone fireplace provide the perfect frame for the massive moose head that presides over the goings-on. And in the unlikely event that the ranch proves too small for you, you can head into Dubois with the other guests for a night of dancing or take in the attractions of Jackson, including an authentic cowboy rodeo.

Just an hour from Jackson Hole and Yellowstone National Park, the Triangle C is perched on a bluff overlooking the Wind River, with views of the Absaroka Range. An ideal spot for photographers!

There is a nice mix of traditional and contemporary activities. You can learn the ancient art of archery with an instructor (bow and arrow provided), travel back in time with the mountain men and learn how to shoot a black-powder rifle and throw a tomahawk, or take a guided canoeing trip.

Guests who like more contemporary outdoor sports can schedule a tee time at the nine-hole course in Dubois, or make a day of it and try the Arnold Palmer–designed championship course in Jackson Hole. Rafting is another option, and many guests choose to take a scenic float trip down the Snake River (white-water raft trips are also available with area outfitters, at additional charge). Mountain biking on the ranch is another popular pastime.

The Triangle C has been owned and operated by the Garnick family for only a few years, but the family has been involved in the Wyoming guest-ranch business for more than three decades. They take great pride in their ranch and have striven to help it retain its heritage (the ranch was established in 1909), while providing it with modern comforts and genteel frontier elegance. The recently added Pinnacle Cabins, for instance, are two-story log complexes with king and queen suites, fireplaces, and Jacuzzi bathtubs. Each has a different theme—Indian, Trapper, Cowboy, and The Ranch House. The lodge features the Tie Hack Bar, whose polished knotty-pine bar, old-timey furniture, and artifacts seem to have been lifted from a Clint Eastwood western. This is truly a showcase property!

Although the Triangle C is very kid-friendly, twice a year the ranch is turned over to fun-seeking single adults. Each spring and fall, singles converge on the ranch for these special "country singles weeks." Dine and dance in Jackson Hole, tour the Yellowstone Park, go floating on the Snake River, fish, hike, bike—and perhaps meet the cowboy or cowgirl of your dreams!

**Triangle C Ranch**
3737 Highway 26
Dubois, WY 82513
Phone: (800) 661–4928; (307) 455–2225
E-mail: info@trianglec.com
Web site: www.trianglec.com

**Owners/Managers:** The Garnick Family

**Accommodations:** Capacity, 50. Guests stay in original 1920s log cabins and in the new Pinnacle Cabins. Take your pick, from rustic tradition to modern comfort. The Pinnacle Cabins are 2-story log complexes, each decorated around a western theme; the original cabins are set in the woods and vary from honeymooner suites to double bedrooms with bunk beds for the kids.

**Meals:** The Triangle C's resident chef, Sallie, serves up fresh, healthful, ranch fare. Sallie has been cooking homemade goodies at the Triangle C for several years, baking homemade breads and specialty desserts. Prime rib, trout almandine and Cornish hens are just a few of the dinner entrees. Breakfast rides, old-fashioned picnics on the deck, and barbecue ribs and New York steaks at the campfire cookout. Special diets can be accommodated, with advance notice.

**Activities:** Summer dude-ranch activities include horseback riding, mountain biking, hiking, canoeing, black-powder shoot and tomahawk throwing, archery, campfire cookouts, scenic float trips on the Snake River, Yellowstone tours, fishing, pack trips (inquire for details), and more. Winter snowmobiling, snowshoeing, cross-country skiing, alpine skiing. Fall hunting trips and fishing trips.

**Amenities:** Conference rooms with computers, copiers, Internet access; 2-table pool parlor, home theater, library, dining room with 65-person capacity, Tie Hack Saloon, archery and shooting ranges, guest laundry, hot tub.

**Special Programs:** Twice-annual "singles weeks" for adult singles. Included are trips to Jackson and Dubois, hiking, riding, rafting, social events. The youth programs are among the best in the country, with a complete naturalist program, a teen program, and a children's program. Typical teen activities include cookouts, horseback riding, personal watercraft riding on Brooks Lake, dances, mountain-bike rides, and more. A great place for kids of all ages to make new friends and learn new, confidence-building skills.

**Rates:** $$ Full American Plan. Reduced children's rates, off-season rates, and nonrider rates. Some off-site activities are extra.

**Credit Cards:** VISA, MasterCard, American Express. Personal and traveler's checks.

**Season:** Open year-round. Dude ranch (spring and summer), hunting and fishing (fall), snowsports activities (winter).

**Getting There:** Located 18 miles west of Dubois, 65 miles north of Jackson. Nearest airports: Jackson, Dubois, Riverton. Ranch shuttle available; rental cars or personal transportation recommended for guests wishing to take part in off-site activities such as golfing.

**What's Nearby:** Dubois, Jackson Hole, Yellowstone National Park.

# TRIANGLE X RANCH

## Moose, Wyoming

A true all-season ranch, the Triangle X is a great place to visit whether you are planning a summer get-away or a winter vacation. This is an authentic working ranch where haying, branding, and raising livestock are the order of the day, but this doesn't mean it's all work and no play.

Guests enjoy everything from horseback riding to river-float trips to square dancing and barbecue cookouts. The winter schedule includes cross-country skiing, snowmobiling, snowshoeing, and off-site alpine skiing at the famous Jackson Hole Winter Resort.

The Triangle X is situated in the heart of the Grand Teton National Park, offering guests mountain views and backcountry wilderness unsurpassed anywhere in the Lower 48. The ranch has been the pride and joy of the Turner family, who have welcomed adventurous guests through three successive generations. The Triangle X is the only dude ranch still in operation within Grand Teton National Park.

Around 1928, J. C. Turner of the Triangle X Dude Ranch moved dovetailed logs from neighbor John Fee's partially completed homestead cabin to the Triangle X Ranch, where the logs were used to form the first ten courses of Turner's new barn. This historic landmark still distinguishes the property.

One of the Turner family's specialties is backcountry pack trips in the Grand Teton and the south Yellowstone wilderness areas. The Turner brothers—Harold, John, and Donald—have been in the outfitting business their entire lives and represent one of the most respected and experienced teams in the industry. They know where to find wildlife, how to make guests comfortable and safe on the trail, and, most important, how to show guests a really good time! Vacationers looking for a backcountry adventure or a superb Wyoming hunting trip will definitely want to inquire about this year's offering for extended wilderness pack trips and guided hunts led by these outdoor experts.

Persons looking for a somewhat more "civilized" trip will want to find out more about a proper ranch stay. Ranch vacationers stay in generous one-, two-, and three-bedroom log cabins with indoor plumbing (sometimes a luxury on a real working ranch), polished wood floors, and attractive western-motif interiors. You'll have a post-card-perfect view of the Teton Range from the comfort of your covered porch.

The Triangle X also serves as the perfect place for "river rats," people who thrive within earshot of the rushing rapids and burbling brooks. That, of course, means river rafters and fishermen. If you're looking for both scenic beauty and exciting adventure, you'll want to get on the list for a rafting trip on the Snake River. Next to horseback riding, it's the favorite activity at the Triangle X.

Fishermen will find themselves in a piscatorial paradise. The Jackson Hole area has literally hundreds of miles of streams and numerous lakes where you can pursue a variety of trout species. The ranch can provide you with a raft and guide for a day of float fishing, or they'll show you some of their "secret spots," which they've ferreted out over a lifetime of fishing the region.

For those individuals looking for a traditional western guest ranch with a wide variety of summer and winter activities, a true working-ranch atmosphere, a congenial staff, and unsurpassed views, the Triangle X is the ideal choice.

## Triangle X Ranch
Star Route Box 120
Moose, WY 83012
Phone: (307) 733–2183
Fax: (307) 733–8685
E-mail: trianglexranch@wyoming.com
Web site: www.trianglex.com

**Owners/Managers:** The Turner Family

**Accommodations:** Capacity, 75. Guests stay in 1-, 2- and 3-bedroom log cabins, each with bathroom and covered porch. Spectacular views!

**Meals:** Meals are served in the main dining room of the lodge. Dinner service is elegant western, with elk-horn chandeliers and linen tablecloths. The ranch owners tout their four-star cooking staff, which mixes up the menu but always serves up homemade breads, fresh vegetables and salads, and exceptional main entrees. Outdoor cookouts and trail-ride cookouts are a big part of the ranch dining experience. Children dine in a separate seating except on family nights.

**Activities:** Fundamentally a riding ranch, the Triangle X maintains an extensive trail-riding program with mountain-savvy horses. Riders of all abilities will be matched to appropriate mounts. The riding here is especially scenic, and you are likely to encounter numerous native animals, so be sure to take a camera in your saddlebag. Backcountry wilderness pack trips (2 days to 2 weeks) where guests can rough it in established camps with sturdy sleeping tents. Fall wilderness hunting camps. Guided fishing in area lakes and streams. Snake River float trips. Winter snowmobiling, cross-country skiing, snowshoeing, and alpine skiing at several nearby ski areas. Evening excursions to Jackson, where dancing, dining, shopping, and melodrama can be found. Daytime rodeo action near town. Evening "social," square dances, local history lecture, cowboy singing and folklore.

**Amenities:** Ranch gift shop, outdoor Jacuzzi, ranch transportation to various activities, old-fashioned swimming hole.

**Special Programs:** Children 12 and under take place in the Kiddie Wrangler program of supervised riding, arts and crafts, swimming trips, and more. Summer backcountry pack trips, winter activity packages, guided fishing and hunting trips.

**Rates:** $$ Full American Plan. Off-season rates, pack trips, winter rates available. 1-week minimum stay in summer.

**Credit Cards:** None. Personal or traveler's checks.

**Season:** May to November, mid-December to April

**Getting There:** Nearest airport, Jackson (25 miles). Located near Teton Village, north and west of Jackson.

**What's Nearby:** Jackson, Yellowstone National Park.

# UXU RANCH

## Wapiti, Wyoming

Hamilton Bryan can relate to his guests' dreams of becoming cowboys. As a kid growing up in Oakland, Bryan spent summers and weekends on his parents' cattle ranch. His hero, he says, was the ranch foreman.

From those beginnings, "Ham" went on to have a successful adult career in business. But the idea of "getting back to the land" lingered in his head, and finally he decided to find the ideal place to return to his ranching roots. He found that place, the UXU Ranch, an eleven-cabin property not far from the borders of Yellowstone National Park on a stretch of highway once described by Teddy Roosevelt as "the most scenic 52 miles in the United States."

The UXU had a colorful history. As local lore has it, the ranch was bought by an estranged husband ,whose wife lived just down the road. To vent his feelings, he named it the "U (expletive) U" so that he could let his ex know his feelings each time she passed by. But Forest Service officials didn't take kindly to a swear word being used within the boundaries of the Shoshone National Forest, and so the ranch became the "UXU."

Since taking over the ranch, Ham has brought his refined sense of western style to the operation, renovating the property with his own quirky touches. In the lodge and cabins, Bryan hung his own photos of the West, along with paintings by notable western artists. Keeping much of the ranch's original Old Hickory furniture, he also contracted furniture designer J. Mike Patrick of Cody, Wyoming, to create some whimsical western furniture reminiscent of the style of the famed furniture maker Thomas Molesworth.

Patrick built beds, mirrors, ottomans, sconces, night tables, and dressers. The furniture is replete with Chimayo cushions and carved images of moose, fly fishermen, and cowboys.

Bryan is definitely a hands-on owner. He joins guests each evening at the dinner table, sharing conversation and stories over gourmet nouveau-western cuisine. "It's sort of producing a movie, and I am the producer," Bryan says. "I really try to present an honest western experience."

And while the accommodations are great, that experience mainly takes place in the spectacular outdoors. It's said that the best way to see a ranch is on horseback, and the UXU accommodates its guests with an excellent horse program. In addition to guided rides, guests enjoy guided fly fishing in area creeks and rivers, mountain biking, river rafting, guided trips to the Yellowstone, and a trip to the Buffalo Bill Historical Center in Cody and the Cody Nite Rodeo. The ranch hot tub overlooks the Absaroka Mountains, and there's an underground sauna for guests who need to relax tense muscles. Bryan likes to host softball games, and if your timing is right, you may get to drive to the field in his vintage Woody station wagon. Golfing and shooting are nearby at the Cody Shooting Complex.

The UXU has been reviewed in dozens of magazines, from travel publications to food magazines, daily papers, and architectural digests. One thing reviewers never seem to tire of is the two scenic outdoor showers in the Hollister Log Cabin, which Ham moved piece by piece and then rebuilt on the property. If you stay, be sure to ask about the unique, and some would say heavenly, plumbing.

## UXU Ranch

1710 Yellowstone Highway
Wapiti, WY 82450
Phone: (800) 373–9027; (307) 587–2143
Fax: (307) 587–7390
E-mail: uxuranch@aol.com
Web site: www.uxuranch.com

**Owner/Manager:** Hamilton Bryan

**Accommodations:** Capacity, 34. 1- and 2-bedroom cabins. Daily maid service.

**Meals:** Chef Rab McKie presides over the western-style gourmet cuisine. Special dietary requests honored with advance notice. "Honor" bar with more than 40 wines.

**Activities:** Horseback riding with instruction, guided fishing, hiking, mountain biking, river rafting, guided Yellowstone trips, visits to the Buffalo Bill Historical Center and the Cody Nite Rodeo. Softball games, nearby golf and skeet shooting.

**Amenities:** Sauna, hot tub, rooms complete with bathrobes and bath supplies, cabins with private porches and swings, daily maid service, meeting rooms for conference/business meetings.

**Special Programs:** Children's program for kids over 6 includes horseback riding, archery, and games.

**Rates:** $$$$–$$$$$ Full American Plan. Rates based on accommodations; the most luxurious and expensive, the Hollister Cabin, is $6,100 for the first adult and $1,075 for each additional person. Reduced children's rates, off-season rates.

**Credit Cards:** VISA, MasterCard. Personal checks, traveler's checks also accepted.

**Season:** June 1 to September 27

**Getting There:** Guests fly to Cody, Jackson, or Billings, Montana. Inquire about special rental-car rates or use the free ranch shuttle service.

**What's Nearby:** Yellowstone National Park, Cody, and Jackson Hole, Wyoming.

# CANADA

# BREWSTER'S KANANASKIS GUEST RANCH AND GOLF RESORT

Banff, Alberta

With Banff National Park at their backs, the Brewster family began accommodating tourists on its ranch operation in 1923. Missy Bagley Brewster recognized that the family's homestead on the shores of the Bow River would be an ideal place for people to rest and stay on their way to Banff. The venture met with fabulous success, and over time the Brewster family was able to greatly expand its ventures. Now, along with the guest ranch, the Brewster properties include a 9-hole mountain golf course with spectacular Mount Yamnuska rising up in the background and Brewster's Mountain Lodge in Banff (another great place to vacation).

This is a spectacular part of Canada, rivaling its stateside equal, Jackson Hole, Wyoming, as a gateway to a fantastic national park. Brewster's location in Kananaskis is less than an hour's drive from ultramodern Calgary, a bustling city with a wonderful, laid-back Western ambience. Less than half an hour's drive west of Kananaskis lies Banff National Park, with its soaring mountains, crystalline lakes, and dozens of recreational opportunities. Travelers who've never visited Alberta owe it to themselves to vacation here. And with the strong U.S. dollar making a Canadian vacation a relative bargain, there's never been a better time for those who live south-of-the-border.

The ranch is a landmark property with 2,000 acres of forest mixed with wide-open pastures and cool, pleasantly shaded glades. Horseback riding, of course, is the main activity. Expect expert guidance and instruction from the staff. Half-day rides satisfy many guests, but if you don't mind waking up saddle sore the next day, the full-day ride to the ridge of Mount Yamnuska offers a splendid and unforgettable overview of this especially scenic area. You may even get to play a game of polo with guests on your own ranch-raised thoroughbred!

Vacationers looking for even more adventure should inquire about mountain pack trips. These rides take guests over the historic Horse Drive Trail, which the Brewsters have used for more than a century while driving horses to and from winter pasture. You'll ride to one or both of the ranch's cabin camps, which provide a much more comfortable place to lay one's head than the camp tents provided by most outfitters.

Back at the ranch, guests can enjoy swimming in the Bow River (an icy experience, but nice on a hot summer afternoon). Those who prefer their water hotter can take a relaxing dip in the fifteen-person whirlpool.

Other activities include hiking amid the wildflowers and wild berry bushes, hayrides, canoe trips, singing songs and sharing stories around the campfire, and fishing for cutthroat trout and Dolly Varden in the lakes and streams adjacent to the ranch.

An especially good time to visit is July, when the annual Calgary Stampede comes to town. Founded in 1912, the rodeo boasts of being "the greatest show on dirt," and, indeed, it is. Stampede Park is a vast area of agricultural displays, horse shows, carnival midways, and commercial exhibits. Be sure to check on the dates if you plan on a July vacation.

The Brewster properties are bustling places, but the flexible schedule allows visitors to do as much, or as little, as they wish.

## Brewster's Kananaskis Guest Ranch and Golf Resort

Box 2606
Banff, Alberta T1L 1C1
Canada
Phone: (800) 691–5085; (403) 673–3737
Fax: (403) 673–2702
E-mail: kgr@brewsteradventures.com
Web site: www.brewsteradventures.com

**Owners/Managers:** The Brewster Family

**Accommodations:** 60-person capacity. 33 cabins and chalets located on the banks of the Bow River. Rooms feature aromatic cedar interiors, full shower/bath, antique furnishings, and daily maid service.

**Meals:** Wholesome foods served family style on long tables. The eggs, butter, cream, milk, meat, and vegetables are strictly fresh. Fresh fruits in season. Homemade breads a ranch specialty.

**Activities:** Horseback riders are assigned their own horses and "rigs" (tack). Rides near the ranch lead to high-mountain vistas or through the foothill country on the Stoney Indian Reservation. Several all-day trips take place throughout the week, with evening campfire cookouts and beautiful sunsets. Gathering the horse herd is a favorite "special" activity for willing guests. Pack trips and overnight rides also available. Fishing in local lakes and streams; Calgary Stampede trips; visits to local Native American reservations with cultural events and native crafts; golf at the ranch's 9-hole mountain course (soon to be 18 holes).

Evening and off-time activities include reading in the library, pool playing, and parlor games.

**Amenities:** Recreation room, library, piano, golf shop with power carts and club rentals, snack bar.

**Special Programs:** No special kids' programs, although there are plenty of family activities that kids can take part in with their parents. Children must be 7 years of age or older to ride horses. Ideal for conference groups, weddings, and large family gatherings, a barbecue pavilion allows as many as 300 guests to be seated. Inquire about special packages: Romance package, Spikes'n'Spurs golf and riding package, Corporate Getaway Days.

**Rates:** $$ Modified American Plan. Breakfast and dinner included in the daily lodging rates. Box lunches available, by request. Activities such as golf, overnight pack trips, and horseback riding are charged separately. Be sure to inquire about packages, such as the Spurs'n'Spikes golf and riding package, as well as rafting, canoeing and other activities.

**Credit Cards:** VISA, MasterCard, American Express. Traveler's checks accepted.

**Season:** June through September

**Getting There:** 28 miles east of Banff National Park, approximately 45 minutes west of Calgary just off the Trans-Canada Highway. Nearest airport: Calgary.

**What's Nearby:** Calgary, Lake Louise, Banff, and Banff National Park.

# THE HOMEPLACE RANCH

Priddis, Alberta

When the only people living in Alberta's western foothills were the Stoney and Sarcee Indians, they referred to the area as "Paradise." If your idea of paradise is one of timbered forests, lush green pastures, blue, blue skies, and wonderful seclusion, then the Homeplace Ranch is paradise indeed.

A small ranch with a capacity of only fourteen guests, the Homeplace lives up to its name. Guests feel like family, and a stay here is guaranteed to make you good friends with the ranch owners, the MaKenny family.

Homeplace Ranch operates year-round and is a genuine working cattle ranch. Located just a half-hour south of Calgary, the ranch lies at an elevation of 4,900 feet (1,500 meters) in the foothills of the snow-capped Canadian Rockies. The ranch is surrounded by thousands of acres of federal forest lands that harbor a wide variety of wildlife species including bears, deer, coyotes, various birds of prey, elk, and many more. Small group rides virtually ensure that you will see plenty of critters large and small during your stay.

Guests stay in the main lodge or coach house in private rooms, each with its own bathroom and shower. A common western-style living room and the main dining room are where guests and ranch employees tend to congregate and socialize.

After a filling breakfast, riding is the usual order of the day at the Homeplace. Each guest is assigned a horse for the week, with a careful pairing of rider skills to the horse provided. Safety and a good rapport with your horse are stressed, and guests are welcome to join in the early-morning grooming and saddling of their mount, if they so desire. Most of the horses were born and raised right here on the ranch, and their familiarity makes them steady and reliable mountain horses no matter their breed.

After riding, guests gravitate toward the Jacuzzi bath or head to the creek to cool their feet. The ambitious can also hike the many local bridle paths and trails or try their hand fishing for grayling and rainbow trout in the nearby streams. Seasoned anglers will want to explore the world-renowned Bow River, a trophy trout-fishing destination just twenty-five minutes from the ranch. Weekends offer a number of entertaining diversions such as rodeos, polo games, and the urbane but still very western nightlife and fancy dining in Calgary, a modern and delightful city much like Denver.

If your vacation goals include "playing cowboy," you can ask to join the resident cowboys and spend time checking cows and "circle riding" the ranch. If you want to squeeze in some sight-seeing, the Homeplace can serve as your base camp to explore Banff, Calgary, and the Head Smashed in Buffalo Jump. Equestrians will want to check out Spruce Meadows, a world-class show jumping facility located just south of Calgary and a mere 20 kilometers east of Homeplace. There, you'll see top-drawer jumping horses, western stock horses, and perhaps catch a polo match. (Ask about special Spruce Meadows event packages, as well as the Calgary Stampede Days rodeo packages.)

The staff will be happy to help you plan and coordinate such excursions, and if this is your desire, it is recommended that you bring or rent your own car (Budget Car Rentals at the Calgary Airport offers reduced rates to ranch guests, so be sure to ask). Golfers can arrange tee times at the Winter Green Country Club, just 7 miles from the ranch.

## The Homeplace Ranch

Site 2, Box 6, RR 1
Priddis, Alberta T0L 1W0
Canada
Phone: (403) 931–3245
E-mail: homeplace.ranch@cadvision.com
Web site: www.homeplaceranch.com

**Owners/Managers:** The MaKenny Family

**Accommodations:** Capacity, 14. Guests are housed in individual rooms in the main lodge and the carriage house. Guest rooms have individual bathrooms and showers.

**Meals:** Typical ranch fare served family style in the main lodge. Guests dine with employees. 3 daily meals, plus snacks, coffee, and fresh cookies always available. Steak cookouts (at least one a week).

**Activities:** Horseback riding is central to ranch activities; careful matching of horse and rider plus experienced wranglers to teach guests ensures a safe and enjoyable experience. Due to small group rides, guests do not follow a prescribed nose-to-tail type of trail riding but are encouraged to master the walk, trot, and canter where appropriate. Cattle work may be available to guests expressing an interest. Instruction with written evaluation available. Trout fishing on the ranch, trophy fishing in nearby Bow River with outside outfitter, informal recreational games, nearby golf. Winter alpine skiing nearby and cross-country skiing and snowshoeing on the ranch. Inquire about rodeo excursions to the famed Calgary Stampede and special events at Spruce Meadows.

**Amenities:** Jacuzzi bath, comfortable guest lounge in the main lodge, tepee site for overnight campouts, and lots of artifacts, photos, and memorabilia that highlight this ranch's almost 100-year history.

**Special Programs:** No formal children's program, although children over 7 are allowed to ride.

**Rates:** $$ Full American Plan. 3-, 5- and 7-day packages. Inquire about the various special-event packages centered around the Calgary Stampede Rodeo and the events at Spruce Meadows. Early in spring, the ranch offers a trail-clearing expedition in which guests help prepare the trails for summer riding; this trip involves lots of riding and plenty of good, outdoor work, as well as extended rides into the high country to gather cattle.

**Credit Cards:** VISA. Personal checks accepted.

**Season:** Year-round

**Getting There:** 30 miles south of Calgary off Route 22. Shuttle service from the airport available at additional cost.

**What's Nearby:** Banff National Park, Calgary, and Spruce Meadows.

# CHILCOTIN HOLIDAYS
# GUEST RANCH
### Gold Bridge, British Columbia

Chilcotin Holidays Guest Ranch is a wilderness experience like no other, short of a visit to Alaska. Located in the northern corner of Canada, Chilcotin's 2,000-plus square miles of guide territory is virtually a wildlife preserve. Here, you can encounter hundreds of species, from mountain sheep to moose, deer, elk, and even grizzly bear. (Don't worry, the guides know how to safely manage wildlife encounters.)

Due to an unique outfitting arrangement, the ranch has almost unprecedented outfitting rights to this huge chunk of mountain territory that ranges from lowland Douglas-fir forests up to the delicate alpine tundra, where visitors encounter unusual wildflowers and vegetation that grows only in these isolated islands of high-alpine land. The ranch is run by Kevan Bracewell and Sylvia Waterer, whose experience encompasses all facets of guest-ranch operations, adventure travel, tourism, and resource management (Sylvia actually has a postgraduate degree in the latter two fields of study.) Since 1990, they've made it their goal to use their diverse skills to create the ultimate "once in a lifetime" adventure experience for their guests.

At the center of this philosophy are guest participation and involvement. On a ride, you may take part in counting wildlife for population studies or collect grizzly hair from a rubbing tree, which will later be used for genetic testing to study the migration and habits of the native bears. You'll be passively and actively learning about the fascinating ecosystem of this region of North America.

Located on the leeside of the Pacific Cascade Mountain Range, the ranch is situated in a "rain shadow," which means that the dreary days the Pacific Northwest is known for aren't a problem here. Typically, the summer weather is warm and sunny, whereas in winter the skies are often blue, with just enough precipitation to make cross-country skiing and snowmobiling pleasurable. Another benefit of this idyllic, dry climate: very few bugs!

*Chilcotin* is an Indian name that means "People of the Blue Water." Glaciers in the region give the lakes throughout the territory a pleasing turquoise color. In the past, the area was a trading region where inland tribes met with coastal Indians, and some of your riding adventures will likely take you over the old trade routes. You may also encounter signs of a thriving gold mine, now abandoned. At one time, this area was one of the richest gold-producing areas of British Columbia.

Carrying you to these historic sites are Chilcotin's unusual mountain Cayuse horses, a mixture of breeds that create a horse well-suited to the rugged mountain environment. These horses have great stamina, strength, and energy but are also gentle and capable of carrying anyone from the most seasoned rider to young children taking their maiden horseback rides.

The Chilcotin Ranch offers guided backcountry hikes, pack trips, and mountain bike trips. Guests are matched by abilities, interests, and ages. Families, for example, are matched with families, and not with single adults. More experienced individuals (avid hikers, for instance) will not be put with novice outdoorsmen. This attention to detail makes a Chilcotin Holidays trip truly special.

## Chilcotin Holidays Guest Ranch

Gun Creek Road
Gold Bridge, British Columbia V0K 1P0
Canada
Phone: (250) 238–2274
Fax: (250) 238–2274
E-mail: adventures@chilcotinholidays.com
Web site: www.chilcotinholidays.com

**Managers:** Kevan Bracewell and Sylvia Waterer

**Accommodations:** Capacity 18. Ranch guests stay in the 2-story ranch house, which has 9 comfortably furnished guest rooms. Shared baths, daily maid service. Adventure guests stay in the permanent base camps in either log or tent cabins, with heating and bathroom facilities.

**Meals:** At the ranch or on the trail, you'll be surprised and pleased by the appealing and creative cuisine. Unlimited fresh fruits and vegetables, home-baked goods, and hearty main courses such as candied salmon, barbecued ribs, tomato salad with balsamic vinegar and olive-oil dressing, chickpea and spinach salad, baked cookies, and oatmeal squares. Sumptuous!

**Activities:** A low guest-to-guide ratio allows Chilcotin Holidays to focus on education as well as guest safety. Groups are matched by ability, age, and family groups. All-inclusive adventure packages include such activities as daily riding, riding lessons, guided hiking, mountain-biking tours, fishing, gold panning for kids, horse-logging demonstrations, horseshoe-throwing competitions. Additional activities include pack trips (often teamed with ranch stays) and mining-town tours. Winter activities include ice fishing, horse-drawn sleigh rides, target shooting, horseback riding, wildlife viewing, cross-country skiing, and snowmobiling.

**Amenities:** The ranch building is comfortably simple. Rooms have feather duvets; big, soft pillows; and queen and double beds.

**Special Programs:** Most trips involve prescribed activities or "adventures," as the ranch literature refers to them. Choose from a number of formal adventure packages and participate in numerous informal activities that take place on the ranch and on the trail.

**Rates:** $$$–$$$$ Full American Plan. Inquire for package specifics and rates. Bring 6 or more, and the person who organized the trip pays nothing.

**Credit Cards:** MasterCard. Traveler's checks and cash accepted.

**Season:** Year-round

**Getting There:** Ranch shuttle service available from Vancouver-area hotels. Nearest airport, Vancouver. Drive time is approximately 4½ hours.

**What's Nearby:** This is an isolated ranch destination; good dining and shopping in Whistler, British Columbia, about 2 hours south.

# ECHO VALLEY RANCH & SPA

## Jesmond, British Columbia

Echo Valley Ranch & Spa is a premier facility; you'll find its equal, but none better in North America. This is a working ranch and much, much more. It is also a sanctuary, a spa, a place for western adventure, and a gourmand's paradise, all amid first-class decor and accommodations.

The ranch was the dream of resident owners Norman and Nanthawon Dove, who purchased the property in 1995. The 160-acre property is augmented by 10,000 acres of leased cattle land and a seemingly endless wilderness owned by the Canadian people. Despite being "in the middle of nowhere," the ranch has a menu of activities that rivals that of any guest ranch described in this book. Here's a quick, but certainly not exhaustive, list.

Daily horseback riding, riding lessons, and clinics; guided hiking; natural history walks; white-water river-rafting trips; 4 x 4 tours; gold panning; fly fishing, spinner and bait fishing in local lakes and streams; "flight" seeing trips; spa treatments, tai chi and yoga classes. Or, for the traditionalist, you can throw in with the working cowboys and help with everyday ranch chores. Move 'em out!

Women will especially appreciate the Baan Thai spa, a traditional Thai house and pavilion designed by famous Thai architect Dr. Pinyo Suwankan. Full-time resident aestheticians and spa therapist offer a complete array of health-spa services. The facilities include beauty and massage salons, exercise equipment, outdoor hot tubs, sauna, steam rooms, jet showers, hydrotherapy-treatment room, and a heated indoor pool. Daily Ruessn dat ton, meditation, and fitness classes (seasonal—inquire about availability).

As you might have guessed, this is an adult-oriented destination, with an age floor of thirteen years. From mid-July to early August, the age restriction is lowered to eight years of age, and more kid-friendly activities and family-oriented events are available. You can, of course, book the whole ranch for a family reunion or other get-together, and you can bring young children.

The evening entertainment is every bit as diverse as the daily activities. There are weekly cookouts with live music performances, Native American drumming, chanting, and dancing. You'll actually be able to visit a Native American camp on the High Bar Reservation, where you can enjoy a traditional Native American meal and watch indigenous dances before bedding down in a real tepee.

On quieter nights, guests may enjoy a big-screen television with VCR and DVD, or satellite programs. You can join in karaoke, group sing-alongs, dancing, billiards, shuffleboard, darts, or board games, or just find a quiet place to read the newest best-selling novel.

The ranch riding program is pretty special. The ranch uses Tennessee walking horses, stately animals known for their ground-covering stride and Cadillac-smooth ride. If you've never ridden one, you will be amazed at how quickly and easily they move, and you may find yourself less sore at day's end, too! (For those riders who wish, there are also a few horses of traditional western breeding, such as quarter horses, as well as two Belgian draft horses.)

It's hard to imagine a ranch that offers so much. You'll simply have to go there and see it for yourself. This is a great property, a place where the Far East meets the Old West, thanks to the wonderful owners who have realized their dreams of an inviting and truly special guest ranch.

## Echo Valley Ranch & Spa

P.O. Box 16
Jesmond, British Columbia V0K 1K0
Canada
Phone: (250) 459–2386
Fax: (250) 459–0086
E-mail: info@evranch.com
Web site: www.evranch.com

**Owners/Managers:** Norman and Nantha-won Dove

**Accommodations:** Capacity, 40. 2 deluxe lodges, 4 cabins, a traditional Ban Thai (Thai house). The Dove Lodge is a log-cabin structure with 6 guest bedrooms, all with large baths and great views. This is the centerpiece of the ranch, where guests meet for meals and games or to dip in the outdoor hot tub. The Lookout Lodge has 9 large bedrooms, all with baths; 4 rooms feature lofts; all rooms feature porches or balconies. The Baan Thai complex features traditional Thai architecture. A penthouse suite with teak furniture from Thailand is the "jewel" of the property. Across from the suite is the Baan Thai Spa. Additional cabins include 1- or 2-bedroom floor plans, with sitting areas and private bathrooms; some have private Jacuzzi hot tubs.

**Meals:** Full-time professional chef Kim Madsen prepares lavish gourmet meals. Emphasis is on healthful foods (real organic foods are used extensively), including wild mushrooms, herbs, and berries. Special diets accommodated with advance notice. Wines and beers served.

**Activities:** Riding, riding lessons, white-water rafting, nature hikes with naturalists, lake and stream fishing, airplane tours, overnight stays in indigenous Native American tepees. There is also a complete spa, with a broad assortment of spa services.

**Amenities:** Conference facilities with audio equipment, computer networking, and Internet access; separate "breakout" rooms. Baan Thai Spa with in-house spa service providers; luxurious rooms with typical resort amenities; satellite TV and media room; guest recreation room, hot tubs, heated pool, and more.

**Special Programs:** No specific children's program. Kids 8 and over are welcome from mid-July to early August; otherwise, kids must be 13 or older. Groups of 20 or more can "book the ranch" and bring along younger children.

**Rates:** $$$ Full American Plan. Prices vary depending on packages chosen. Guests looking to exert themselves will want to try the Echo Valley Ranch Experience, which includes outdoor adventures and "soft" adventures, whereas spa lovers may wish to choose the Echo Valley Spa Experience, which is oriented toward spa treatments, fitness, and health. Check the ranch literature for detailed descriptions of the different package offerings.

**Credit Cards:** VISA. Personal checks and traveler's checks accepted.

**Season:** Year-round

**Getting There:** Nearest airport: Kamloops, British Columbia. Private airstrip on the ranch. Located 270 miles north of Vancouver, 100 miles from Kamloops.

**What's Nearby:** This ranch is situated in the heart of the Canadian wilderness.

# THE HILLS HEALTH RANCH

## 108 Mile Ranch, British Columbia

Among the many guest ranches listed in this book, we've included a select few renegades that break from the traditional template. The Hills Health Ranch is one of them. As much a chic health spa as a spectacular guest ranch, The Hills will appeal to persons who not only want a western vacation but who also want a richly pampered one.

This is a place where fitness classes are as important as horseback rides, and where the ol' watering hole is a hydrotherapy pool! Guests may choose from a variety of packages, usually a delightful mix of standard guest-ranch activities coupled with spa services. For instance, the five-night "ride'n'spa" combines daily horseback riding, an all-day cowboy cookout ride, and a hayride sing-along party but adds on two relaxation body massages, facial, manicure, pedicure, hyrdrotherapy treatment, and access to the many spa amenities such as saunas, weight rooms, Jacuzzis, and the indoor pool.

Similarly, the six-night Connecting with Horses program emphasizes extensive daily riding combined with a bit of horse psychology to help you better understand and relate to your four-hoofed friend. Also in the package are a variety of spa services, such as a fitness assessment, lifestyle consultation, specially tailored meal plans to help you reach weight goals, private riding lessons, exercise classes, massage, hydrotherapy, and much, much more.

Sounds great? It gets better. Since the emphasis of the ranch is on encouraging and supporting healthful lifestyles, the cuisine is a bit different than one might expect at a typical dude ranch. The Hills boasts a full-service country dining room with an excellent gourmet menu, serving healthful ranch, vegetarian, and low-fat spa cuisine; and, of course, you can still enjoy traditional cowboy cookouts and early-morning cowboy breakfasts.

Guests who want to shed a few pounds may opt for a thirty-night, a ten-night, or a six-night "weight loss" or "inches off" program. Don't worry, you won't starve: The meals are calorie-controlled but filling, very nutritious but wonderfully delicious—the kind of meals you'd make yourself, if you only had the time (and a nutritionist's degree). If weight loss isn't your goal, you can opt for the relaxing stress-busting Spa Retreat (ideal for guests who prefer to spend their time luxuriating and working out in the health spa instead of on the trail).

If all this sounds a little fancy, well, it is. But the ranch is also a wonderful place to experience nature at its finest. The ranch is surrounded by 20,000 acres of Canadian wilderness and ranchland amid a true working-cattle ranch. On a bike, a hike, or a mountain horseback ride, you'll experience great views and the clean, fresh scent of coastal evergreens.

The activities don't end with the summer season, either. Come winter, the emphasis shifts to snowsports, including cross-country skiing, snowshoeing, downhill skiing, and snowboarding. The ranch has 200 kilometers of trails for cross-country skiing.

Each guest is guided, nurtured, educated, enlightened, and supported as he or she begins to make lifestyle changes and choices that will improve their state of wellness and health. This is truly a vacation that will stay with you long after the pictures have been put away. It may even be a life-altering experience.

## The Hills Health Ranch

P.O. Box 26
108 Mile Ranch, British Columbia V0K 2Z0
Canada
Phone: (250) 791–5225
Fax: (250) 791–6384
E-mail: info@hillshealthranch.com
Web site: www.spabc.com

**Owners/Managers:** Patrick and Juanita Corbett

**Accommodations:** Capacity, 150. Guests stay in lodges with hotel-style rooms (great for couples and singles) or in chalets well suited to families and groups. Lodge rooms feature either a queen-sized bed or a queen and a double bed, a private bathroom, and cozy bathrobes for each guest. Each chalet features 3 bedrooms, a full bath, living room, patio, fully equipped kitchen, including a full-sized stove, refrigerator, and microwave oven. Beds are both queen sized and doubles.

**Meals:** Healthful spa cuisine emphasizes low-fat, natural foods with carefully calculated nutritional balance. Ranch-style cookouts, cowboy breakfasts, and health-conscious ranch cooking make it easy for guests to ease into the dietary swing. For persons interested in losing weight, special reducing diets are created. A typical day's menu: breakfast of banana pancakes with berry syrup; lunch of chicken stir-fry on 7-grain pilaf and home-made bread, salad nouveau; dinner of Moroccan-style chicken brochette with couscous pilaf and toasted pecans, grilled eggplant and fresh herbs, and frozen yogurt crepes. Vegetarian and special diets accommodated.

**Activities:** Ranch activities include horseback riding, hiking, fishing biking, golfing, canoeing. Horseback-riding lessons for novice riders to very experienced riders. Equestrians, ask about special horse care and safety seminars and the Communicating with Horses workshop. Spa activities include spa services, fitness classes (pilates, taibox, yoga, step/circuit train-

ing, aquafit, aerobics, street defense, and more), swimming. Nearby championship golf courses and 5 tennis courts. Wintertime Nordic skiing, snowshoeing, alpine skiing, and snowboarding on the facility's own slopes and terrain park. Also, inner tubing, ice skating, dogsledding.

**Amenities:** Full-service spa with certified and highly trained staff. Massages, facials, manicures and pedicures, waxing, reflexology, nutritional and fitness counseling, fitness instruction and classes, and more. Facilities include weight rooms, exercise studios, aerobic exercise machines and weight-training equipment, saunas, indoor pool, 2 hydrotherapy baths, gift shop, winter ski shop, 15 separate treatment rooms. Banquet and meeting facilities for conferences. Socializing and dining in the Swiss Fondue and Hot Rock Restaurant, the Victorian Tea Room, and the Coffee Saloon family lounge.

**Special Programs:** Children are welcome but are their parents' responsibility. No specific children's programs, but kids may participate in many on-ranch activities.

**Rates:** $$–$$$ Full American Plan and Modified European Plan. Prices go down as the number of individuals in the party increases. Be sure to consult with your booking agent about package prices, what they include, and the cost of additional services not charged as part of the package. Children's rates. No minimum stay.

**Credit Cards:** VISA, MasterCard, American Express

**Season:** Year-round

**Getting There:** Located 8 miles north of 100 Mile House, British Columbia (about 300 miles north of Vancouver). Nearest airport is Williams Lake via the Vancouver Airport.

**What's Nearby:** Nearest community at 100 Mile House, British Columbia (8 miles).

# SPRINGHOUSE TRAILS RANCH

### Williams Lake, British Columbia

Many people enjoy the freedom of trailer and car camping in summer. Springhouse Trails Ranch is one of a handful of guest ranches with its own campground, enabling the gypsy camper the chance to enjoy a dude-ranch vacation in their own home-away-from-home. In addition, this Canadian guest ranch offers the more traditional cabins as well as apartment-type lodgings.

The campground is the full-service type, with full hookup RV sites, bathrooms, showers, and laundry facilities. There is even a playground and a trampoline for kids!

Flexibility is the rule at Springhouse Trails. Campers can take advantage of the relatively inexpensive camping rates (especially affordable for residents of the United States, given current exchange rates). Vacationers looking for accommodations can rent rooms by the night or as an American Plan package that includes lodging and two- or three-meal-a-day options. Activities such as horseback riding can be paid for a la carte or as part of an inclusive package that includes lodging, horseback riding, three daily meals, and use of all ranch facilities. This level of flexibility makes Springhouse Ranch appealing to people who wish to stay for a night, a week, or a month—an arrangement that's hard to find at most guest-ranch destinations.

The ranch is located in British Columbia's Cariboo Mountains at an elevation of 3,000 feet. The forests have abundant stands of pine and fir, which give the air a refreshing and clean scent. Broad, open pasturelands and glades invite lots of exploration on horseback. Guided riding is informal, with lots of opportunities to range out and explore the surrounding wilderness and lots of opportunities for family vacation photos.

The property was revitalized by Werner and Susi Moessner, a German couple who left Stuttgart in the late 1970s in search of land. They opened Springhouse Ranch to guests in 1980 and developed quite a clientele of European guests who appreciated the bilingual nature of the ranch as well as the excellent German cuisine that was mixed in with the more standard western ranch meals served in the dining room. At present, the ranch is run by the Moessners' daughter, Eve, and her husband, Herbert Winkler, in the tradition of their family.

Springhouse Ranch is situated near a small lake amid open pastures and rolling hills. Activities are informal, with horseback riding, hiking, and canoeing on the lake being the principal draws. A nearby bird sanctuary is an ideal place for nature observation (be sure to bring along a pair of binoculars and a guidebook to Western birds). Casual lake fishing is also a popular pastime, so plan to bring along a rod and tackle if that interests you. Guests wishing to play a round of golf or work on their tennis swing can take advantage of public facilities in nearby Williams Lake. River-rafting excursions may also be arranged through Chilko River Expeditions, which has a good relationship with the folks at Springhouse Trails.

A flexible schedule also leaves time to explore several nearby gold-rush towns (this area of British Columbia once formed the heart of a major gold rush) and a chance to take in local rodeos or take an airplane tour of this lovely region of the West. Your hosts will be glad to help you coordinate excursions, and be sure to inquire about upcoming community events and celebrations such as the Williams Lake Stampede Rodeo.

## Springhouse Trails Ranch

Box 2, RR 1
Williams Lake, British Columbia V2G 2P1
Canada
Phone: (250) 392–4780
Fax: (250) 392–4701
E-mail: eve@springhousetrails.com
Web site: www.springhousetrails.com

**Owners/Managers:** Eve and Herbert Winkler

**Accommodations:** Capacity, 40. Guests are housed in rustic, individual log cabins with kitchens and in apartment-style guest rooms in 2 large lodges. Also available is a full-service campground with a dozen RV spaces with hookups and laundry and shower facilities.

**Meals:** Guests dine in the lodge's main dining room/restaurant. The menu is a mix of standard western ranch items as well as German specialty items such as schnitzel. Weekly outdoor barbecues. Full bar and imported German beers.

**Activities:** Horseback riding, hiking, fishing, informal outdoor games and recreation. Nearby golf, tennis, and river-rafting excursions (extra). The Williams Lake area offers many opportunities for sight-seeing, so be sure to plan accordingly.

**Amenities:** RV campground with full hookups for 12 vehicles; restaurant with bar; children's playground.

**Special Programs:** No special kids' program, although children are welcome.

**Rates:** $–$$ Packages with Full American Plan and horseback riding. Children's rates.

**Credit Cards:** VISA, MasterCard

**Season:** May to September

**Getting There:** Located 11 miles southwest of Williams Lake; 6 hours northeast of Vancouver by car. Airport service to Williams Lake via Vancouver International Airport.

**What's Nearby:** Williams Lake, with golf, tennis, and seasonal rodeo events.

# THREE BARS CATTLE & GUEST RANCH

## Cranbrook, British Columbia

Located on the western side of the Canadian Rockies, Three Bars Guest Ranch shares much in common with the guest ranches located in the land of its southern neighbor, Montana. Persons familiar with the Glacier National Park will find themselves right at home in this beautiful stretch of Canadian backcountry. The summer weather here is moderate and mild, with clear, cold mountain streams, wide-open pastures and parklands, and forests that run to the far horizon.

Amid all this natural splendor is a handsome, modern log lodge with peaked-roof awnings and a broad, inviting front porch that emphatically says, "Relax—you're on vacation." Whether your idea of time off means relaxing with the latest *New York Times* bestseller or taking a soothing trip down the mild St. Mary's River, the Three Bars is a great place to find your bliss.

As an actual cattle ranch, the Three Bars promotes an excellent riding program. The ranch boasts of more than ninety riding horses, which works out to two horses per guest. That makes matching every guest to an appropriate horse quite easy and ensures that no horse in need of a little time off is pressed into service. Your horse will be yours for the week, but on the off chance that you don't get along, another will be ready to step up and become your new pardner.

With so many mounts, the riding is unlimited at the Three Bars. Take off for a few hours or spend the entire day in the saddle, going deep into the endless system of trails. After a couple of days in the saddle, guests may opt for the "fast ride," where they get the opportunity to do some trotting and galloping during a ground-covering guided tour. (Guests who are really avid and enthusiastic horsemen will want to inquire about special "horsemanship" weeks.)

Riding lessons are available in the arena to help gunsels (newcomers) attain sufficient proficiency in the saddle and to review the essential points of safety on horseback. Even children get in on the action, with riding programs for kids as young as six years. There are daily activity programs and a Junior Wrangler riding program for kids, too.

The nearby St. Mary's River is not only a good place for a float trip, but it's also a blue-ribbon trout habitat ideal for anglers. Just a short walk from the ranch, the St. Mary's is the ideal place for first-timers and fly-fishing veterans alike. Basic fishing tackle is available at the ranch, or you can bring your own custom carbon-fiber fly rod. If you require a guide, the ranch will be happy to help you find a local outfitter who knows all the best spots. For the less demanding, a stocked pond in Cranbrook provides a great place to spend time fishing with the kids. The ranch will be happy to outfit you with spinning rods and a local map.

The Three Bars is fairly upscale, with a nice complement of amenities such as an indoor pool, outdoor hot tub, and tennis court. Children will enjoy the children's play area and petting zoo, and everyone seems to have fun playing volleyball and pitching horseshoes.

The Three Bars is home to the Beckley family—Jeff, April, and their two sons, Tyler and Jesse. The Beckleys love sharing their rural western lifestyle with guests, and it shows in everything they do.

## Three Bars Cattle & Guest Ranch

9500 Wycliffe Perry Creek Road
Cranbrook, British Columbia V1C 7C7
Canada
Phone: (250) 426–5230
Fax: (250) 426–8240
E-mail: info@threebarsranch.com
Web site: www.threebarsranch.com

**Owners:** The Beckley Family

**Accommodations:** Capacity, 40. A fairly upscale facility, with modern guest cabins featuring private entrances, sun chairs, log furniture, queen-sized beds, full private baths, and sitting areas. Linens and bath and pool towels provided; daily maid service. Inquire about the different cabin floor plans, which vary to accommodate a variety of family situations.

**Meals:** Western ranch meals, predinner cocktail hour. Special diets with advance notice.

**Activities:** Horseback riding with expert instruction, ideal for guests who want to learn. Guests join in cattle driving, when needed. Guided hikes, fishing in St. Mary's River. Weekly float trips during the spring and early summer runoff. Swimming, tennis, hiking, mountain biking. Nearby golf.

**Amenities:** Hot tub, indoor swimming pool, tennis court, lounge, media room (TV/VISA, VCR, DVD, etc.), meeting rooms for conferences. Nearby golf, downhill skiing, and helicopter tours (additional).

**Special Programs:** No formal kid's programs, although children over 6 may ride on supervised rides with wranglers. Baby-sitters available.

**Rates:** $$ Full American Plan. Reduced spring and fall rates; stays shorter than 7 days available. Reduced children's rates.

**Credit Cards:** VISA, MasterCard. Personal or traveler's checks accepted.

**Season:** May through September. The ranch is available October through May for conferences.

**Getting There:** Courtesy shuttle from Cranbrook Airport provided. Three Bars is located between Cranbrook and Kimberly in the southeastern corner of British Columbia. Canadian Airlines and Air Canada offer regional airport services with connections to Vancouver, British Columbia and Calgary, Alberta. Drive time from Spokane, Washington, is 4 hours; from Calgary, 5 hours via Banff National Park. Request a map for specifics.

**What's Nearby:** Glacier National Park (east of the ranch, in Montana) and Waterton National Park, in Alberta; also, Banff National Park (2 hours north) and Calgary. Nearby Cranbrook, British Columbia hosts an annual rodeo. Step back in time and visit the gold-rush days at Fort Steele, a restored Canadian Mounted Police outpost, located just a few minutes away from the ranch.

# WILD ROSE RANCH

## Kimberly, British Columbia

Wild Rose Ranch is a small, intimate family property nestled in the mountains of eastern British Columbia. If you think of the northwestern Canadian province as a wet, heavily timbered area of dense vegetation, the Wild Rose will come as a pleasant surprise. Like eastern Washington, northern Idaho, and Montana, this region is shadowed by the peaks farther west and is considerably more arid than the coastal regions of Canada and the United States. Although the land is still lush with vegetation, visitors tend to enjoy clear, sunny skies, especially in summer.

The motto at the Wild Rose is "adventures for the soul." It's an apt description of what visitors can expect: challenging adventures and an environment that helps one recharge one's inner batteries.

The adventures center around a variety of organized programs at the Wild Rose. The General Ranch program, for instance, includes horseback riding, hiking, self-guided bird-watching, and fishing in Wolf Creek, as well as white-water rafting, when river water levels allow. In spring, the ranch shifts focus and "goes to the birds" with its bird-watching intensive program especially for birders and wanna-be birders. This program takes advantage of an area of the ranch that has been created and protected as bird habitat by the ranch owners and the conservation group Ducks Unlimited. (Birders, be sure to ask about the two international bird festivals, the Creston Valley Osprey Festival and Wings over the Rockies.)

This region is also a fine place for fishermen, with a wide range of excellent trout-fishing habitat in the East Kootenay mountains. The stream, rivers, and lakes here offer rainbow, cutthroat, brook, and bull trout. Many areas are catch-and-release, and guests can choose from bank fishing to wading to float trips. The ranch can outfit you with boats, motors, canoes, life jackets, float tubes, nets, and enthusiasm. Fly rods and spinning rods are also available for guest use.

The Wild Rose has recently switched to an adult-oriented philosophy. The minimum age here is twelve, so bring the teens along if you wish. Just make sure they are enthusiastic about horseback riding, as that constitutes the main daily activity here. The program is very good, with daily rides lasting anywhere from two to seven hours. There is also an outdoor riding arena where guests can practice the finer points of equitation and get to know their mount a little better. Guests who wish can try their hand at the exciting western rodeo sport of barrel racing.

In late spring and early summer, you can experience the grandeur of the Canadian Rockies while rafting the thrilling white water or on a milder float trip on the calmer sections of the local rivers. And after a day of adventure, soak in the natural hot springs along the banks of Lussier or Ram Creeks, just a forty-five-minute drive from the ranch.

In winter, guests can still enjoy this special region. Nearby ski areas include Kimberly Alpine Resort, Panorama, and Fernie. These three ski areas are a well-kept secret offering dry, light powder conditions, short lift lines, and a friendly and international clientele. If you wish, you can even book a helicopter ski excursion, likely to rank as the adventure of a lifetime. To cap off your winter trip, schedule a massage and personal spa package (skiers and snowboarders, be sure to ask about these).

## Wild Rose Ranch

P.O. Box 181
Kimberley, British Columbia V1A 2Y6
Canada
Phone: (800) 324–6188
Fax: (250) 422–3149
Web site: www.wildrose-ranch.com

**Owners/Managers:** Barry Rogers and Shannon Langley

**Accommodations:** Capacity, 14. Guests stay in the modern cedar-log lodge or cabin. All rooms have private baths.

**Meals:** Meals are served family style in the dining room or outside on the deck overlooking Wolf Creek. Home-baked breads, fresh fruits, and vegetables complement the home cooking. Wine is served with afternoon appetizers, and guests are welcome to bring their own liquor.

**Activities:** Horseback riding, canoeing, whitewater rafting, trout and lake fishing, hiking, bird-watching, hot-springs visits. Entertainment includes local rodeos, cookouts, campfire sing-alongs, and visits to nearby Fort Steele.

**Amenities:** A small, intimate, and cozy ranch offering comfortable rooms and a friendly staff that will assist you in planning and enjoying a restful and adventurous vacation in Canada's lovely Kootenay Range. A variety of sport-fishing equipment available for loan.

**Special Programs:** No organized children's programs. Mature children 12 and older are welcome to participate in activities alongside their parents.

**Rates:** $$–$$$ Full American Plan. Short stays of 3, 4, and 5 nights also available. Off-season discounts. Special package prices and reduced winter rates and stays.

**Credit Cards:** VISA, MasterCard

**Season:** May to November, December to April

**Getting There:** 30 miles north of Kimberley, 209 miles north of Spokane. Nearest airport in Cranbrook, 30 miles south. Guests typically make connections from Spokane, Calgary, or Vancouver, British Columbia.

**What's Nearby:** Fort Steele, a refurbished outpost of the Royal Canadian Mounted Police. Be sure to visit the local hot-springs baths as well.

# ABOUT THE AUTHOR

Gavin Ehringer's writing has appeared in dozens of equestrian and Western-lifestyle publications, including *Cowboys & Indians, America's Horse, New Country,* and *Western Horseman.* He is the author of the Western Horseman book *Rodeo Legends* and co-author of *Rodeo in America* published by the University of Kansas Press. In addition, he has contributed to several guidebooks about ski resorts in his home state, Colorado, and a guidebook to Aspen, Colorado.

Before embarking on a writing career, Ehringer worked as a wrangler at several guest ranches in Colorado, including the award-winning C Lazy U Ranch which is featured in this book. He also apprenticed on working-cattle ranches throughout southern Colorado.